MAKING
MONEY

....

TEACHING
MUSIC

DAVID R. NEWSAM AND BARBARA SPRAGUE NEWSAM

WRITER'S DIGEST BOOKS

Cincinnati, Ohio

99 98 97 96 95   5 4 3 2 1

Library of Congress Cataloging-in-Publication Data

Newsam, David R.
  Making money teaching music / David R. Newsam and Barbara Sprague Newsam.—1st ed.
      p.   cm.
  Includes index.
  ISBN 0-89879-657-1
  1. Music—Instruction and study—Vocational guidance. I. Newsam, Barbara Sprague. II. Title.
ML3790.N49   1995
780'.7—dc20   94-37927
                                                               CIP
                                                               MN

Edited by Julie Wesling Whaley
Designed by Brian Roeth
Cover Illustration by Julie Baker

ABOUT THE AUTHORS

David R. Newsam is a member of the faculties at Berklee College of Music, Dartmouth College and the University of New Hampshire. He has taught private music lessons in studios and in his home for more than fifteen years. David has also taught in public schools and in a number of specialized summer performance programs. In addition to his teaching experience, he has an extensive performance history. He holds a bachelor's degree in music performance from Berklee College of Music.

Barbara Sprague Newsam is an educator and lifelong music enthusiast. She received her master's degree from Harvard Graduate School of Education and currently directs a student assistance program in Manchester, New Hampshire. Barbara is the author of the *Complete Student Assistance Program Handbook*. Her musical experience includes songwriting and performance.

Dedication

To Maya Rachel

ACKNOWLEDGMENTS

A great many musicians, educators and professionals helped in the completion of this project; to name them all would be impossible. However, we'd like to thank Gail Galiant, Kathleen Kanaley and Marilyn Williams for their time, expertise and encouragement.

We'd also like to thank the people at Writer's Digest Books: Mark Garvey for having confidence in the project and Julie Wesling Whaley for her stellar editing job.

We want to thank the gifted teachers we've encountered throughout our lives who have blessed us with their wisdom and encouragement. It is their example that guided us to the teaching profession and motivated us to undertake this project.

• Budgeting for an Inconsistent Income • Bartering: A Different Kind of Income • Insurance: Covering Your Axe, Violin or Piano • Retirement Considerations • Taxes: Face Your Fears and File an Early Return • A Final Word About Finances

INTRODUCTION

MAKING THE DECISION TO TEACH MUSIC

You love music, and you think you might want to teach lessons and share some of your skill and enthusiasm with others. Maybe you have been teaching for some time and are looking for ways to recharge your batteries, or perhaps you are just starting out. You probably have had some very good and maybe a few not-so-good teachers yourself to use as models in developing your own teaching style. A few outstanding (and lucky!) teachers are simply born great, and the rest work hard at becoming great. The first step in becoming a great teacher is deciding if it's what you *really* want to do.

TEACHING IS A LIVING, NOT A LAST RESORT

Teaching music privately is challenging and exciting, but it is not necessarily an easy way to supplement a performance habit. While many musicians teach lessons to supplement their income or to make a living, if you don't want to teach, you don't have to. It is not a foregone conclusion. And if you don't enjoy teaching, your potential students will be better off if you leave the teaching to those who love doing it. Many great musicians over the years have chosen to do other things to make a living: accounting, waiting tables and carpentry, to name a few. Teaching is demanding and different enough from performing that some excellent musicians feel that they're simply not cut out for it, and you may be among them. Not all good players make good teachers. If you have the bug to perform and see teaching as playing the ultimate second fiddle, pursue more performance opportunities rather than becoming a cynical and bitter teacher.

If you've never taught, however, or are new at it, you may wonder whether there is a great teacher lurking beneath your skin. The world may be deprived of one excellent teacher if you don't test the waters, so we encourage you to make the attempt. If you are nervous about teaching, be reassured that every great teacher was at one time an inexperienced one. Every new teacher has tossed and turned the night before a first-ever lesson hoping that the student won't know more than the teacher. Also, if you taught years ago and didn't like it but suspect that you may feel differently now, we really encourage you to give it a try.

On the other hand, maybe you're already a good teacher and in the process of becoming great. You'll reap great personal and financial rewards if you take time to perfect the craft of teaching as seriously as you pursue excellence in playing your primary instrument. Clearly, if you are reading this book, you are displaying your commitment to the process of becoming a great teacher. We hope you'll pick up some ideas to further hone your craft or get some validation for the good things you're already doing.

LIVING WITH IRREGULAR PAYCHECKS AND BEDTIMES

If you already work in the music business, you are probably accustomed to the odd hours and the unpredictable pay schedule and won't have any trouble adding more uncertainty. If you (and perhaps your partner) have the intestinal and financial fortitude to live with this inconsistent arrangement, teaching lessons will fit right in. But if you need a ten-o'clock coffee break, a regular performance evaluation and a steady raise, you may have to secure some additional, predictable income while teaching lessons part time. Chapter nine covers the financial details.

The only predictable thing about the pay from lessons is that it varies. There is a certain rhythm to it, however. Young students tend to be very organized during school days and fall completely apart during school vacations and during the summer. If you live and teach in an insular community, you may do well, in fact, to give lessons to kids only when school is in session. Adults tend to back out of lessons during the holidays and when their children are on school vacation. Ways to minimize these difficulties are discussed in detail in subsequent chapters.

For the most part, music lessons take place after traditional working hours for adults and after school gets out for kids. That means peak lesson hours fall in the late afternoon and evening. This may be a perfect arrangement for you, too, if you teach lessons in addition to holding down a regular "day job." Just remember that on the nights you teach, you may "get off work" as late as nine or ten in the evening.

FINDING SPACE TO TEACH LESSONS AND STUDENTS TO TEACH

The issue of finding space in which to teach is so important that we've devoted a whole chapter to it. In general, if you have a great space, great. If you don't, and really want to teach anyway, don't let your lack of a high-tech or spacious studio stop you, because there are many workable alternatives. Good teachers can be found teaching in their living rooms, rehearsal spaces, garages, a friend's or family member's living room, offices, music stores and teaching studios. Some teachers use practice rooms at colleges and high schools, and some travel to students' homes or conduct group lessons at community centers or in adult education programs. Chapter one contains specific advice pertaining to each situation.

The wider your criteria for students, the more students you attract. A teacher who can comfortably teach students of all ages at most levels in various styles has no trouble filling out a lesson schedule. Don't sell yourself short, but, at the same time, be realistic about your limitations. If you are an expert classical guitarist, for instance, you can teach all beginning guitar students, most intermediate students in most styles and advanced classical players. You might get frustrated with an advanced player who wants to learn heavy metal, and you'd do better in the long run to refer that student to a teacher who specializes in that style.

Take an honest look at your own education and performance history, and determine reasonable parameters for your student population. Evaluate your patience with children. At family reunions, are you the one making balloon animals for the little ones in the family room, or are you under the buffet table hiding from your nieces and nephews? Teaching children requires specific techniques (see chapter five), and if you are a good teacher of young children, you are sorely needed. On the other hand, some people can really connect with teenagers and can inspire them to great musical heights. Other people think teenagers are dreadfully unkempt creatures and can't imagine why anyone would bother with them. Most people think adults are the most civilized population, but others find them self-conscious learners and actually prefer to work with children. Search yourself to discover what gifts you have and which students would benefit the most from them.

EVALUATING YOUR MARKETABILITY

Most private music teachers are marketable once they make the decision to market themselves, which is sometimes a great psychological hurdle to get over. Tips on marketing, promotion and visibility are covered in great detail in chapter four. In evaluating your marketability, you must consider the current popularity of the instrument(s) you teach, the geographical area you live in, the hours you have available, the population you want to teach, and the level of cooperation you can expect from your loved ones. While guitar teachers may be inundated with calls, bassoonists may be sitting by the phone. So, if your pool of potential students is small, you may have to travel or do more work to gain referrals. When you are deciding whether to teach lessons, consider the energy you may have to expend doing self-promotion, and ask yourself whether you are willing to do it.

SOME FINAL WORDS ABOUT MAKING THE DECISION TO TEACH

The teachers we know teach music lessons for a number of reasons, ranging from needing a little extra money to staying connected to the music scene to wanting to be involved in music full time. Some reasons seem more noble than others, but the truth is that any reason is good enough if you are going to feel good about teaching. You need to be happy and satisfied with your choice, and musicians are often torn. Most are bright, disciplined and expressive people who could excel in any number of fields, so it's important to *decide* that teaching is something you want to do. A few teachers end up teaching by default; if that is your situation, you should rethink and recommit yourself to the process.

Once you have made the decision to teach, this book contains all the tools you'll need. We hope you will reach into this toolbox, chapter by chapter, and use what you need to customize your teaching style. If you are already teaching, use what you can to streamline, refine, and make your life easier. If you are a novice at teaching, use our experience as a basic field survival guide as you begin your journey. We wish you luck!

CHAPTER ONE

FINDING TEACHING OPPORTUNITIES

I f students don't break down your door to get to you, you may have to send out a search party for them. Don't be discouraged by the prospect, because there are many hidden opportunities to teach music lessons and special classes, although not all of them come to mind immediately. If you want to fill a lesson schedule completely, you have to look in several places or work in different venues until your "net" stretches across a sufficiently large pool to gain enough students. Think of this process as an investment in your future. This chapter outlines different places you can teach lessons and classes and discusses the challenges specific to each setting. Because the subject of teaching at home deserves special attention, it is covered separately in chapters two and three.

TEACHING IN PUBLIC SCHOOLS

Schools represent a tremendous teaching opportunity. In a brief jog around your neighborhood, you'll likely pass elementary schools, middle schools, and junior and senior high schools full of ready learners. Getting your foot in the door at schools may be intimidating, however, and for this reason many would-be teachers avoid the process. Putting the intimidation factor aside, there are different ways of being involved with teaching music at schools. Not all positions require teacher certification or a full-time commitment to the school. If you do not want to work in a school but you are looking for lesson referrals, it benefits you to be in contact with the schools in your area.

Becoming a School Music Teacher

The most familiar way of being involved with a school's music program is to serve as a traditional music teacher. In many schools one person teaches all music and music appreciation classes, directs a band

and a chorus, and provides musical accompaniment for any number of seasonal productions, musicals and ceremonies. Most musicians were first influenced and inspired by one of these committed individuals. Having served in this capacity, we can say on good authority that these positions require boundless energy and tremendous dedication to young people and music itself.

In public schooling, most states require that a teacher become certified as an educator, though some states make concessions for noncertified personnel to get started and then get certified along the way. Other states allow professional people to turn a portion of their work experience into credits toward certification. If you hold a music degree and are willing to go through the educational certification process eventually, you may want to apply for these rigorous positions.

As a full-time music teacher in a school, you are usually given a teacher's contract and all the associated benefits and responsibilities. If you are interested in pursuing a music teaching position, peruse the newspapers for teacher vacancies and apply, knowing that competition may be stiff from certified, master's level teachers who have been laid off during budget crunches.

Considering half-time or traveling positions. Many cities, towns or districts post half-time music positions, which sometimes require a great deal of traveling from school to school. In this arrangement, you may be responsible for basic music classes at any number of levels; sometimes these positions include students from kindergarten through high school or several schools within a region or district. If you can supplement such a half-time position by giving private lessons in the schools or elsewhere, this may be a workable way of doing music full-time. Positions that require traveling or are located in rural or inner-city areas may elicit less competition from experienced educators, so if you are just starting out and want to make an investment in your experience, you may choose to apply for these positions.

Making the most of being a music teacher. Music teacher positions are what you make of them. Teaching twelve sections of sixth-grade recorder classes can make the most dedicated musician weep. For this reason, it is important to have realistic expectations about these positions. You probably are not going to fulfill your performance fantasies playing "Pomp and Circumstance" to an auditorium full of teary parents. Nor are you going to be whisked from your bandleader podium to Carnegie Hall. On the other hand, teaching in schools has other, less stellar but perhaps more lasting, rewards and provides great experience.

In a small school system, you may have the freedom to design an entire music curriculum or to start an innovative program. In a large system, you may have the opportunity to work with veteran teachers and/or teach more specialized classes in your area of expertise. A school music teacher inspires children to express themselves musically, and you may make a real difference in the lives of your students. If you can remember that while you rehearse the marching band in a torrential downpour or duck flying peanut butter sandwiches during lunchroom duty, you belong in the schools.

Working *With* the Schools Without Becoming a Music Teacher

Other, less familiar ways to infiltrate the hallowed halls of schools don't require you to become a traditional music teacher. The school may act as a referral agency for you for private lessons, or they may hire you to teach lessons right in the school, either during school or after school hours. Most schools do not require educational certification for such ancillary positions, so you may be a ready candidate for these opportunities.

The first step: getting into the schools. Getting your foot in the door is often the most difficult step. Although slick promotion, updated resumes and good references (see chapter four) all contribute to your chances, your best bet is to get to know the principal, the faculty and, most important, the music teachers in the schools where you want to teach lessons. Even if you don't get to teach *in* the school, music teachers are good people to know if you are looking for students for private lessons. Music teachers (and band directors especially) tend to be incredibly energetic, busy people, so you have to be patient and determined to get to know them. Don't think that you're going to start dropping in on them in September and have a full lesson schedule by October. If you want long-term results, make the decision to put some long-term work into developing a relationship with your schools' music departments. At the very least, drop off a stack of your business cards to the music teacher and the guidance department in your local high school so you can get some referrals. In a more aggressive scenario, you may want to sell your services directly to the school.

Volunteering guest spots, lectures and classes. Part of promoting yourself and making yourself known in the schools is volunteering your time. We know you want to make your living doing music, but there is often profound fiscal potential in acts of volunteerism. People get to know and trust you and then hire you for events in the future. Again, school music teachers tend to be extremely busy people who can use some help from time to time. By offering your services to the music department, you win points from the teacher and increase your visibility to the school and to the students. Some suggestions for classes, workshops and guest spots include:

• Offer to direct an additional band or ensemble in your area of expertise (chamber music, jazz, rock, choral music) for students who are sufficiently motivated and skilled. You can meet with this group at the school or in some other community building once a week, once a month, after school or on weekends. Try to showcase such an ensemble during school concerts and community events to connect your work with the school. Always give credit to the school's music department for the fact that the students were motivated and prepared enough to engage in this special endeavor.

• If the school offers a music appreciation or music history class, offer to give a lecture, presentation or demonstration. Music teachers are responsible for designing a curriculum for 180 to 200 school days. They appreciate the help if you are flexible and willing to fit into their system. Even if the music teacher can't use your services the first time you offer, always leave the door open. Don't hound the teacher, but let him or her know that your offer is sincere. Be sure to leave a phone number where you can be reached.

• Become a substitute teacher (often no certification is required). Ask to substitute for music positions. If you are substituting for band directors or music teachers who are going to be absent for days at a time (for field trips and events), contact them to discuss their lesson plans. Do a conscientious job, and eventually they will request you as a substitute in their absence and you will be a known entity in the department.

• Offer to run a workshop on some aspect of performance or theory. Music teachers get tired of hearing their own voices. Be extremely flexible. "I can come talk about the history of blues to any size group of any level of students on any Tuesday in March" is a real help. "I'd like to talk to your upper-level choral students about madrigals next Tuesday at 11:00" is a demand, not an offer, and belies ignorance of the way schools do business.

- Ask for a formal internship. If you really want to learn the business of school music departments, one way is to get in there and roll up your sleeves. You meet a lot of talented students and learn the ropes this way. Note: Don't jump at an unpaid internship where a paid assistantship is a possibility.

Giving Private Lessons in Schools

Progressive school systems and proactive music departments like to offer additional music lesson services to their students. The teaching arrangement may be that students pay the school and the school hires a private teacher on a consultant basis (you!). It works this way most often when students are taking lessons for course credit.

Usually the arrangement is less formal: The school simply offers the lesson service to those students who want it, and students are responsible for paying the teachers directly. In a system with a well-respected and active music department, lesson arrangements with outside teachers may seem ordinary, and the positions may be posted. In more traditional systems, the idea of offering music lessons at school may seem *revolutionary*. If you want to teach lessons at local schools, find out whether you will be vying for existing positions or introducing an entirely new concept.

If you can arrange to give lessons at a school (or several of them), think in advance about your challenging role and how you want to handle it. For instance, what are the school rules? Are you responsible for enforcing them? What if, the first semester, only one student wants lessons? You must decide whether it is a good use of your time to travel to the school to give one lesson, betting on the odds that next semester you might have more students follow.

Teaching for credit. If you teach private lessons and the school plans to give your students credit for it, you must fill out some sort of evaluation to grade students on their progress. Find out if you are responsible for designing a final exam or if there are proficiency guidelines already in place that you should guide your students toward. If the school wants you to devise your own evaluation, draw up a rough draft of your evaluation tool before your lessons begin. Also, find out when evaluations, midterm comments, warnings and grades are due and to whom you must submit them. Record these deadlines in your datebook, and get them in on time.

Schools and timing private lessons. Schools pose special challenges because they are on a different clock from the rest of the planet. School personnel often have to "translate" real time into school time. "You want to come in at 10:30? That's right in the middle of period C. It would be better if you could come at 10:52, right before period D." If you give lessons during the school day, your best bet is to schedule a number of students right in a row and give a whole day per week to the attempt. That way you can just go to the school and surrender that day to the time warp.

If you have only a few lessons to schedule, be sure to ask about assemblies and special classes that may interfere. If you teach after school, find out about all early release days. Ask the school secretary for a school-year calendar and mark your personal calendar with vacations and holidays. Pay special attention to any days off you might not think of, such as teacher workshop days. At the junior and senior high levels, ask about midterm and final exam schedules and how you can best work within or around those. In cold climates, ask about how snow days are handled and what radio and TV stations are informed first if school is canceled.

Developing a fee structure for private lessons in schools. You may have no input to how students are charged for lessons if the school handles it. There may be a flat fee for the semester, of which you and the school receive a percentage. Consider this: Is the school going to pay you substantially less per hour or per student than you could make in a studio or at home? It's likely that these are the same students that you would have in your studio. The reasons you want to teach them in the school include convenience, generating more individual lessons, not having the space to teach where you are, and making a reasonable amount of money. If teaching in the school means you will take a considerable loss, don't do it, but do promotion there anyway.

If the school is going to pay you adequately, find out how and when. Are you paid for students who don't show up? What if a student is ill? What if a student drops out halfway through the semester? How do you arrange for makeup lessons? It is important to know that, like coaches, additional music personnel often get checks at the end of the semester in one lump sum. This is all right if the money is extra, but if you are counting on some money every two weeks, you (and your mortgage company) don't want to be surprised.

If students are responsible for payment, you should establish a relationship with the parents right away. You may want to offer parents the option of paying weekly, biweekly, monthly or for the semester, or you may settle on a single payment plan that feels comfortable to you.

Develop a policy for missed lessons; the simplest is to require that students pay whether they show up or not. The stricter the policy, the more consistent attendance you enjoy. Offer makeup lessons to students who have a reasonable excuse, but make it the student's responsibility to contact you in advance. Price yourself after finding out what the going rate is. Don't overcharge or you may discourage students; don't undercharge or you may feel resentful and used. Keep very accurate records of payment.

One way to ensure that the music director will dislike you is to have parents trying to get messages through the director to you (especially if they are complicated or angry messages!). To avoid this, give each student, or mail each parent directly, a letter of introduction that includes a phone number where you can be contacted directly. Clearly outline the terms of payment and makeup lesson policy. Ask for and record the name and address of each student's paying parent; remember that Johnny Jones's mother may be Betty Smith. Just as a precaution, you might want to run your letter by whoever hired you, in case there is existing protocol about letters going out from school personnel.

Dressing the part. Working (and keeping a job) in a school in any capacity means playing and dressing the part. While you might rationalize that you only see kids, that it's after school hours, etc., it is always smart to present your best professional self. We are certainly not fashion consultants or image experts, but we can say from experience that it's easier to loosen up once you are respected than it is to draw in the reins once you've let them out too far. If you're comfortable in casual clothing, try to strike a balance. For instance, black jeans topped with a blazer presents a more professional image than blue jeans and a sweatshirt. Especially if you appear young, distinguish yourself from the students with adult accessories (a tie, a scarf, a briefcase). If you're young, spandex is a no-no; if you *think* you're young, spandex is a definite no-no.

Learning the language of schools. Schools are little societies unto themselves, and when you work in them, it's best to understand all the ins and outs.

• Students who take lessons are often involved in band and may have specific pieces they should be working on. You look like a better teacher if the students who are sent to you return with better knowledge of their band pieces. It's a hard balance to strike, but you want to give the students some of what they want and some of what their band directors need them to have (especially if you want the band director to give you more referrals).

• Understand the role of the music department at each school. In some schools, the music department is highly regarded while in others, unfortunately, music is seen as a frill. Investigate the climate before you say too much. This is not a call to indifference, or censorship, but simply a reminder that forewarned is forearmed. You can be very opinionated (as we are) about the importance of music in the school curriculum, but don't be caught by surprise.

• Think about what you want to be called. It's nice to be on a first-name basis with students, but in most systems it sets you apart from other faculty and may mean that you are not taken as seriously.

• Be aware of, though not paralyzed by, our litigious age. Don't touch students; no matter how innocent, touch can be misinterpreted. Don't socialize with students unless their parents are present (at a concert or recital, for instance). Maintain appropriate demeanor with students at all times.

TEACHING IN PRIVATE SCHOOLS

Most issues pertinent to public schools are pertinent to private schools as well. One significant difference is that private schools do not have to hire state-certified personnel, though many prefer to. Therefore, if you are uncertified, you may want to look into private schools. Another difference is that private schools often have *less* money to spend on music than public schools. Because they do not have to meet state or federal standards mandating curriculum, some choose to eliminate music programming altogether, instead counting on parents to secure private music instruction for their children. This situation can create two distinct opportunities for musicians who want to drum up business.

The first strategy in private schools is to promote yourself rigorously and try to generate business through referral. If you have students who go to private school, give them a stack of your cards. At the very least, give your business cards and promotional package to guidance counselors and teachers. Private school parents tend to be involved, and you may get a lot of referrals by asking to speak to a parent group. If you are very motivated, you might want to generate a list of private music teachers to give to private school parents. (Make sure that you are first on the list!)

The second tack, which requires some work ahead of time, is to try to sell yourself to a small private school as a complete music program, on a part-time consultant basis. Covering the cost of a full-time salary plus benefits is very costly, and if you can propose music instruction at a reduced cost to the school, they may take you up on it. Taking grade levels and number of students into consideration, design a limited and workable curriculum; perhaps you can go into the school for one day per week and run two sections of vocal music, an ensemble, and three or four private lessons. You can also offer referral services for students who want lessons on instruments other than your own. (Prepare a list and ask the teachers you put on it to supply you with business cards. With luck, that relationship will be reciprocal and you will gain almost as many referrals as you give out.) You may even end up coordinating lessons with other teachers for students and perhaps taking a small commission.

Some private schools have well-established and prestigious music programs. If you want to get into these music departments, you have to do the same self-promotion that you must do in the public school setting. Get to know the chair of the music department and consider the techniques outlined previously.

TEACHING AT COMMUNITY MUSIC SCHOOLS

Many localities enjoy community music schools, academies or institutes. Sometimes these schools have buildings of their own, and sometimes they meet in community buildings. Some are conglomerations of very good music teachers who have a common method or theory, and some are essentially referral agencies for local private music lesson teachers. If there are such music schools in your area, read the section on working in schools and the section about working in music studios because the situation contains elements of each. In some of these schools, you are a member of a bona fide faculty, and in others you are more like a member of an association of teachers. Both are good situations, and you must either qualify for the association, or apply to the school. Before jumping into any teaching situation, ask around town to find out the school's reputation.

TEACHING LESSONS IN MUSIC STORES AND STUDIOS

Many music lessons take place in the back rooms of music stores and in studios designed for this purpose. Some operations are primarily music stores, with a few lessons being given here and there, and some operations are primarily music studios with ten or twelve practice rooms, with the storefront serving as a small supplier of the necessary accessories. Another way music stores and studios make money is to rent and/or sell instruments to high school band members; when they rent a student a trombone, they try to sell some lessons as well.

The clear advantage of teaching in a store or studio is the number of potential students. Lessons in stores tend to be scheduled every half-hour or hour, served rapid-fire. From right after school through dinner time, you can expect to see six to eight students without a break. For many musicians, stores and studios present a ready opportunity for giving music lessons and for staying in contact with other musicians.

Applying for a Teaching Position in a Store or Studio

Some stores and studios have a "head teacher" to whom you must apply to get a teaching position. In a large store or studio, this head teacher is usually responsible for finding new faculty and for keeping the practice rooms and studios occupied as much as possible. In a small store, the owner/operator usually handles all teachers and scheduling.

When applying for a position in a store or studio, you may have to undergo a very formal interview and audition process, or you may be able to to get to know the owner/operator on an informal basis and get a teaching position that way. (This is also true of community music schools.) The best approach is to be as professional as you can from the start. Make an appointment to talk with the person in charge of hiring, even if the store or studio is not currently hiring, so you can get a sense of the place. At an informal store or studio, they may tell you to stop in anytime, and you may feel a bit stodgy for asking for an appointment, but if they run things formally, you will not have eliminated yourself from the running for being too casual.

Don't try to make friends with the staff of the store and then launch a surprise attack at the end of the conversation by adding, "Oh, by the way . . . I'd like to teach here." Another bad idea is to play one of their instruments, hoping to impress the staff with your incredible skill, then ask for a job. A better and more professional approach is to state your purpose at the beginning ("My name is _____. I'd like to talk to someone about teaching lessons here"). You'll have plenty of time later to showcase your knowledge and play their instruments. Come to the store dressed appropriately and bring an updated resume (see chapter four), references and a demo tape. If the owner/operator can't speak to you, or is trying to rush you out the door, try to find out a less busy time when you can check back, and leave your materials at the store so the owner can look them over.

Follow up the initial meeting. Often you hear from such contacts months later, especially at the start of the school year and right after the holidays when stores and studios are overwhelmed by requests for lessons. The basic lesson in positioning yourself for any employment is that no one faults you for being overprepared. Unfortunately, the converse is not true.

You may encounter a music store that doesn't offer music lessons. In this case, you have the opportunity to convince the owner that it may be profitable to house your teaching business. The benefit for you is that you have a captive audience in the store's clientele; the benefit for the owner is that you are increasing the potential for sales. The more popular your instrument is, the more lucrative the arrangement may be for both of you. Collaboration is the key. Offer to clean out the back room for or with the owner to make room for your equipment. If the owner seems reluctant, offer the arrangement on a trial basis.

Recruiting Students for a Store or Studio

Once you have been accepted as a teacher by a store or studio, the question of getting students may arise. This is not an issue if the store hired you because they have a waiting list of students who need lessons. There may not be a list, however, and you may be the one in a waiting position at first. If the store or studio advertises through radio or print media and mentions that lessons are available, you benefit from their advertising. Without being pushy, encourage the store to advertise in school papers and community "free presses," and publicize the fact that you teach there by telling everyone you know. You win points when a student comes to the counter asking specifically, "I want to take lessons with Bob Smith, and I know he works here."

It is important to display your versatility to gain referrals. One guitar teacher we know also teaches bass, banjo and mandolin lessons, thereby positioning himself to receive a great many more students than the instructor who plays only one instrument. Within the store, be generous with referrals to people outside of your instrument. The next time someone says, "I always wished I could take piano lessons," you can respond by saying, "There's a woman who teaches piano in the next studio over from me at the store, and she's great with adult learners. Let me write down her name for you." Having given out hundreds of referrals, we can say that what goes around eventually comes around.

Scheduling Students

Once recruited, students in stores usually are scheduled in one of two ways. The first is that the store gets calls for lessons, and schedules teachers accordingly. You might have some say about which days you want to give lessons, but the store is responsible for scheduling you and may also be responsible for securing payment from the student. After taking some percentage for administration and space rental, the store or studio pays you the remainder. In a very small neighborhood music store there may be two people working at any given time, one staffing the counter and one giving a lesson and the two may switch off.

The second way students are scheduled gives you more control. Interested students call the store for lessons, then you are given the potential student's phone number and the scheduling responsibility. In some cases, the private lesson teacher is responsible for securing payment from the student and then paying a percentage per student (often expressed in terms of "rent") to the store or studio. (For tax purposes, keep track of the rent you pay—see chapter nine.) With some arrangements you can rent one studio space on a monthly basis and it becomes *yours*. The benefit to this is convenience; you can personalize the studio space and can keep lesson materials and an instrument there. If you teach a lot of lessons, monthly rental agreements are usually a good idea, since they cost less and give you greater convenience.

Establishing a Fee Structure

The fees for lessons and the percentage you must pay the store may be established by the store. Some places charge a flat fee per student. Never try to squeeze more out of a student than the going rate. If you get caught, you'll probably be fired. If you discover that it's not worth your while to teach there at the going rate and that you're becoming frustrated and tempted to surreptitiously raise your rates, think about changing venues; or, if you think it's worth the risk, speak to the owner/operator.

In other situations, you are responsible for setting your own fees, but you must still pay a flat fee to the store for rent. In this case, make sure that you cover your own costs. On the other hand, you don't want to price yourself out of range. Consider the average income of people in your area, your experience and education, and the rates of your competitors. Fee structure options are discussed at length in chapter three. An easy way to manage payment is to charge your students the way the store or studio charges you. If the store requires payment by the month, charge students by the month as well, thereby reducing your financial busywork.

Generally, teaching lessons in a store or studio is a great "gig." The only consideration is whether you could do better giving the lessons on your own. Some stores take such a significant chunk from your pay that it may be better to try to give the lessons elsewhere, if you have the promotional energy, space and inclination. If you don't feel like drumming up the business yourself, however, working in a store can cut out that part of the work for you, providing you with an invaluable service.

Commissions, Endorsements, and Encouraging Students to Buy

Sometimes music teachers in a store are responsibile for trying to get students to buy things there. Clarify your role early on. It helps you and the store if they already stock products you feel you can recommend to your students. It won't be looked upon too kindly if you are always sending your students elsewhere to buy competitors' products. If you are partial to a particular method book or series, for instance, and the store doesn't carry it, try to convince the owner/operator to order it. You do yourself, the store and your students a favor when they can do "one-stop" shopping at the store or studio. Try to strike a balance so you can give the store some business while maintaining your integrity.

In this age of endorsements, some stores carry one line of instruments exclusively and try to encourage their students (either directly or indirectly) to purchase these products. Think through whether you are willing to endorse the products sold at the store. In some stores the arrangement is really very explicit, and you may be lent an instrument from this line on which to teach. If part of your job is to encourage students to buy from this line of merchandise, find out if you will receive a commission.

Leaving a Store or Studio

Most stores and studios have clear contracts about what happens when you leave. Generally, since students came to the *studio* for lessons (and not to you personally), you are not permitted to take the students with you when you leave. Some stores and studios require that you sign a contract when you first start working there stipulating that you will not teach any lessons to students you encountered there for at least one year after you leave the store. At the time you start, you may not give this arrangement any thought, but when you are about to leave, you discover what a difficult position this puts you in and how delicately it must be handled.

When you decide to leave a store or studio, do not take on any new students who are referred to you through the store; refer them to other teachers there. Especially if you are trying to build up an at-home teaching business, be very clear about referring students to the store. Assure the owner/operator that you are doing your own promotion outside the store or studio. If you have a student who has been with you for a long time and who refuses to take lessons with anyone else, you have to work with the student and your conscience to hammer out some suitable arrangement.

Working the Counter; Counting on Work

Another way to make the break into a music store or studio is to work there as a salesperson. In some cases, you might be able to teach lessons part time and work the counter part time. If you are interested in teaching lessons at a store or studio, and you are offered a counter position as a consolation prize, it is wise to state your wants explicitly. You could tell the proprietor, "I'd like to work here, but I'd really like the opportunity to teach some lessons sometime in the near future." Too many very good musicians are frustrated by having to hand out guitar picks all day.

On the positive side, working the counter in a store or studio can provide very good work experience as you get to know the products and the people who frequent the store. As you establish yourself, you may indeed get the opportunity to teach lessons. If you are a performing musician, it is very likely that you can pick up jobs with other staff members, as well as get to know other musicians who are working in the area. Most music stores and studios have a bulletin board of bands who are seeking additional members, local club performances, etc., so you have your finger on the musical pulse of the local area. Another plus is that you have hundreds, maybe thousands, of new and used musical instruments at your disposal from which you can learn a great deal. If you simply enjoy being in and around music and musicians all the time, working in a store or a studio is for you.

Using Your Discount Wisely

One obvious benefit of working in a music store or studio is that you often are given a discount on products from the store. Here are a few points to remember so that if you have a discount, it remains a benefit and not a liability.

- Limit your purchases. Unless you plan on working in a store simply to add to your collection of instruments and accessories, don't spend your entire paycheck on new equipment. It's like not having a job at all. Even with 10 to 30 percent off, something you don't need is still something you don't need, and buying it is no bargain.
- Assess your musical equipment needs without regard to your discount. Then assess whether buying something with the discount is really the best bet. Consider brand, price, condition, etc. For instance, if you need a keyboard, but it doesn't have to be the latest technology, you might be able to get a much better deal on a used one than on a new one by using your discount.
- Don't transfer your discount privileges to anyone. It's always tempting to pass along a good deal, but most stores have clear rules about playing middleman with your discount, and if you are caught you may be reprimanded or fired. If you just make a rule that you won't do it for anyone, you won't have to agonize over the decision each time someone asks you (which, by the way, students, parents and friends will).
- Buy your basic equipment in bulk, at discount prices. If your store carries what you like to use, buy in bulk anything that doesn't deteriorate too much over time. Manuscript paper, valve oil, picks, strings, reeds, books, sheet music and music stands are all wise uses of a discount.
- Use your discount to make your life easier. If you've always wanted a second instrument to keep in another location, or to travel with, maybe your discount will finally let you do it.
- Use your discount to promote music in your family. You can wrap up the holidays with gifts from a music store. Give a favorite niece or nephew a musical instrument and you've started another musician on the way.

TAKING YOUR SHOW ON THE ROAD

Because people's lives are so busy these days and they are protective of their time at home, teaching lessons at students' homes is becoming big business. You can capitalize on the changing times by taking your show on the road. But before taking this leap, consider the geographical area you hope to cover to see if it is feasible.

You recruit for lessons in students' homes much the same way you do for private lessons in your own home (see chapters four and nine). After speaking with the parent or student on the phone, send any promotional package you have. If you have anything with your picture on it, send it along, since people feel more comfortable if they recognize you when they first open the door.

Because you are bringing a lesson to the student, you can charge a little more for that convenience. One positive aspect of teaching at a student's home is that you meet with the parent every time and can secure payment at the time of the lesson, either on a weekly, biweekly or monthly schedule. As a general rule, you should not teach children in their homes when a parent is not present. It sets you up to be responsible for a lot more than a music lesson.

Meeting Students and Parents on Their Own Turf

While at first it is intimdating to teach on someone else's turf, you are providing a much-needed service to busy families and your effort is appreciated. When first meeting with parents, present yourself as professionally as possible. Not only are these parents trusting you with their child, they are letting a complete stranger into their house. Expect a few awkward moments initially as they introduce you to the student, apologize for the mess, keep the huge dog from pawing you to death, and finally ask you where you want to teach (unless you teach piano, in which case they will lead you there). Ideally, you want to teach in a common room on the main floor that doesn't get too much traffic (avoid students' bedrooms). Dining rooms, recreation rooms, living rooms, dens and family rooms are good. It is psychologically important for you to give the lesson in the physical location where the student practices, thereby carving out a "music space" in the house. Doors should remain at least ajar unless the parent requests that they be closed.

Being on the student's turf has both benefits and drawbacks. On the pro side, parents feel comforted because they can watch you and their child interact and can feel they are keeping him or her safe. In addition, when parents are nearby they may glean some of what is required for practice and be able to remind their children what is expected. Some teachers like to call the parent in at the end of every lesson for a minirecital and a once-over of what should be practiced during the coming week. (This is good idea for young children, the kiss of death for teenagers.)

Most parents assure you that they won't interrupt the lesson, but you should tell them they're welcome to come in anytime. The same is not true for siblings, who tend to make faces. If you are teaching adults, try to discourage their children from sitting in, as they are extremely distracting.

Now for the drawbacks. Small children, especially, are often distracted when they are in familiar surroundings. Bear this in mind from the beginning and use specific techniques to hold their attention (see chapter five). Encourage the parent to create a "working" atmosphere when you are there, so the child is not missing out on anything else. Perhaps other siblings can be outside or upstairs doing homework. With teenagers, make some firm suggestions that they should not take any calls while you are there. Televisions should be off, pets kept in other rooms, and distractions kept to a minimum. Talk promptly with the parents about any problems or distractions that arise. Because the parents are there, in all likelihood staring at their kitchen clocks, make sure you start and end on time, giving the student his or her money's worth.

Bringing Materials With You

If your car is to be your office, plan how to organize your materials so that when you use the trunk of your car for other purposes, you don't lose what little organization you've found. Keep often-used handouts and method books in a file box (milk crates work well) and extra supplies in another box (see Example 1-1).

During lessons, use an individual student folder to jot down things you want to bring for next week. Then, at some set time every week, fill the folders with the supplemental materials you've promised. It looks sloppy if you consistently say, "Oh, I forgot to get you that piece we talked about last week." Set up a procedure that you follow every week so it becomes automatic.

Since you travel to the student, you may want to provide a "store" of very basic supplies that students can buy from you at your cost. For horn players that may mean keeping a supply of valve oil, for guitar players having a stash of strings and picks. If you use one method book or series consistently, have a few of those on hand, to save students

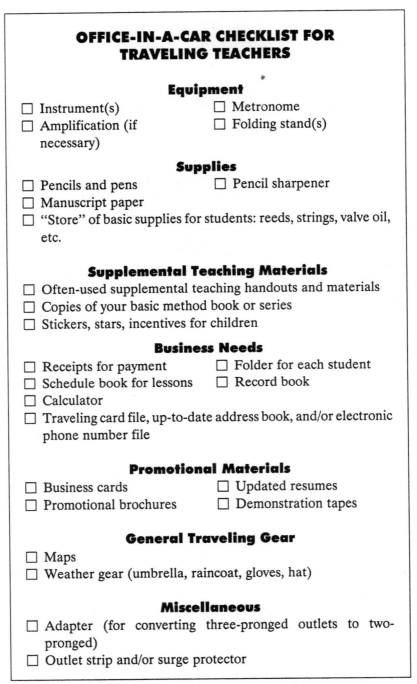

OFFICE-IN-A-CAR CHECKLIST FOR TRAVELING TEACHERS

Equipment

- [ ] Instrument(s)
- [ ] Amplification (if necessary)
- [ ] Metronome
- [ ] Folding stand(s)

Supplies

- [ ] Pencils and pens
- [ ] Manuscript paper
- [ ] Pencil sharpener
- [ ] "Store" of basic supplies for students: reeds, strings, valve oil, etc.

Supplemental Teaching Materials

- [ ] Often-used supplemental teaching handouts and materials
- [ ] Copies of your basic method book or series
- [ ] Stickers, stars, incentives for children

Business Needs

- [ ] Receipts for payment
- [ ] Schedule book for lessons
- [ ] Calculator
- [ ] Folder for each student
- [ ] Record book
- [ ] Traveling card file, up-to-date address book, and/or electronic phone number file

Promotional Materials

- [ ] Business cards
- [ ] Promotional brochures
- [ ] Updated resumes
- [ ] Demonstration tapes

General Traveling Gear

- [ ] Maps
- [ ] Weather gear (umbrella, raincoat, gloves, hat)

Miscellaneous

- [ ] Adapter (for converting three-pronged outlets to two-pronged)
- [ ] Outlet strip and/or surge protector

Example 1-1. Office-in-a-Car Checklist for Traveling Teachers and parents a trip to the music store. You may also offer to pick up other supplies for students, if you have easy access to a music store.

Other Traveling Options

When you decide to travel, other options arise. One teacher we know started giving one student piano lessons at the student's home. After a while, several of the student's neighborhood friends wanted to take lessons as well. Since they lived in a fairly rural area, this teacher worked out a deal with the original student to give her lessons at reduced cost in exchange for the space to teach the other students. In this case, what began as one lesson became an entire afternoon's worth.

Entertain the possibility of group or family lessons. Particularly in difficult economic times, families may jump at the option of having two children take lessons for a reduced fee. Think about lumping together lessons at large apartment complexes, condominium developments and neighborhoods. Don't forget retirement communities, since many retirees are finally enjoying enough leisure time to take the music lessons they've always wanted.

TEACHING AT COLLEGES AND UNIVERSITIES

Getting onto a college teaching faculty is almost always done by interview and audition, even for a position teaching private lessons. Because the requirements may be more stringent than in high schools, take an honest look at your experience and education before applying. Most colleges want at minimum a bachelor's degree in music and extensive performance experience, and most prefer a master's degree. However, you never know who else will apply, so even if you don't have these qualifications, and you are willing to risk rejection, send your materials anyway. The worst they can say is no.

College Interviews and Auditions

If you plan to apply for a college position, expect to be interviewed and perhaps auditioned by the chair of the music department. (In a music college, you will be interviewed/auditioned by the chair of your particular instrument's department.) Be sure to bring all your updated materials with you, and make sure they are impeccable. An otherwise qualified musician will not make the cut if there are misspellings or omissions in his or her resume. In some cases the dean or a committee makes the final decision.

If you are hired as a mainstream faculty member, you may be responsible for teaching any number of music courses, from basic appreciation for non-music majors, to sight-reading, ear training, etc. What you teach is similar to whatever you learned in your own college music program. When you are new on a faculty, you usually teach whatever course is hated the most. You might be called upon to serve on juries for admission, placement or scholarship recipients, and you may have some hand in conducting, rehearsing or directing various ensembles.

Teaching Lessons at the College Level

As in high schools, if you are hired to teach private lessons, you may be paid by the school per student or per credit hour. You may be considered a bona fide part-time faculty member, or the college may have less concrete ties with the "lesson faculty" — and you may feel that subtle separation. In some cases the students are responsible for paying you while in others the school pays the private lesson teacher for a limited number of students to take lessons for credit. Usually, you are responsible for auditioning the pool of applicants and deciding who can take the lessons for credit. The remaining students may simply be out of luck, or the school may allow you to give lessons there on your own schedule without granting credit. As in high school teaching, find out right away what proficiency examinations and evaluations your students are headed for and tailor your lessons so your students are prepared. Find out when grades are due and what the procedures are for submitting them.

College music students tend to be highly motivated, skilled people. Some of them may have earned music scholarships. Even at big schools, music departments tend to be fairly insular — everyone knows everyone because they are in some ensemble or band together — so it is easy to feel overwhelmed or "out of it" when you first land such a position. Be open and innovative. Try to work on projects with other faculty members, to avoid isolation and its companions, self-doubt and/or grandiosity. Being connected with a college faculty can offer some incredible performance opportunities with other faculty, guest artists, or your own performing ensemble. These performances help increase your visibility within the department.

Teaching at Community Colleges

Some community colleges offer music courses for credit and may not have as difficult employment requirements as universities. Community college programming often is a combination of adult education (offering some percentage of classes in the evening) and traditional college curriculum. As in other settings, you may be able to teach private lessons or a music course or two, depending on their needs. Many community colleges offer group lessons.

TEACHING AT COMMUNITY-BASED PROGRAMS

In your search for suitable teaching opportunities, don't overlook the variety of programs in your community. These programs may not even know how badly they need you until you tell them! Although the program itself might not be able to "hire" you on a long-term basis, and you might have to volunteer your time initially, you may get access to potential students and increase your visibility. Think about tapping the following community-based programs and others not mentioned here.

• Adult education programs are always looking for teachers to teach "enrichment" classes and group lessons. Think about offering a "listening series" or "music appreciation" course and a couple of group lessons. Sometimes adult education programs offer such courses in their brochures and note which ones fill up. You are always better off to suggest a few classes, so if enrollment is thin you can try to get students to take another of your courses as a second choice.

• YMCA and YWCA run any number of programs for youth, men, women and senior citizens. Though many people associate "the Y" with physical exercise, these organizations offer ever-widening programming. You could become part of an after-school program, handle one lecture in a stress management series (Music and Stress Reduction), or simply post your promotional materials on their community bulletin board.

• Think about local youth programming: Boys' and Girls' Clubs, Boy Scouts, Girl Scouts and after-school or latchkey programs.

TEACHING OPPORTUNITIES AT PRESCHOOLS, DAY CARES AND KINDERGARTENS

When you work with very small children, "teaching" is a word used loosely. Not that there isn't learning going on, but little ones generally don't let you proceed on the path you so carefully worked out prior to your arrival.

There are a couple of distinct opportunities for musicians in day cares and kindergartens. The first is simply to come in once a week or so for a music "class" for the kids. Some preschool and kindergarten teachers are music phobic and appreciate a small break once in a while. Money for such services may be nominal, but they can open up the second opportunity: You may be able to promote private lessons, particularly if the parents are relatively affluent.

Here are a few points to remember when you work with groups of small children:

• Bring an instrument that you don't mind having to wipe down later. Little children want to get "up close and personal" with whatever instrument you bring. So bring your "second string" instruments and let the kids (gently) paw them to their hearts content. They also want to get close to you. Don't be surprised if a child plops down in your lap.

• Little children do not sit still or stay quiet. Expect interruptions and diversions.

• Plan several five- or ten-minute activities rather than one that lasts a half hour: counting with a metronome, clapping, singing one song, dancing to another, listening (for a minute) to several different instruments, telling a story using musical "sound effects," and making musical instruments out of everyday objects.

TEACHING AT SUMMER MUSIC CAMPS

Because summer vacations can be so disruptive to your teaching schedule, it may be more work to hold your schedule together during summer months than it's worth. If you have a consistent clientele that is basically unaffected by school and summer vacations, then by all means adjust your schedule accordingly and deal with the minor rescheduling hassles that occur during these periods. One option is to consolidate your teaching. If you teach three afternoon/evenings during the school year, maybe you could move all your students to one full day. (School-aged students who continue during summer months can often fill those hard-to-schedule morning hours.)

If you do cancel or cut back your lessons over the summer, consider teaching at summer camps. Many camps are delighted to include a music teacher on their staff to lead fireside choirs and assist with musicals and other camp activities. Although at small camps you may have to double as a lifeguard or rowing instructor, larger camps may hire a full-time music instructor.

A minimum knowledge of guitar is an absolute prerequisite—it's difficult to lead the camp in "Home on the Range" while playing the oboe. Most trained musicians can learn a few basic chords on the guitar in a few short lessons, so don't let this discourage you from what could be a very rewarding experience.

Remember that most camps are in isolated regions and require that you reside there for the duration of the program. The change of scenery and lifestyle can be stimulating and life-affirming for most. If you are a city-dweller with a fear of raccoons and large insects, however, you may want to consider a specialized summer music program.

Specialized summer music programs have become more and more popular in recent years. Many are housed on private school and college campuses. Some run for a few days while others may run the entire summer. Certain camps are offered for a specific instrument while others are open to all band instruments. Well-known artists sometimes offer special courses or master classes.

Most music camps require an endless amount of energy. Classes usually run from breakfast to dinner with rehearsals, ensembles and concerts scheduled well into the late night hours. The pace is demanding but the rewards are often well worth the effort. You may have the opportunity to meet (and perform with) great visiting artists. You can network with many excellent teachers who give you insights into teaching methods, promotion, student recruitment and performing. Most of all, you are exposed to a population of dedicated, open-minded and serious young musicians who benefit from your expertise.

Most summer camps are advertised in magazines. If you are specifically interested in music camps, check music magazines such as *Guitar Player* or *Modern Drummer* that target younger musicians. Once you've found a camp that interests you, send a resume and promotional package to the director. Be sure your demo tape contains music representative of the style taught at the camp.

SOME FINAL WORDS ABOUT FINDING PLACES TO TEACH

If you want to teach music, we can assure you from experience that there are many places to do it. Generally, when people think about teaching music, they consider only one place to do it—such as a public school, a college or a teaching studio. Limit your thinking this way, and you limit your teaching potential. Instead, consider all the options and make inroads in each. By doing this, you reach the potential students. Combine these efforts with the proper marketing, promotions and teaching skills, and you'll be on your way to making teaching music a full-time, lucrative profession.

CHAPTER TWO

TEACHING AT HOME— SOME THINGS TO CONSIDER

W hen you are a successful professional teaching musician, it is bad enough that you may spend several nights every week performing in a club or traveling to private engagements. Add lessons during the afternoons and evenings and you may find yourself away from home for as many as six or even seven nights per week. At this point many teachers give up and become nine-to-five computer technicians or telephone operators. If you find that, all other musical frustrations aside, you are simply tired of being away from home, you may want to consider changing your promotional material to read "lessons in your home or mine."

Making the decision to teach in your home, however, is not quite as simple as changing your promotional materials. It is a matter of changing your mind-set a bit. When you take the leap into teaching at home, your livelihood truly becomes a family affair. Unless you live alone, it means sharing your place of business with others, and that can mean difficulties with overlapping roles. It is important to establish clear rules for your business, family and social responsibilities, for your own sake as well as for those who live with you.

MAXIMIZING THE BENEFITS OF WORKING AT HOME

Very few people are lucky enough to wake up every morning looking forward to going to work. But you can be one of them if you do your work at home. While teaching at home has a few minor drawbacks, they can definitely be outweighed by the benefits. Obvious financial incentives, such as reduced travel, mean reduced wear and tear on your automobile or less bus or subway travel. Eating meals at home cuts down on expenses too, especially if you eat out while on the road.

If a student cancels a lesson at your home, the unexpected time off allows you to take care of family business, make business calls, or relax in a familiar setting. Even while you are working, your family feels that you are "at home." The fact that you can't be disturbed because you are with a student does not diminish the feeling that you are home and therefore safe and part of the family. Working at home, you feel that you are in touch with what is happening in the lives of your family members.

Most important for your teaching, being at home in your own studio or teaching space gives you the advantage of easy access to your materials, recordings, equipment, etc. When you're on the road you may only be able to bring the bare essentials. At home all your trappings are at your fingertips, making you a much more effective teacher. And, perhaps best of all, you have the freedom to create an environment that truly reflects you as a teacher. You can create a space, an atmosphere and a teaching style that showcase your musical interests and skills to their fullest. This freedom ensures that you are more relaxed and confident in your approach and this is reflected in the enthusiasm you bring to each lesson.

Creating a Workweek Around Your Rhythm

If you teach at a studio or school, your schedule often depends on what studio or classroom time is free. Most teaching studios expect you to be available to teach whenever they have times or studio space available, not necessarily when it is convenient for you. This can obviously pose serious problems or even prove impossible if you are trying to balance your teaching career with other careers or activities. In general, if you are teaching for someone else then you lose a lot of flexibility.

Teaching at home frees you to choose your own hours based on your rhythm and weekly commitments. You can maintain your regular band rehearsals, take your children to swimming lessons, and teach on the evenings that *you* are free. (You can even decide *which* evenings you are free!) You can get home from your day job and begin teaching after you have had time to eat and relax.

Establish a schedule that best fits your style. Early in your teaching career, the temptation is to schedule every student you can into every available nook and cranny of time, from the retiree who wants to meet at 7:00 A.M. to the rocker who wants a lesson just before he hits the club at 11:30 at night. Take it from ones who know: When you have the student base to do it, choose your teaching times carefully. It doesn't benefit you at all to have students traipsing into your house when you are unprepared for them or at any time that makes your family feel invaded. If you don't function well in morning hours, wait until after lunch to begin your workday. If you have children who attend school, then use the morning hours for teaching and give your children your full attention during after-school or evening hours.

Remember, though, that when you limit your teaching to specific hours, you limit the pool of prospective students. Not all students are free during the hours or days you choose to teach. If you have decided that this is how and when you would like to commit to teaching, however, then we are confident that by employing the methods we suggest for advertising and promoting yourself, you will have little trouble filling your home schedule. If you are uncertain what your own rhythm is, try scheduling several days differently to determine which works best for you.

Teaching at home allows you to feel more positive about scheduling breaks in your teaching day because you are not left hanging around some studio with nothing to do. For instance, if you are commuting several hours to teach at a college, you may schedule lessons straight through from early morning to lunchtime, take a half-hour break, then resume teaching until dinner. Finally, you drive home and gobble down a sandwich, fries and a shake from Burger World. While this may be a lucrative and busy day of teaching, it isn't the best routine for your arteries or your peace of mind. Do this over and over again, and the wear and tear starts to show.

Being at home allows you to set a more relaxed pace for your daily teaching. Because you avoid many miles of travel you can schedule longer, more frequent breaks to ensure that you can eat, relax, and still be fresh by evening's end. Scheduling small breaks is a wonderful way to relieve the stress of teaching many back-to-back lessons. You can schedule a short break after every three or four lessons. This gives you the freedom to have a lesson go longer than usual without "running behind" for the entire day. If you have no scheduled breaks, then running over even a couple of minutes each lesson can put you off schedule for the rest of the day. Knowing that you can get caught up and back on schedule after your scheduled break makes your teaching go much more smoothly.

You could do as many therapists do and schedule fifty-minute "hours." That way you can give yourself a little time between lessons to make notes, catch your breath, grab a quick snack, and be ready for your next student. We find it best to have lessons start on the hour or half hour, and end fifty minutes later. If you ask students to come at 5:10, they interpret that as 5:15 or, knowing you're free at five, they come early to chat.

Being Your Own Boss

Whether you are out recruiting students, making contacts, going to an interview or teaching, you should maintain a professional look at all times. If you are trying to sell yourself as a professional music teacher and a respected member of the community, then dress and act the part at all times. You never know who you will run into while out in public. Unfortunately even a trip to the grocery store or to the post office can turn into a business trip if you meet a prospective student or the parent of a current one. (Super Bowl Sunday might be the one day you can hit the supermarket for chips 'n' dip in your sweatpants and sneakers.)

If you were employed as an instructor in a school or studio, you would be representing someone else's interest. Since your appearance would reflect upon your employer's reputation, you might be asked to adhere to a dress code. As a self-employed teacher working out of your own home, you are your own boss and can set your own code of dress, conduct, etc. So while you may dress in a suit and tie to travel to a private school or university to teach, you may kick back in jeans and a tee shirt as you invite your students into your home for lessons. This is not to say that you should not consider dressing professionally when teaching at home. Certainly a new student or parent of a new student judges you as if you were teaching for someone else. Greeting a new student in sweat pants and a Beavis and Butt-head tee shirt is probably not a good idea. You want to dress to impress whenever you are dealing with new clients. If you have an established clientele and have gained their respect through your teaching skills, however, then they won't care if they show up to your home and you are dressed casually. It may even help your students relax if they see you more relaxed.

Remember also that when you teach in a studio, the students' first impressions of you are based almost entirely on your appearance and manner. Dressing respectably, acting confident, and carrying yourself in a professional manner directly influence your students' initial perceptions of you. When you teach at home, the student is influenced not only by your appearance but also by your environment. Your house, and especially your studio, tells the student a great deal about who you are as a teacher. This relieves some of the need to dress the part because you are in a place that constantly reflects who you are as a person. You have the freedom to let down your hair a bit and to fall into a more relaxed routine.

WORKING IT OUT WITH YOUR SPOUSE AND FAMILY

For your home teaching business to be a success, you need the cooperation of everyone involved in the home. Every time the phone rings or someone steps into your home, how your family reacts can determine the effectiveness of your business. Only with the encouragement and the complete cooperation of these people can your home business succeed. Be thorough and complete in letting your family know how your business affects every aspect of family life. Take the time to discuss what this means with everyone involved and be patient in getting everyone coordinated and working toward the same end.

Making Room for Your Music

Make sure that the space you use to teach is one that can be spared or easily shared with the family. If you teach in the dining room, what happens at dinner time? Does your family have to eat in the kitchen or in the living room? Is that all right with them? Do you have to break down your studio every time you have people over to dinner? If you use the guest bedroom for your teaching, how will this affect your business when your mother-in-law visits? Do you foresee constant tension because one family member wants to have guests over more often than others? If these situations seem workable, then go for it. If they seem unreasonable, then consider alternatives right from the start. (Forcing your mother-in-law to sleep in the garage may not be the best alternative.)

We encourage you to create a permanent space in your home that is designated as your studio and does not double as anything else. That way you can really personalize the space without worrying about having to "strike the set" when you need to entertain or when someone comes over to stay. It also helps your family understand what is business and what isn't. The ideal situation is to have a separate room on the first floor close to an entrance, so students don't have to trudge through your living space. However, terrific studios have been fashioned out of far less than ideal situations. Some basements, garages, guest rooms, dining rooms, dens, breakfast nooks, etc., have made terrific studios. Another possibility is to visually "split" a larger room using tall bookcases, furniture or screens to create a smaller semiprivate space for lesson-giving. It also depends, of course, on the instrument you teach. Pianos, harps and drums command their own space, while horns and woodwinds require very little. Even with a smaller instrument, we'd hate to see you using the kitchen sink as a music stand.

Having your own space also reduces the possibility of resentment from family members. It is like having your own room when you were a teenager: You could always shut the door so you didn't have to deal with your parents, and they didn't have to deal with the mess.

Consider how much your business actually intrudes in the home. If you teach only on Saturday mornings when the family is at basketball practice, then the impact may go relatively unnoticed. (Except for the added cash, of course.) If you teach fifty students throughout the week, then the impact is considerable. Determine the amount of time you can devote to teaching with your family's needs in mind. For instance, if you have a newborn baby then teaching late into the evening might not work too well.

Discuss your plans with your family and be flexible, considering their concerns and needs at all times. If it is impossible to have both business and family under one roof then business has to move. It should not be necessary to make a choice, however. If the right balance is achieved, you can teach in your home studio and still meet all your family responsibilities.

How to Leave Work When It Is Always There

For most people who work outside the home, the mere act of leaving an office or work space and traveling home allows them the mental separation they need from their work. They can leave the worry, trouble and stress associated with work behind. When your work space is in your home that separation is often very difficult.

It may take time, but it is important to establish methods for leaving work in your studio and not let it carry over into your family. For most self-employed people this is difficult because it can seem that you are always "on the job"—networking, taking calls, or doing advertising/promotion of one sort or another. This is compounded when your business is under the same roof as your family.

Keeping Work Time and Family Time Separate

One method for leaving your work behind is to have specific times for family that are completely uninterrupted by work. It may be as simple as not taking phone calls in the morning while you prepare for the day ahead. This allows for family responsibilities to remain consistent. If getting the children ready for school is passed to your spouse each day because you get business calls each morning, then resentment may begin to creep into your family life. Let the answering machine take the calls and you can return them after the children have left for school. This gives you and your spouse equal time with the responsibilities and gives you important time with your children. Some families try to eat dinner together every evening. Even if you have lessons in the early evening, you might consistently reserve one hour per evening to eat with your family. We suggest not taking calls during this time either.

You can facilitate this system by giving students specific rules with regards to your home/personal life. You can specify hours during which you accept calls. While it is important to give students extra time when they have special problems or questions, it should not interrupt other lesson times or your family time. Set up times when students can call with questions the same way you would have office hours at a college or university. You don't need to sound rigid about this either. Simply say, "Call anytime with questions. There are times during the day when I can't take calls, but leave a message and I'll get back to you."

Put the same emphasis on family time that you do on teaching time. If someone calls during a student's lesson you may either not take the call or else briefly explain that you can't talk now and reach the caller later. If you give similar consideration to your family time, then students learn to respect the boundaries you've established. You are actually more likely to stretch those boundaries than students are. Except in extreme circumstances, resist the urge to compromise "just this once." If you don't, soon you are scheduling students through dinnertime every night.

Decide What Space Is Private and What Is for Business

Decide early on which area or areas are included as part of your business and which are exclusively private space. Set down clearly defined rules and have all members of the family adhere to them religiously.

If students use your washroom, be sure to work out specific rules with your family. If you have two bathrooms, assign one to students and one to family members during your teaching hours. If only one room is available and your children are too young to understand privacy, be sure to have a good lock on the door to avoid embarrassing moments for students. It's just good sense to keep the washroom clean, keep private toiletries in cabinets, and keep the laundry in a hamper instead of in a pile on the floor.

If students use a common area like the living room or front hall or foyer for a waiting space, then decide whether this area is to be shared with your family or to be used exclusively by your students. Having alternate space for your family to "live" in may avoid conflicts between family and students. Creating a basement family room with an additional television or play area gives family members the privacy they need without forcing your students to wait outside in the inclement weather.

Cleanliness as a Business Proposition

Once you decide to do home teaching, your home becomes more than just your humble abode. The general appearance of your entire home now reflects on your business. It does little good to have a state-of-the-art teaching space in pristine condition if students must wait in a living room strewn with dirty laundry and last night's dinner plates. An important part of your business is having your home in a condition that reflects positively on your teaching reputation.

It may not be necessary to maintain a spotless home twenty-four hours a day to succeed as a home instructor. It is a good idea, however, to clear a path of general cleanliness in those areas that are exposed to students. If your studio has a separate entrance and waiting area, then it is your job to keep those spaces clean and tidy. If your studio is within your living space and students are waiting in your living room, passing through your hallways, or using your washroom, then cleanliness is an important part of your business presentation.

If you are not prone to consistent (or compulsive) cleaning, carefully consider the alternatives. One alternative is not to worry about it and let your true colors show, but this reflects poorly on you and your business. The second alternative is to leave the housecleaning to your spouse or other family members. Tread carefully, however, because housework is a sensitive issue in many homes. Constant cleaning for *your* business might not go over too well with those doing the chores. Avoid putting additional stress in your relationships over responsibilities that really belong to you. If you truly cannot deal with the cleaning tasks, consider hiring a professional to maintain the cleanliness of this business/home space. (If it is only for your business space, the cost may be deductible; check with your tax professional.) You may find setting up a barter situation with one of your students a reasonable solution to this dilemma (see chapter nine).

How to Handle Mealtimes

Mealtimes can be difficult for any family. The days of the entire family sitting down for the evening meal together may be just a memory from "Leave it to Beaver." Dinnertime can be important family time and you may consider working your schedule to accommodate this evening activity with your family.

The hardest decision may be whether or not to give up prime teaching time in the evening. Most of your teaching may take place between 3 P.M. and 9 P.M., and to forfeit an hour each night might take a considerable bite out of your weekly earnings. Still, it is important to maintain a sense of family, so consider taking a scheduled evening break to eat dinner with your family.

Besides, teaching straight through the evening from three to nine o'clock without a break can really put some stress into your life. Scheduling a break helps you feel refreshed and prepared for every student. Otherwise by evening's end you may be without energy, humor or patience and those students scheduled later in the evening can suffer.

So why not schedule an hour off at dinnertime and have the break serve a dual purpose? It gives you the respite you need to remain fresh for the rest of your students and it also affords you the chance to spend some important quality time with your family. Establishing this routine certainly helps the stability of your family and directly influences your abilities as a strong, supportive teacher as well.

Your Family's Role in Your In-Home Music Business

Having your home invaded by students is something that undoubtedly affects your family members. Including your family in the responsibilities of your business adds to the positive natures of your family *and* your teaching business. Working together ensures a smooth operation as your family and teaching roles overlap. *Not* working together adds stress to your family life and often negatively affects your business.

Teaching your family to represent your business benefits you in big ways. Whether it is answering the door or the phone, welcoming students into your home, or conversing with them on their way out the door, a positive experience in your home includes more than just what goes on inside your teaching studio.

On the other hand, if you don't return phone messages or if a student trips on toy trucks and cars while traversing your living room, then no matter how effective a teacher you may be, that student's impression of you as a teacher may be clouded. Encourage, train and rely on your family members to be extensions of your personality when it comes to business in the home. Answering calls, taking messages, greeting and welcoming students, and making each student feel comfortable, well liked and important are all elements of a well-rounded home-teaching business.

Answering the phone and door and taking messages. If you have a separate business phone, you can let an answering machine or business secretary take calls when you are not available. You can leave specific information about when you will be available to take or return calls. If you are expecting a call, you can leave a message pertinent to that particular caller. If you are doing business on your home phone number, however, your family must realize the importance of the business calls.

If your children answer the phone and the door in the normal course of their daily lives, then the common courtesy you teach them should carry over to their dealings with your students. You may need to supplement how they handle normal calls and visitors to fit the specific needs of your business dealings.

It is crucial for you to return all calls received when you are away. If you also teach away from home, it may be difficult for students and others to reach you at home. Be certain that all calls are noted and that any messages are relayed to you quickly and accurately. Many people don't leave a message unless one is solicited, so be certain that family members ask each caller if they would like to leave a message. At the very least they should try to get the caller's name, phone number, and the best time for you to return their call. Always inform your family of your schedule so they can let the caller know when you will return home should they care to call back. Knowing the nature of the call is helpful too. Does the caller want information about lessons? Do they need to tell you they can't make their lesson?

Because of the society in which we live, it is important to teach your children what information they should and should not give out over the phone. You may want them to say that you are unable to come to the phone at this time as opposed to letting people know that you are not at home. Be careful about giving people too much information without first ascertaining their true motives. Ninety-nine percent of the people you deal with are honestly interested in taking lessons. The one percent who are interested in less honest pursuits should not occupy your thoughts constantly but should not be overlooked completely either.

Is your spouse your secretary? Your accountant? Relying on your family and/or housemates to assist you in your business endeavors certainly helps you in the short run. But in the long run it may cause resentment and become destructive to your primary relationships. Nowhere is this more critical than in dealing with your spouse.

Your spouse or partner may have a business. A partner who works full-time outside the home may work different shifts each week. Perhaps your spouse is the primary caretaker of your children or the primary wage-earner. Whatever the specifics, it's safe to assume that your spouse has certain, and probably full-time, responsibilities. So expecting your spouse to suddenly volunteer all free and available time to take your calls, schedule your lessons, and figure your tax records seems really quite unreasonable. Asking your spouse to take on or to share certain tasks, however, is not unreasonable, especially if it benefits your business efficiency (and, in turn, your family finances).

Your relationship with your spouse or significant other should be first priority at all times. If within the framework of that relationship you are able to work together toward a common goal (your teaching career) then both of you reap rewards. The more success you experience in your business, the more comfortable and confident a person you become. You should be able to achieve a balance so that both business and personal relationships develop and are strengthened.

There are dangers to having relationships and business mix. Ask your spouse or partner into your business only after you have put a great deal of thought into it. A dynamic developed in a relationship over years can be destroyed in one business encounter. Obviously, some degrees of involvement require much less trepidation than others. If the extent of your spouse's involvement is answering calls while you are in lessons or away from home, then it should not differ any from you taking your spouse's messages. If your spouse actually books lesson times, gives out information about your teaching, or keeps records of your business transactions, then a different level of understanding is necessary.

Difficulties arise when misunderstandings occur. Misunderstandings are bound to happen if clear and distinct roles are not set down ahead of time. If your spouse fails to take down an important message or "double books" a lesson time or loses an important sales receipt, who is to blame? Ultimately, you are responsible. If the importance of these things is not spelled out prior to their happening then how can your spouse be at fault? You wouldn't hire employees and expect them to understand their roles without your explanation!

For your spouse to become part of the solution and not part of the problem, you should sit down and discuss the role you would like your spouse to take in your business. Explain the significance of your business and the specific areas where you need help. Be sure that whatever your spouse agrees to do does not take away from his or her own way of life or contribute to more stress in your daily routines. If stress from your business creeps into your partner's life, then resentment is sure to follow.

Working on your relationship with a significant other is crucial to your well-being. Deciding to involve this person in the day-to-day activities of your teaching business is likely to add to the pressures of that relationship. If the bond is strong between you, then the assistance you receive should help strengthen your relationship as well as benefit your business. Whether your partner becomes your personal secretary, does all your accounting and taxes, or simply records your messages when listening to the answering machine, a successful business often results from the understanding and assistance of those closest to you.

Dealing With Your Children While You Work at Home

If your children are at home when you are teaching, establish rules for them. This helps ensure that you can devote your full attention to your students and not be distracted by your children.

Having a separate teaching space that is off-limits to children is part of ensuring your privacy. If you teach in a space shared with the rest of your family, it is more difficult to establish clear boundaries.

Having a consistent teaching time also helps establish boundaries for children. Work time is a time in which daddy or mommy cannot be interrupted. If you teach each evening from five to eight o'clock your children learn that they must wait until after eight for you to join them in the family again. *You* must be very clear and set the tone because students (at first) try to warm up to your children and they reassure you (not meaning it) that they don't mind if the children are around during lesson times.

To hire or not to hire a baby-sitter while you are at home. One dilemma that may arise is trying to determine whether you need a baby-sitter when you are at home teaching. This is determined by many factors, the most obvious being the ages of your children. Having a newborn is a twenty-four-hour-a-day, seven-day-a-week responsibility. Deciding to stay home to teach *and* care for a newborn child is completely unrealistic. Leaving young children unsupervised while you are trying to teach a lesson is also completely unworkable. You must constantly excuse yourself to mediate some dispute or get another glass of apple juice. While you apologize, your student thinks of ways to politely quit taking lessons from you. If you have older children who come home from school while you are teaching lessons, however, it is conceivable that they could entertain themselves without disturbing you. A lot depends on the maturity of your children. If you try it and are consistently interrupted, then consider the experiment failed and seek alternatives.

One practical alternative is to hire a baby-sitter to come into your home while you are teaching. You can earn a much higher wage teaching music lessons than what it costs to hire child care. If you charge thirty dollars per hour for music lessons and only pay a few dollars per hour for child care you still end up ahead by over twenty-five dollars an hour. You obviously lose out on important time with your child, but if students out there are waiting for lessons you may want to weigh the benefits of bringing in a baby-sitter and earning that wage. At least your child is in your home. You have some control over the type of child care received and can monitor that care to some degree. Compared to sending your child to day care, this option is much better.

An ideal situation is to find a student who can baby-sit on lesson day. That way the baby-sitter is already in your home and it is someone whom you trust with your child. You may even consider some type of barter arrangement, trading off lessons for child care. An hour lesson may be worth the equivalent of four or five hours worth of child care. Another option is to hire a younger teenager whom you might not want to leave completely alone with your children, but feel all right about when you are there in case of dire emergency.

You may think you can leave your kids to their own devices while you teach and train them to only interrupt the lesson in the case of emergencies. However, you'll have to sort out with your kids what constitutes an "emergency." You'll probably discover that your eight-year-old thinks it is an emergency when his seven-year-old sister wants to play with his Sega system, and he may not consider it an emergency when the four-year-old is making a plastic garbage-bag playhouse. For this reason, we encourage you to hire a baby-sitter so you can maintain a professional atmosphere in your lessons.

BUYING (OR RENTING) A HOME THAT ACCOMMODATES YOUR MUSICAL NEEDS

Whether or not you plan on teaching in your home at the time you begin searching for a house, it's a good idea to consider specific music/teaching needs your new home should accommodate. Even if you have a steady teaching position outside the home, choosing a home that affords you a space to develop your craft should be on the top of your list of priorities. This space should be as essential to your life as a bedroom, bath or kitchen. If you plan to teach in your new home then a music studio should head the list of new home needs.

When we purchased our first home together we searched for months and months before finding a home that suited our needs. We were looking for a home that would accommodate a music studio big enough for equipment and comfortable enough for teaching. We also wanted something that had easy access (first floor or basement) and had an adjoining waiting area. Our search ended when we found a home that had a master bedroom and an adjacent living room on the first floor. Our first project was to design the studio so we could begin teaching in our new home as soon as possible.

While each person's needs and wants differ, make it a priority to decide what your needs are and to accommodate them in your search for a new home or apartment. Compromise is common in many areas, but you may not want to buckle too much when dealing with your music studio. Decide what you want and continue the search until you find it.

Certainly there are alternatives to purchasing a home with a perfect set-up already established. If you are looking for a new apartment, look for one with an additional bedroom that could be made into a studio. You may have to compromise a little on location to get a slightly larger place at an affordable price. Adding on to an existing building or converting a workroom or basement into a music studio may be an even better solution if you are handy with a saw and hammer. You can personalize the design and development of your studio and such things as shelf or desk space can easily be designed into your new room.

Purchasing (or renting) a new home or condominium is a big decision. You can't predict every need in advance, but from experience we can say that deciding to insist on a studio area before beginning our search was the wisest move we made. Our search was more difficult, but it paid off in the long run. We've been satisfied with the studio space we have and it has proved to be a financially and artistically rewarding part of our lives and careers.

Considering Location, Parking and Zoning

In addition to specific concerns about the indoor aspects of setting up studio space, there are other important considerations. If students cannot find your home, or a place to park when they arrive, then your chances of keeping students coming back are greatly reduced. If you set up shop and have the town shut down your business because of complaints from neighbors, then your new home was not a great investment. It is tremendously important to troubleshoot all the possible areas of conflict ahead of time. Don't sign on the dotted line until you are certain you can run and maintain a successful business from your new home studio.

Many people fantasize about a dream home in a secluded, wooded area. That log cabin by the stream may be good for peace of mind but it may not bring you a piece of change. In fact, you probably want to consider a populated area that is easy and safe to travel to and from. Having to spend ten minutes on the phone getting directions to your home may discourage a prospective student from making the trip to your studio for that first lesson. If your home is easy to find but in a neighborhood that is unsafe after dark, you may have difficulty convincing students to book evening lessons. Check with local police or crime-watch groups to satisfy any concerns about safety issues (for your students and your family).

Unless you live in an area that has reliable mass transit, you need accessible parking also. Parents and students become easily discouraged about driving to lessons if they must circle your block every week in search of a parking space. On-street parking, a large driveway, or access to a public parking lot or garage is an important buying consideration for your new home.

Once you have found a home or area that you are interested in, be certain to check zoning laws in that area or town. If you plan to conduct business in your home you may fall within guidelines or restrictions established by these zoning laws. Most rural areas allow businesses to be established in the home. Many towns, however, restrict business in the home. Constant traffic in and out of your home or noise from your studio could elicit complaints from neighbors, so be certain to investigate the legality of your operation before deciding on purchasing a home. (Call the town hall.)

Even if your teaching business *is* legal, be sure to respect your neighbors to ensure cooperation from everyone in and around your business.

A FINAL WORD ABOUT PLANNING FOR HOME TEACHING

We think teaching at home combines the best of all possible worlds. You get to participate in your home life while still making a living doing what you love to do. Teaching at home should enhance your life, rather than detract from it. We've offered these observations and suggestions in the hopes that your home-teaching experience will be as fulfilling as ours has been.

CHAPTER THREE

SETTING UP A WORKING HOME BUSINESS AND STUDIO

Once you establish a place to set up your studio, you must tend to the many details of initiating the business side of your home-teaching enterprise. You must take the business side of your teaching very seriously, even if you don't consider yourself the "business type." This means devoting many hours to creating a working style that fits your personality while still being efficient and productive. Many teachers are unprepared for the extensive time and energy necessary for establishing and maintaining a smooth business operation. Businesses of any kind only succeed with proper planning and lots of hard work.

We also want to remind you to have fun! One of the biggest rewards of being successful in your own business is having fun and making money doing something that you truly love to do.

STUDIO POLICIES

Many policy issues need to be dealt with before you set up shop. The more carefully you think through these issues ahead of time, the fewer snags you run into.

Scheduling

Keeping and maintaining an accurate method for scheduling student lessons is key to a well-run operation at home. When conflicts arise they are likely due to poor record keeping.

The master schedule: post it and update it. The busier and more successful you become, the more difficult it is to keep all your obligations and appointments straight. You may be balancing a performing career with a teaching business, a full-time job and family obligations. No one can possibly keep all their appointments straight without some kind of reminder, so develop a master schedule everyone can see (see

Example 3-1). If you don't want to broadcast your personal appointments, you might keep a separate listing of scheduled lessons in your studio. But somewhere you should also have a master schedule that includes *all* business and personal activities of your household. Many times a doctor or dentist appointment does not get noted on your teaching schedule and conflicts can arise.

Once this master schedule is created, post it in a most accessible place and update it constantly. We use the broad side of the refrigerator, and we post six months at a time. Keeping the schedule thorough, accurate and updated ensures that you avoid embarrassing conflicts. If your spouse or other family members take messages or book lessons for you, make sure that everything gets noted on the master schedule. If a message comes in that affects your schedule, be sure it gets transferred and does not remain on a slip of paper or the answering machine until too late.

Working flexibility into the schedule. Having flexibility within your daily schedule affords you the option of last-minute changes in schedule or makeup lessons. "Hello, Dave. This is Mark. My mother just called and she has to work late so I can't make my lesson at 4:00 today." This is a pretty common type of phone call in our home. But because of the way we schedule lessons, this student may have a lesson after all because we usually try to leave an hour of "float" time open. This student gets his all-important weekly lesson and there is no need to schedule a makeup date. It may mean switching dinner from 6:00 to 4:00, but that seems like a minor concession.

Having a flexible daily schedule definitely benefits you in many ways, some immediate (getting the laundry done), others long-term (lowered risk of burnout). Likewise, having a flexible weekly schedule can benefit you also. Perhaps you can set aside one day a week to accomplish personal business. You may also be able to use this day to do business calls or accounting, or it can serve as a possible makeup day. Having that extra day is useful should you need to cancel lessons for personal, health or weather reasons or for holidays. You can also use this extra day to schedule lessons for those who study on a bimonthly or monthly basis (see page 48).

In creating some flexibility in your schedule, you reduce the number of hours available to do actual teaching. This is well worth it for the teacher interested in long-term teaching and quality results. Having an hour off here or a day free there (or even a week vacation) goes a long way in contributing to your overall health and well-being and

JUNE

Sun	Mon	Tue	Wed	Thu	Fri	Sat
1 SOUNDS GOOD MUSIC 3-9	2 YWCA 12-3 "ON THE ROAD" 4-8	3 JUDO-12:00 HOME STUDIO 3-8	4 YWCA 12-3	5 RED SOX vs. A's 7:00	6 SOUNDS GOOD 9-1	7 BAND REHEARSAL 7-9
8 DENTIST 9:45 SOUNDS GOOD 3-9	9 YWCA 12-3 "ROAD" 4-8	10 JUDO-12:00 HOME 3-8	11 YWCA 12-3	12 SOLO CONCERT LIBRARY 8:00 PM	13 SOUNDS GOOD 9-1 SOFT ROCK CAFE 9-12:30	14 BAND 7-9
15 SOUNDS GOOD 3-9	16 YWCA 12-3 "ROAD" 4-8	17 JUDO-12:00 HOME 3-8	18 H.S. GRAD. REHEARSAL 9:00AM YWCA 12-3	19 H.S. GRADUATION 4:00 PM- 10:00 PM	20 SOUNDS GOOD 9-1 DRESS REHEARSAL 2:00	21 STUDENT RECITAL 2:00 BAND 7-9
22 HAIR 11:15 SOUNDS GOOD 3-9	23 YWCA 12-3 "ROAD" 4-8	24 JUDO-12:00 HOME 3-8	25 YWCA 12-3 ANNIVERSARY PARTY 5:00	26	27 SOUNDS GOOD 9-1 SOFT ROCK 9-12:30	28 BAND 7-9
29 SOUNDS GOOD 3-9	30 YWCA 12-3 "ROAD" 4-8					

Example 3-1. Posted Master Schedule

increases your chances of maintaining an inspirational role as an instructor.

Offering weekly, biweekly and monthly arrangements. It is most advantageous to set up weekly lessons for students whenever possible. Regular, disciplined interaction between student and teacher is best monitored on a week-to-week basis, especially with beginning students and younger musicians who lose momentum when two or more weeks pass between lessons. In some unusual circumstances, meeting even more than once a week is appropriate, for instance when a student is preparing for a juried audition or something similarly high-pressure.

In other instances, however, weekly lessons are out of the question. One common issue is finances. Some students may not be able to afford weekly lessons and seek alternate scheduling. You may encounter adults with work, family or social responsibilities who seek less regular meetings. And there may be professionals who want to meet only when specific problems arise.

You must decide as to whether you want to make lesson times available to students who prefer bimonthly, monthly or irregular lessons. Weekly lessons are easiest to organize, schedule and maintain, but if you have unfilled times, catering to those who desire less regular lesson times can be a great method for filling times (and possibly hooking up with some talented and dedicated musicians). The best scenario is to find two students who want biweekly lessons and can alternate week-to-week in the same time slot. You can also talk students who want weekly half-hour lessons into taking biweekly, hour-long lessons if it uses your time more efficiently. This can work as smoothly as a weekly situation as long as schedules are not thrown off by holidays, missed lessons, etc. A similar scenario can be organized with four students who want monthly lessons. (When a certain day of the week occurs five times during a month then the fifth week can be used as a makeup time.) You can also use the biweekly or monthly plan as an alternate suggestion to a student who may be considering quitting lessons because of lack of time or finances. Better to see them once a month than never again (see Example 3-2).

Be aware that the odds of missed lessons increase with less regular lessons. If a student comes to you for lessons every Monday at 3:30 there is little risk of that student forgetting and scheduling something else into that time by accident. (We find that the incidence of missed lessons is greater after a holiday or vacation week.) If a student sees

Monday	Tuesday	Wednesday	Thursday	Friday
WEEK 1		3:00 JIM Z. 4:00 TOM H. 5:00 BILL F. 6:00 JON A. 7:00 JESSE B.		
WEEK 2		3:00 JIM Z. 4:00 KAREN H. 5:00 BILL F. 6:00 JON A. 7:00 TOM K.		
WEEK 3		3:00 JIM Z. 4:00 TOM H. 5:00 BILL F. 6:00 JON A. 7:00 KIM T.		
WEEK 4		3:00 JIM Z. 4:00 KAREN H. 5:00 BILL F. 6:00 JON A. 7:00 JEFF Y.		
WEEK 5		3:00 JIM Z. 4:00 5:00 BILL F. 6:00 JON A. 7:00		

Example 3-2. Monthly Lesson Schedule
*Note that Jim Z. (3:00), Bill F. (5:00) and Jon A. (6:00) are all weekly lessons.
The 4:00 time alternates between Tom H. and Karen H., while the 7:00 time
involves four different students. This demonstrates bimonthly and monthly
scheduling. Because the month includes five teaching days, two slots are open for
makeup lessons in week 5.*

you once a month, it is much more likely that he or she may not remember the appointment.

One suggestion for these less frequent lessons is to use friendly reminders, either phone calls or postcards, a few days prior to a scheduled lesson. You can have students fill out postcards during lessons, then you can use the cards to notify them of the next lesson. Mail the cards before their next lesson or give the card to them at the end of the lesson, like at a doctor's office. Little organizational touches like these are the things that make students take you seriously. Students who fill out their own reminder cards are much more likely to remember the next meeting with you or at least to think to call if they can't make the lesson.

Deciding on a Makeup Policy

Every business that schedules appointments must deal with people who fail to keep theirs. In home teaching, missed lessons can create specific problems. First, progress slips for certain students and, secondly, you face the possible loss of income from no-show lessons. To ensure that students develop real consistency in their studies and that you benefit from their weekly attendance you must develop and adhere to strict attendance/makeup lesson policies. The more lenient the policy the more abuses you encounter. By contrast, the stricter your policy is the more likely that students remain consistent in their commitment.

Establish a policy that lets students know they are paying for a lesson *time* not for the actual lesson. In other words, they are reserving your services each week regardless of whether they decide to take advantage of your expertise or not. Because they decide to skip a lesson does not relieve them from the obligation of payment for that time slot. This may seem somewhat harsh, but if it is not adhered to, you can count on certain problems in the future.

Most people who do miss a private lesson have some excuse for not being there at their scheduled time. Students may not be too excited about paying for a lesson they missed, so they request a makeup lesson. You need to establish a working policy for makeup lessons that both you and your students can live with.

Not doing any makeup lessons at all, regardless of the excuse, is one extreme. Doing makeup lessons for every missed lesson with or without an excuse is the other end of the spectrum. You should establish a policy that falls somewhere in between. Most businesses allow for a cancelation within a specific time frame. If you are able to rebook a time that a student cannot make, then it benefits you and the student to do a makeup lesson later. You can accommodate another student who may need to switch times, for instance. If you lose the time *and* schedule a makeup, however, you are actually working for half your original rate: a one-hour time slot *plus* a makeup lesson for one price.

With this in mind, you need to establish a specific time frame for calling and canceling a lesson. It may be twenty-four hours' notice, it may be one week's notice. It is your decision what is fair for everyone. If you teach many students or have a few students who are on a waiting list for a permanent time and can easily fill in unused slots then perhaps twenty-four hours' notice is enough time for you to rebook a lesson. We established a one-week notice when our home business was functioning only one day a week. That way we could rearrange lesson times with students one week prior to their next lesson as opposed to calling last minute to see if they wanted to do a longer lesson or move to an earlier time. We felt that most students who had a conflict due to a doctor's appointment or school function would know about it well in advance. Also we simply didn't have time during the week to make the calls necessary to rebook a lesson. Our policy, once implemented, proved very successful and students had no problems abiding by it. Without a consistent makeup policy you may find yourself constantly changing *your* schedule to meet the inconsistencies of your students. This is sure to make your life very unpleasant in the long run.

Once you decide on a policy, write it down and be certain that students receive a copy at their first lesson. Don't wait to explain your policy after a student's first cancellation. Update your policy periodically and redistribute it to students who have been with you for a while. This helps reinforce your standards and fend off any abuses of the system (especially from teenagers). Your makeup policy may be part of an overall policy statement to each student or something separate. Either way, it is important to set something down prior to teaching and to adhere to it religiously once it becomes established (See Example 3-3).

One method for ensuring consistency in attendance is to borrow a technique from other practices. How many times have you gotten calls or cards reminding you of doctor, dentist or hair appointments? A friendly reminder can prove very successful in establishing consistent attendance for your lessons. You may want to initiate this for newer students and forgo it once some consistency is established. Students may be startled by this approach so you may want to warn them. Say,

---

MAKEUP LESSON POLICY STATEMENT

Students must notify Mr. Smith of a lesson cancellation a minimum of 48 hours prior to lesson time. If at least 48 hours' notice is given, then a makeup lesson will be scheduled at the earliest possible date. If less than 48 hours' notice is given, students will be charged for the scheduled lesson and no makeup lesson will be given. There are no exceptions to this policy.

Example 3-3. Makeup Lesson Policy Statement

"I'll be calling you in the middle of the week to confirm your lesson time and to see if you have any questions." You can also use this friendly contact with students to see how their week is progressing or if they have encountered any problems with the lesson material. Parents like this approach because they can ask you questions about their child's progress. You present yourself as a more interested teacher if you show concern for a child's studies as opposed to just calling to make sure the parent shows up with a checkbook.

Deciding on a Fee Structure

Every business must decide the value of the product or service that it offers. As a self-employed businessperson you must assess your service based on quality, convenience, student need and competition.

Finding out what the going rate is. Check out your area to see who your competitors are and what their rates are. If there is no competition in your area then perhaps you could use a surrounding area as a basis for setting your rates. Another strategy is to find out what other types of instructors in your area charge. You could contact dance, art or martial arts instructors to find a competitive rate for your services.

Having determined the rates of comparable instructors, you should consider a number of factors in determining the rates you charge for your instruction. First, you must weigh teaching experience of your competition against your own. Let's say that the only other teacher in town charges fifty dollars per hour for lessons but has twenty years' experience. It makes little sense to charge a similar rate if you are just starting out in the field. Instead you should offer a competitive price and perhaps draw from a pool of beginners who do not require as experienced an instructor. On the other hand, it is a different story if there are several teachers in town who charge twenty-five dollars per hour for lessons but have minimal experience. If you are vastly more qualified than most, you may want to charge a higher rate. This may limit your ability to win beginner students but may also make you more attractive to those looking for an instructor with more knowledge and expertise than the established teachers in town.

Another factor to consider is the current economy of your geographical area. Generally speaking, urban areas have a higher cost of living. In less populated areas, you may have to charge lower rates to stay competitive and attract students from lower income brackets.

The amount of competition you face is another factor in determining your rates. If you face little or no competition for students and there is a real need for instruction, then you may be able to set a good, reasonable rate. If competition is great and you are the new kid in town then your strategy must change. If you can offer a specific talent, ability or quality that your competition lacks, you may be able to compete at similar or higher rates. If you do not necessarily stand out of the crowd then perhaps offering a lower rate will be the selling point that begins to attract those students to you.

Remember that you are pricing your skills, so resist the temptation to undersell yourself. Most people really do believe that they "get what they pay for," so set your rates accordingly. It is much easier to attract students initially by setting a reasonable (though not rock-bottom) rate and find yourself with a full schedule of students. Once you've established yourself as a quality instructor you can gradually raise your rates and maintain your current load of students while attracting others.

Offering a sliding scale. Many businesses charge customers a fee based on a sliding scale. That scale is often determined by what a person can afford. Though it is a bit unusual, you could offer lessons to students for reduced cost.

A sliding scale based on need should take into consideration the earning power of each individual student. It is wise to determine the high and low fees on your scale. An adult who has an established position in the business world could set the top fee on your sliding scale. A teenage student who works part-time to pay for lessons or a mother who has several children taking lessons could determine the low end of your sliding scale. Your job is to determine what each student can afford. This method can be confusing and difficult to maintain at times. It requires that you establish some method of determining need. You may be able to determine that based on a conversation designed to size up the student's need. You may take a more formal route and let students know the high-low fee scale and have them determine what they can afford. Difficulties can arise if you have an unstated sliding scale policy. You run the risk of two students discovering that they pay different rates for the same service. Be very careful to avoid embarrassing situations like this.

One alternate method of creating a sliding scale is to base it on category of student. You can establish separate rates for beginner, intermediate and advanced students. You can also determine rates based on child, teenager, adult categories. Children taking lessons may have brothers or sisters who also study, so a lower rate may apply. Teenagers may be paying for lessons by themselves, so another lower rate could apply. Adults are generally in a better position to afford a higher fee. You may decide to base the fee not on affordability but on amount of work or stress involved in teaching students in each category. Because children require so much more attention and patience, that category may actually require a higher fee than adults who are often more laid back and less stressful to deal with. If you are more comfortable with children and find adults more stressful, then set your rates accordingly. This method of establishing your fee structure actually allows you to attract those students whom you feel most comfortable teaching.

Sliding fee scales can also be a lot more work than just having one standard fee. Problems can arise in bookkeeping, record keeping and accounting. It is one more way to be responsive to students' needs, however, and a creative way to attract students you enjoy working with.

Offering lower-cost lessons for harder-to-fill time slots. Evening hours are always the times most requested by students. Therefore you can demand top dollar for lessons between the hours of five and eight o'clock. Afternoon and later night times are somewhat less desirable so your fee for those times may be slightly lower. Morning times are most difficult to fill, so you could offer low, attractive rates for those hours. Better to teach several morning lessons at a lower rate than not to teach at all. This might be especially attractive to homemakers, retired people, or second/third shift workers, so target those groups when advertising for morning times. Be creative as you attempt to fill your schedule.

Offering scholarships. One final option for lessons is to offer students of exceptional talent a scholarship. This might come in the form of reduced (or no) lesson payment, or a barter system. The reason for offering a student reduced or free lessons could be based on financial need (see sliding scale) or on merit.

Offering scholarships can serve as a powerful form of marketing for your teaching talents. Inevitably a gifted student will be showcased in a performance of some sort. The student's peers usually ask who he or she studies with and "voila," your name resounds like an echo through the Grand Canyon. Word of mouth is always the best form of publicity, and a recommendation from a talented student is better than a full-page ad in *Rolling Stone* magazine. So consider offering scholarships to the most talented students you encounter.

Should you decide to offer free lessons to talented adults, you could request return instruction from them. This type of barter system benefits both of you as you can gain some valuable techniques or materials from your professional students.

Payment weekly, monthly or by semester. Your payment policy is directly connected to your policy for attendance/makeup lessons. If your attendance policy states that students are responsible for paying for each lesson whether or not they attend, it is a good idea to have students pay for lessons in advance. It is much easier to collect for a lesson that a student believes will take place than to extract payment for a missed lesson after the fact. Whether you decide on a weekly, monthly or semester policy, advance payment guarantees your wage and helps establish consistency in your students' attendance.

One of the most common policies for payment among teachers is a monthly system. The student pays for each lesson that falls within that month. Make the payment for the next month due in the last week of the current month. This way every lesson is paid for in advance, including the first week of the month.

Some students can't afford such a large outlay of cash in one lump sum and they may want to pay weekly. This can be accommodated easily. Although monthly payment is preferable, weekly payment can work *if* you can get students to pay for a week in advance. In other words, on the first meeting have students pay for *two* lessons, the first lesson and next week's lesson as well. Then next week they bring a single payment to cover the following week. When students miss a lesson then they are again responsible for two payments. This reestablishes the payment-in-advance policy.

A third system of payment should be considered for teachers or students on a school calendar. If you teach as adjunct faculty to a college or university, then you are likely to be on a semester schedule.

If you teach private lessons to college students, they are on a similar schedule. In these instances, semester payment is most advantageous. Students expect to lay out a large portion of their savings at the beginning of the term and adding music lesson payment to the list seems insignificant at that time. Plus, college students traditionally run out of money as the semester wears on. Get the payment up front for the semester and forgo having to deal with collecting payment for three to four months. It makes your life a great deal easier.

Written policies and materials. Whatever policy you decide on, be sure to state it in writing and distribute it to students before or during the first lesson. The purpose of a lesson policy is to ensure payment for each scheduled time slot. In addition, you are trying to encourage consistent attendance and, in turn, steady progress as musicians.

If you use several options for payment, either list them together or create separate policy statements for each option. Distribute the payment policy statement with the makeup lesson policy (see page 52), since the two go hand in hand (see Example 3-4). If students have paid for a lesson in advance they are less likely to miss that lesson and the need for makeup lessons is diminished.

Developing a collection of materials for your home teaching business not only helps your work go smoothly but also makes your business run more efficiently.

Materials you generate that are business related increase your effi-

---

COMBINED PAYMENT/MAKEUP LESSON POLICY STATEMENT

Payment for lessons will be made on a monthly basis. Payment for each month is due the week prior to the new month. (Example: June lesson payment is due the last week of May.)

All federal and state holidays are observed.

Students must notify instructor of a lesson cancelation a minimum of 48 hours prior to lesson time. If at least 48 hours' notice is given, then a makeup lesson will be scheduled at the earliest possible date. If less than 48 hours' notice is given, students will be charged for the scheduled lesson and no makeup lesson will be given. There are no exceptions to this policy.

Example 3-4. Combined Payment/Makeup Lesson Policy Statement

ciency and present you in a better light as you deal with students. Think of everything you repeat to every student and document these things in a handout that you keep on file. How about making a map with detailed directions to your studio? Mailing this to new students is much more impressive than trying to relay directions over the phone or jotting them down on a dinner napkin. On the map you can include parking suggestions and other pertinent information. On our map we have a note to respect our neighbors by staying out of their driveways. We also ask students to turn their radios down before approaching our home. A letter of introduction to parents of younger children helps that relationship get off to a good beginning. Keep a file of originals and make a monthly trip to the copy shop to replenish your stock of basic materials.

DESIGNING A WORKING STUDIO

Lots of time and careful consideration should go into designing your ideal teaching studio. You spend more time in your studio than in any other room in your home. Your teaching studio should be practical, functional and inspirational. It should have proper lighting and storage and be isolated or soundproofed so you won't disturb neighbors or sleeping babies. Your studio should be furnished with the best equipment and secure from thieves. Most of all, your studio should reflect your personality and interests as a musician and as a person. It should make students light up when they walk in. It should make them feel at home, relaxed and ready to focus on the lesson ahead.

Ensuring Adequate Electrical Capacity

The first call we made when we began designing our home studio was to an electrician. Having purchased an older home, we had the perfect space for the studio but many alterations were needed. The first thing we noticed about our new space was the lone, two-pronged outlet placed against the far wall. Our first vision was of a state-of-the art studio with every piece of equipment plugged into one over-crowded, call-the-fire-chief, wires-running-everywhere outlet. Instead, we had an electrician install high-capacity wall-to-wall power strips. This gives us the flexibility to occasionally redesign our studio and add new equipment. Obviously, if you play an acoustic instrument and don't anticipate the need for stereo equipment, you won't have to worry about electrical supply.

After our electrician completed our wiring needs, we retained him to work on the lighting. Most quality businesses spend a lot of time and money providing the best possible lighting for their trade. Poor lighting can cause reduced concentration, eyestrain, and other stress-related conditions. Because you will spend long hours in your studio, take time to consider the best lighting for your room: overhead track lighting, fluorescent lamps, recessed lighting. Consult a lighting specialist or research home design or architectural magazines to determine what type of lighting best suits your needs.

Adequate Soundproofing

Nothing would be more disheartening than to complete your perfect studio only to receive complaints of excessive noise and be forced to close down your business. Like wiring and lighting concerns, soundproofing your room provides your studio with a foundation for long-term use. Complete this step of the design before any cosmetic work begins. It's much more difficult to add soundproofing later than to install good preventive materials up front.

The amount of soundproofing your room needs is relative to the noise you expect to produce in the room and the level of sensitivity of those around your studio. If you are a flutist who lives alone in the remote regions of Montana then your concerns are minimal. If you have small children, live in an apartment complex and teach drums then you have some major concerns to deal with. For most instruments, a thick carpet, storm windows and solid doors provide ample sound protection. For instruments such as drums, additional material may be necessary. Consult a hardware expert for materials that provide the best protection for your situation. Several low-cost alternatives may provide adequate soundproofing if finances are a consideration. Acoustic ceiling tiles are fairly affordable these days. Hanging rugs on walls or gluing empty egg cartons to the walls was successful in the past when professional soundproofing was beyond our budget.

Storage for Instruments

Sufficient storage space is also important for the efficiency of your studio. If you collect instruments, it may be difficult to teach with those instruments stacked throughout your studio. If possible, you should store all instruments not being used for teaching. This makes efficient use of your studio space and also helps secure your valuable instruments. There is no need to advertise your vintage violin collection to your entire student population.

If storage space is limited, try to be creative in making space for your room. We once hung guitars on the walls when closet space was at a premium; it relieved some clutter in our spare bedroom and became a decorating statement as well. A drum trap case makes a nice coffee table. With a cushion on top, that amp becomes your seat for teaching.

You should consider the maintenance of your instruments. Is the room properly vented or heated so it maintains a consistent temperature? Is the room dry in winter and moist in summer? These points are of particular concern to those with wood instruments. Invest in humidifiers and/or dehumidifiers to ensure the safety of the wood. Keep the temperature moderate and provide additional heating or air conditioning if needed. Choose an inside wall or space for storing of instruments so they're not exposed to drafts or temperature extremes. You have probably spent a great deal of time and money acquiring your instruments. Be sure to provide an environment for them that ensures their safety and quality for a long time.

Having Double Instruments for Easier Teaching

For most music lessons students bring their own instruments. For instruments such as drums, percussion and piano, however, this may be simply impractical. For the instructor on these instruments it is important to have an instrument for you and one for the student. If you do not have a double instrument set-up yet, it is something you may eventually want. Better to plan for it than to be stuck with having to expand your present room or purchase a new space altogether. Having a dual set-up is preferable to teaching with only one instrument. Playing *with* your students is crucial to their growth and understanding of time, feel, and other elements of musicianship.

Storage for Music, Recordings and Books

Another important feature of your studio should be storage for books, recordings and sheet music. Having easy access to musical examples is key to good teaching. Being able to reach for a piece of music or read a quote from a book, look up a definition or pop in a CD goes a long way in emphasizing or solidifying a point. When working on a new song or a phrase with a student, being able to hear the passage or melody from you is important. But that can be supplemented by a recorded performance by a master musician on a classic recording.

As you fill your studio with instruments, books and music recordings, not to mention equipment, stereos and sound reinforcement, you suddenly discover a drastic lack of space. Not to worry. Keep bringing in stuff, just be creative in how you set up your studio. We created a massive desk with shelf space by using file cabinets (for music) and record cabinets as a base. On top of the cabinets sits a wood desktop holding a computer and printer and additional cabinets containing books and CDs. This is covered by shelving that holds stereo and recording equipment. Additional shelves for books and records serve as a stand for a MIDI keyboard station. You get the picture. Let no floor or wall space be wasted.

Establishing a Lending Library for Students

Having easy access to recordings and written music is a great way to supplement your lessons and spark student interest. It's not very practical, however, to spend a large portion of the lesson time playing albums and reading quotes from magazine articles. Because these things can be vitally important but also somewhat time-consuming, a great solution is to establish a lending library using some of your materials.

Obviously you want to keep a lock on your violin collection and on those collector recordings. But making tapes, music, and articles available for your students to borrow is very motivational and helpful to their studies. So much of learning music is hearing it. Time constraints force us to limit how much listening we do during lessons. Listening at home during the week and reading inspirational articles helps students stay focused and motivated. Lending these materials to your students shows them the passion you have for music and for teaching.

Although a lending system is a great benefit for your students, it can be a nightmare for you if you don't approach it with caution and with organization. Not every student who receives material from your library will have the same passion about it as you do. In fact, some may take poor care of things or misplace them. Don't lend anything that you can't replace easily. Establish a system for signing out materials to keep track of who has what and when they took it. Be sure to check the log weekly to ensure that all materials are returned the next week. Retrieving material is more difficult once a few weeks have gone by, so stay right on top of it.

Personalizing Your Studio

We have several unique but nonvaluable stringed instruments that we use as decorations in our music room. Next to them hang music and dance posters, album covers and soccer memorabilia. We have tried to create a studio that is not only functional and inspirational but also reflects the personality, passions and interests of the people who teach there.

Your music studio should take on a look that reflects you and your personality. Perhaps you can hang posters of your band or photos of your family, pets or cars—anything that gives the room a flavor reminiscent of who you are musically and personally. Have fun with this part of your design. Include humor and especially nonmusical interests. Much of your relationship with students is musical but a part should also be personal. They should get to know more about you than just your address and monthly rates.

Creating a Comfortable Waiting Area

In designing and furnishing a music studio you must not only consider space for teaching but also a waiting area for students' parents and for the next student.

One option to consider is waiting space *within* your teaching studio. There are both good and bad points to this situation. The good part is that you can invite parents to be a part of their child's lessons. Often it is the parent who motivates the student to practice and helps organize the practice sessions for the child (see chapter five). Parents who sit in on the lesson are no doubt more conscientious when monitoring their child's musical growth throughout the week. But some students are less relaxed with parents observing their every move. Having some distance between teaching and waiting areas lets the parent observe without obstructing the child's progress.

Problems arise when students arrive early and wait for their lesson. Most students are very self-conscious, and the one being taught often feels as if he or she is no longer in a private lesson but in a public performance instead. Anticipate this and use it to your advantage. Getting students to overcome and deal with their fears, doubts and insecurities is an important part of learning to become a performer. You can even use the opportunity to stage informal recitals for waiting parents and students.

A second option is to have a separate waiting space outside your studio. Ideally this waiting area is adjacent to your teaching space. You can hear when students are arriving for their next lesson and it still allows parents to monitor the lesson from afar. Leave the door to the studio open so they can listen in on their child's lesson. Refer to the previous chapter for a discussion about how to function with waiting students and parents if the waiting area (or teaching area) is being shared with your household.

Provide those waiting with a comfortable area. In colder climates you need a spot to hang heavy winter coats and to leave snowy boots. The waiting space is essentially an extension of your studio; therefore, the personality you have designed into your studio should also be present in the waiting area. Have music magazines for students and other magazines for parents to read. Have music playing on the stereo or the television tuned to MTV. Often we play instructional videotapes for students who must wait for a long time. Have a play area with toys and books for young children to stay occupied. They may be waiting in your home for as long as an hour, so you should extend the same considerations to them that you would to any guests. Some teachers go so far as to have a coffeepot going at all times or a small refrigerator with juice in it for students and their parents. Although this may seem like a huge inconvenience to you, think how it reflects on you as a teacher. A parent who sees music lessons as just another thing they have to do reports to a friend, "It's so relaxing taking Johnny to lessons. He goes in for half an hour, I have a cup of coffee and read a magazine." Be sure students and parents have access to a rest room.

An ideal situation is have two waiting areas, one in the music room for including parents and one adjacent to your studio for keeping them (and others) separate.

Designs for Home Studios

Design for your home studio may be unique in many ways. You can convert a loft or attic into your music space. You can park your car in the street and transform your garage into a studio separate from your home. Whatever you choose, the process and details are similar to many other studios. Here we have outlined three typical studio layouts for you to consider.

Home studio #1 (dining room). One example, a dining room, uses shared living space. Your design should be like a MASH unit that can be dismantled in case of dinner parties. Storage should be concealed, if possible. Equipment, instruments and music should be easy to reach but in closets, trunks or boxes. The dining room table can be folded up, pushed to the side, or used for holding music, stereo equipment, etc. Consider purchasing a dining table with a lot of leaves to increase your options now and in the future.

A waiting area can be fashioned out of any adjacent room. The kitchen or living room would both serve the purpose.

Home studio #2 (first floor bedroom/den). Another possibility is a first-floor bedroom or den. This too could be convertible, shared with family as a guest bedroom. It is tempting to share a playroom with your children, but the children usually want to play pretty much on the same schedule you want to teach. A spare room can be used as a permanent music studio. Waiting space should be provided in the studio or in an adjacent living or dining room.

Home studio #3 (basement, with separate entrance). Our third example is a basement studio with separate entrance. When designing a basement studio from scratch consider a separate waiting area just inside the entrance.

EQUIPMENT NEEDS

In this age of advanced musical technology, computer-generated music and home recording, your studio should be equipped with the most up-to-date electronics in order to stay ahead of the competition. Even if you teach on a traditional instrument, try to incorporate some elements of the advanced technology available today. Electronic keyboards or drum machines, recording and playback equipment and music-writing software can be incorporated into traditional teaching settings.

A Sound System That Does the Job

Electric guitar, bass and keyboards are among the most popular instruments purchased and studied today. Even drums and woodwinds have entered the world on MIDI. If you teach brass, winds, voice or percussion, instruments traditionally taught in an acoustic environment, miking techniques are important to students entering the performing field. In many cases, a quality sound system is one of the first purchases you should make. If you do live performances on your instrument then you may already own a sound system that can double in your studio. If space is a consideration, many high-quality systems are available in small, portable set-ups.

Recording Capabilities

Recording techniques should be included in your curriculum. Easy-to-use, hands-on, four-track recorders are economical and ideal for your teaching studio. These recorders can serve as teaching tools for students interested in entering the field of recording. You can help them prepare for an upcoming recording session by doing a run-through on your machine. Four-track systems are also a wonderful way to create recorded examples and exercises for your students to listen to or work with. Develop a library of cassette tapes of standard tunes and progressions that your students can use to develop soloing ideas.

You can also use recording equipment to help students create audition tapes or simply to hear themselves play. Many students leave the lesson only to get home and forget what was covered. Some teachers record the lesson, or important excerpts such as assignments or complex rhythmic examples, and give the student a copy of the tape on the way out the door.

Playback Capabilities

Recorded music should play an important role in your teaching. Playing old LPs on a turntable you purchased at a yard sale may not get your point across effectively. Most students interested in music place a high priority on the top-of-the-line stereo products. Your studio is not complete without a top-quality playback system. Easy access to your system is important as well. If you teach in a common area in your home, a portable stereo might give you the quality sound and movability you desire. In a permanent setting, a component stereo system is preferable.

Electronics

Besides recording, playback and sound equipment, owning electronic equipment helps make your studio state of the art. Several specific pieces of equipment should head your wish list.

No musician should be without a metronome. While that old pendulum beauty from your early years may hold great sentimental value, your studio could use an upgrade to the electronic age. Many high-tech metronomes are on the market today, some with remarkable features. Check out your local music store and invest in a quality metronome for your studio. Time is such an important element in music. If you can convince your students of the importance of working on time you are certain to see more progress from week to week. The surest way to instill this habit in students is to use the metronome during all aspects of your lessons.

Convincing students to work with a metronome is difficult at times. One method of encouraging the concept in a subtle way is by using a drum machine. Now you can teach time *and* "feel" simultaneously. Have fun while working on a concept crucial to the development of your students; try those Bach inventions to a disco beat, or do those scale patterns to reggae. Even drum set teachers should consider this approach. Students should learn to play along with the machine as they develop steady time.

Save space in your studio for a keyboard station, because no matter what instrument you play, this can aid your teaching style greatly. Technological advances in keyboards have been mind-boggling over the past decades. Check out a demo of the top-of-the-line keyboard if you have any doubts. A keyboard is a necesary part of your home studio. From a basic standpoint, teaching harmonic and melodic concepts on the keyboard is elementary. Nonharmonic instrumental instructors especially want to use a keyboard to teach harmony to their students.

Accompanying students with simple harmonies while they wrestle with reading melodies is one common use of the studio keyboard. A more contemporary approach is to use the keyboard to sequence fully orchestrated play-along progressions. This can be a very effective tool for students who have not had an opportunity to perform with other musicians. The sequencer simulates a live band and drives home the importance of time, continuity and feel. Sequencers are a feature on many of the newer keyboards. You can purchase them separately and connect them to your keyboard or to a sound module. You can purchase a monitor or keyboard amplifier for your keyboard station or connect it to your sound system. Once you have written a progression for the sequencer, you can record it and add it to your cassette library to use in developing improvisational techniques.

Computers

Computers are so much a part of our society today that most businesses, schools and homes use them. A computer for your music studio can serve so many purposes that not owning one seems risky. In chapter four we discuss creating resumes and advertising materials on your home computer. The computer is for doing the administrative aspects of your home business, including creating your own materials for lessons, creating handouts and writing letters. Software can transform your computer into the sequencer you use to create play-along materials or compositions. The computer also can be your biggest ally in organizing your tax information.

In short, life without a computer seems nearly impossible. Purchasing a computer for your studio should be a given. Decide what your needs are and what you can afford. Like keyboard technology, computer technology is advancing rapidly. It may make good sense to consider used equipment from someone who is upgrading to the newest model. This can save you thousands of dollars and still provide you with the essentials. You can also upgrade the memory and software on your current computer to handle the extra roles for your business.

HOME SECURITY

Having spent large amounts of money and time in designing and completing your home music studio, you want to protect your investment with several security measures. Crime is a reality today so while precautions should protect you if they're implemented well, theft is still a distinct possibility. Chapter nine discusses insurance. Best to be protected before and after a theft of your valuable property.

Locking Everything

Building proper storage for all your instruments and equipment is an important design element for your studio. Besides simple storage, you should include secure locks for anything of value you leave in your music room. Closets and crates should be installed with locking systems. Your studio itself should have locks on doors leading into and out of the room. Be sure to engage these locks anytime you are away from the room.

You have a great deal of traffic through your studio and perhaps through your living areas during the course of a business day. Students, prospective students, family, friends and parents all travel in and out of your room. Be certain not to invite crime into your life. Don't show off your valuable instruments or equipment to anyone whom you do not trust implicitly. Even when you feel you can trust a student completely remember that the student's friends may be less reliable. They may see your studio while sitting in on a lesson or hear of your studio through a conversation.

Use caution at all times. Never leave valuables lying around the room. If you receive payment for lessons be sure to place it in a safe location. It is conceivable to leave your studio, even for seconds, only to return and discover something missing. Creating trust with students is a key ingredient to a successful teacher-student relationship, but you still owe it to yourself to take every precaution when dealing with your livelihood.

Using Light-Timers and Radios

When you are away from home, several easy deterrents can keep those potential thieves outside your home. Make your home look occupied at all times. This can be as simple as turning on lights throughout the house. A dark home is an invitation to a thief. If you are away from home for an extended period of time, use security timing devices. These are available affordably at hardware stores and provide further protection. Timers are set to go on and off at various intervals to create the illusion of activity within the home. Turning on the radio is also a deterrent. Talk radio or a ham radio can create the illusion of conversation in the home and be more effective than music.

Alarm Systems

No system of prevention is foolproof, and certainly turning on a radio when you leave does not keep a professional thief from entering your home. To better insure your business against theft, consider investing in a home alarm system. Security systems are more affordable than ever. Services range from a simple alarm to a silent alarm that notifies police or security forces. Consult your local police department for recommendations.

A Big Dog

Using man's best friend as a security precaution can be another effective deterrent to thieves. Whether Fido protects your home from inside or out, the threat of an animal attack frightens away many criminals. Think carefully, however, about keeping an animal for protection when you have many students coming to your home for lessons. It isn't overly welcoming to have a large dog licking his chops at you when you arrive for a lesson.

SOME FINAL WORDS ABOUT YOUR HOME BUSINESS

Setting up a business of any kind requires a lot of forethought and hard work. Even with careful planning, you learn some things through old-fashioned trial and error. Though it's easy to become discouraged by the logistical details, it is important to keep your sights on your goal: a successful teaching business in the familiar comfort of your own home.

CHAPTER FOUR

MARKETING YOURSELF AS A TEACHER

Whether you've decided to teach in a store, in a studio or in your home, you need to find students who are eager to be taught. For some teaching musicians, a first contact happens fairly naturally when a younger or less experienced player asks, "Do you give lessons?" You want to be ready for this question with an emphatic *yes*, whether this is your first student or the latest to be added to your waiting list. The key is to tap all the right places and techniques to elicit students and to keep on tapping until you have a full schedule and a waiting list.

The single most important aspect of increasing your ability to find (and keep) students is to become as visible as possible in the music area of your community. (There is a hidden or not-so-hidden music culture within every community. It is just a matter of accessing it successfully.) Of course, this single aspect takes on many angles and works differently from person to person and from community to community. But regardless of your approach or your goals, you must get your name out to the public. It is essential that when your name comes up in conversation people say, "Oh, I've heard of her," or "I hear he's a terrific teacher."

No matter how insignificant each gesture may seem at the moment, every hand you shake, every business card you exchange, every concert you perform increases your marketability as a teaching professional.

LOCAL MUSIC STORES: THE MEETING PLACE

In addition to its obvious function as a place to check out new equipment and purchase your musical supplies, the local music store can also become an important networking place. Here you may meet the area music educators purchasing instruments or music for their band programs. You may run into the leader of the area's heavy metal band dropping off copies of his latest CD for sale. You may see that sixteen-year-old blues phenomenon taping up a poster for his upcoming show. Regardless of the time of day, the music store is often the hub of activity and the place to begin networking in your musical community. If there are several local music stores in your area, your first order of business is to stake them out to find out where the real action is. You may have to access all of them for different purposes.

Finding Students in a Store or Studio

In chapter one we discussed giving lessons in a music store. If the local store doesn't offer lessons or have an arrangement with a studio, working in the store may give you the opportunity to offer your teaching talents to the store's clientele. While making the sale of that new five-piece drum kit, you may ask the person purchasing the set if they are taking music lessons. (Tell parents that you use a progressive and *quiet* method of teaching drums and watch your students pour in.) If the purchaser does have a teacher, it gives you a sense of who is out there teaching in your area. Networking is essential, so it's wise to consider this teacher a colleague rather than "the competition." Referrals from teacher to teacher may lead to a large part of your student pool in the future.

Using Bulletin Boards

So you don't have what it takes to sell sheet music for "The Wedding Song." Perhaps you've heard enough bad versions of "Stairway to Heaven" plunked out on neon-colored guitars for one lifetime. Then you should simply stop by the music store instead of spending forty hours a week there. You may feel that your time is better spent finding students in other ways than through the store's employment.

Stopping by the store is one way to make the contacts necessary for building your reputation and finding students, but you can't hang around long enough to meet or see everyone who comes through the doors. One way to try to reach those people you miss is to use the store's bulletin boards. An ad describing you and what you offer is one way to attract potential students you don't get to meet.

Many stores require ads to be on a 3″×5″ index card, so try to be brief but informative. You may choose to be extremely general (see Example 4-1), very specific, (see Example 4-2), or eye-catching (see Example 4-3). You can speak to the customer: "Do You Want to Play in a Band but Lack Skills?" Or, you can describe yourself: "B.I.T. Grad

---

GUITAR LESSONS

- All Levels
- All Styles

In my home or yours.

All evenings:
(203) 555-5555

Example 4-1.

ATTENTION SHREDDERS

Guitar Lessons in All Contemporary Styles

METAL * THRASH
PUNK * GRUNGE

—2-Hand Tapping —Sweep Arpeggios —Bending
In the Style of Vinnie Moore, Paul Gilbert, Steve Vai

Contact: Shane Diamond
           (217) 555-5555

Example 4-2.

DRIVE YOUR PARENTS
INSANE

Tell Them You Want to Take
Guitar Lessons With
Aleckz From the Band Moat's Art
Leave a Message at 555-5555

Example 4-3.

with Ten Years' Teaching Experience Seeks Students." If the store lets you display a flier, then these ideas can be expanded upon with more information and creativity (see page 75). Put some serious thought into what you really want and don't be afraid to advertise for it. If you want adult learners, be sure to specify that you specialize in that area.

If the music store offers private lessons, chances are they won't allow you to advertise yourself as a teacher. As we've mentioned, however, there are many other networking opportunities in the store that you can take advantage of. Additionally, the bulletin board can serve as an indirect source of student recruitment by using it to advertise any local performances or nonteaching services you can offer (studio musician, arranger, etc.).

Making Connections With the Store Owner and Salespeople

With the tremendous number of opportunities available at and through local music stores, one of the most important connections you can make in your quest to find students is gaining the confidence of the store's owner and salespeople. Taking the time to present yourself in your best light helps build your image. Be sure to let the staff know of any events you are involved in or other skills you possess, because they may get specific requests from customers. Above all, treat these people with respect without hounding them.

While the owner may have the most contacts in the established musical community, the salespeople in the store have the most contact with musicians in the area. More important, most salespeople are often the very first contact with beginner musicians. When a person makes the decision to take up a musical instrument, the first step is usually to head to the local music store to buy or rent an instrument.

While the initial sale of an instrument is important, most good salespeople think about future sales as well. A beginner (or the paying parent) typically buys a student-size, low-budget instrument. After a period of learning, the decision to move up to a quality instrument is made. So most dedicated salespeople have a vested interest in seeing their customers succeed in the learning process. This is where the teacher-sales staff relationship can work to full advantage. New students need a good teacher to help them move to the next level of musicianship. The relationship that you develop with that salesperson can lead to many referrals for beginner students.

The salespeople can serve as a quick judge of ability when the customer is trying out a piece of equipment. The piano student who is shopping for a first synthesizer needs a tutor in MIDI, sequencing or music software. The rock player who is buying an acoustic bass for the school's jazz combo needs a good teacher in swing and improvisation. Parents buying traditional orchestral instruments appreciate a referral to a reliable and well-prepared teacher experienced at meeting the challenges of teaching younger children. Even if you teach lessons part-time, the more you can do to let these salespeople know of your abilities, both as a person and as a teacher, the more likely you are to get a referral from them for new students. Give salespeople a stack of your business cards so they can be generous in giving them out.

FINDING STUDENTS THROUGH YOUR LOCAL SCHOOLS

Many children are first exposed to live music through their school. Thankfully, most states require schools to include at least minimal music education as part of the curriculum, so by the time students reach elementary school they have been exposed to music in some form or another. Making connections at all levels of your schools helps locate students to fill your teaching schedule.

In the elementary grades, often it is the parents who want their children to take up an instrument, so cater promotional efforts to a parent's needs. Most parents believe (and it is true) that studying music can provide enjoyment, a sense of accomplishment, self-esteem, learning and discipline. Parents like those words a lot, so be sure to use them when advertising the benefits of music lessons. As students grow into adolescence, however, they begin to form their own identities around the music they listen to and, for student musicians, the type of music they play. Many musical adolescents discover in high school that their musical ability can land them in a specific social group at school (the band, for instance) or even get them into college. You attract more students at the junior and senior high school levels by appealing to them directly. It is absolutely the kiss of death to tell a teenager what his or her parents want them to do.

Getting to Know Music Educators and School Administrators

In an ideal situation, a school department or district has a general music teacher, an instrumental/band director and a choral teacher for elementary, middle and high school levels. In addition, many schools employ adjunct faculty and guest lecturers. It goes without saying that if you are looking for students, you need to look to the schools. Meeting with and forming positive relationships with school administrators, guidance counselors and, most important, music faculty provide you with the opportunity to seek employment within the school system or use your association with these people to recruit students from the schools in your area. (For an in-depth discussion of public and private school opportunities see chapter one.)

Advertising in Schools

As in the music stores, the bulletin boards of many schools (especially at the college level) are a meeting place for the exchange of information, products and services. Using bulletin boards in a school allows you to reach out to a population that may not make it into the music stores, since many schools provide instruments and supplies to their students. Your ad could be the motivating factor for a student who has been considering lessons but has been unable to make a definite decision to begin playing. Flashy, eye-catching and humorous ads are just the thing for school bulletin boards where you want to attract a student audience. Obviously, your ad should look a little different if you are running it in the PTA's newsletter. The music department in the school may have its own bulletin board that would be a high priority for any ads you post.

Some junior high and most high schools have a school newspaper and a yearbook that take advertising. Consider purchasing an ad in the newspaper or yearbook to promote your teaching business.

Many school groups and organizations (both student and parent) have newsletters or run special events with programs that sell advertising space. Check with the music faculty about concerts, musicals or fund-raising activities where you could buy an ad in the program. Not only are these ad opportunities generally very affordable, they increase your visibility and indicate your support of school music programs, a feeling you want to foster.

On page 74 are some sample ads that may work well in schools.

CREATING AND USING EFFECTIVE FLIERS

Music stores, universities and schools are obvious places to reach an audience of prospective students by using ads, posters, fliers and brochures. However, often the places that are not so obvious yield the

Woodwinds

Alvin Bailey
private instruction

ALL LEVELS
ALL STYLES

Los Angeles
(818) 555-5555

**Best of Luck
to the
Class of '95**

Example 4-4. Yearbook Ad

Woodwinds

Alvin Bailey
private instruction

ALL LEVELS
ALL STYLES

Los Angeles
(818) 555-5555

- Tutor for all concert/jazz band music
- Specializing in theory/improvisation
- College audition preparation
- Day/evening/weekend lessons available
- Affordable rates

Example 4-5. School Newspaper Ad

most surprising returns. We have found amazing results in the most unlikely locations.

Public Bulletin Boards

Try to place your fliers in locations with a great deal of public traffic. One place that often has a bulletin board for public use is the local Laundromat. Everyone has to wash their clothes, and in a big city so many people rent that few have their own washer and dryer. We have received many responses from ads placed in Laundromats and similar public places. Bus stations or public transit stops, libraries, banks, credit unions, shopping malls and supermarkets are places traversed by hundreds of people each day. In trying to reach a specific market you may want to look for places near schools, concert halls and conservatories. Some small clubs that feature music have bulletin boards announcing upcoming events. Especially in a smaller establishment, when you are hanging your flier take the time to chat with the person on duty. Don't slink in and out without a word, since this person may become an important referral source.

A well-done flier campaign can really work. Recently we addressed a classroom full of music students who were interested in a career as music instructors. The subject of advertising came up, and the students were discussing the topic of fliers. I said I didn't know who Jim Smith was but I knew he was a "unique music teacher." The class responded with laughter because it was a line from Jim's flier and everyone in the class had seen the flier at one time or another. He had them posted everywhere. There may be a point of overexposure, but if you're trying to build a full load of private students, it's a long way before you reach that point.

Advertise to the Right People

Your fliers must include detailed facts about you and what you have to offer prospective students. Include a phone number where you can be reached. You may want to have tear-off sheets that include your name and phone number (see Example 4-6). Include "music lessons" or something similar so if the little slip of paper sits in the person's wallet for two months they'll know what the number is for and remember to call you. (Also this helps avoid suspicious looks from spouse or significant other when a mysterious name and phone number falls from a potential student's shirt pocket.) Include day and evening phone numbers if you work and can receive calls without affecting your job.

Robert Wolfe

A Piano Teacher
Who Makes a Difference

- Bachelor's in Music Performance,
  University of California
- Ten years' teaching experience
- Extensive performing career
  including performances with the
  Wellesley Symphony,
  Boston Opera Company
- Master classes with
  Claude Bolling and Andre Previn
- Reasonable rates
- Group and family discounts available
- Certified educator
- First lesson free
- References available upon request

Call Evenings @ (999) 555-5555

Robert Wolfe (999) 555-5555 Piano Lessons	Robert Wolfe (999) 555-5555 Piano Lessons	Robert Wolfe (999) 555-5555 Piano Lessons	Robert Wolfe (999) 555-5555 Piano Lessons	Robert Wolfe (999) 555-5555 Piano Lessons	Robert Wolfe (999) 555-5555 Piano Lessons	Robert Wolfe (999) 555-5555 Piano Lessons	Robert Wolfe (999) 555-5555 Piano Lessons

Example 4-6. Flier with Tear-Off Sheets

Do not include a home address in your ads. You may design a poster that details information about your extensive knowledge of MIDI, computer technology and electronic keyboards. Then you include a home phone, work phone and your home address. To a professional thief, your ad reads like this: "Tons of expensive equipment available. Stop by during daytime hours when I am at work. Help yourself." If you teach at home you eventually give directions to your home to any new student. But by that time you have talked to the student and/or the parents and can make a better judgment as to the sincerity of the individual and whether or not you are being set up.

Bumper stickers are another form of displaying your interest in music or the nature of your profession, but consider them carefully. "I've Got SAX Appeal" might get a laugh and let people know of your musical interests. Displaying a sticker in your rear window from New York Conservatory of Music will undoubtedly elicit a wave from a fellow "alum." Unfortunately, you may reach the wrong audience with your message. Having a "Kiss a Musician" bumper sticker on the back of your van, which is weighted down with equipment, may be a clear invitation to thieves to "rip off a musician" instead. Even if your van is empty (when you're performing, for example), really vicious types may wait until you return to rip you off up close and personal.

If you are a piano teacher who travels to students' homes then you probably aren't transporting a piano in your trunk, so it can't hurt to show off a sticker from your alma mater. However, if you're carrying around a guitar, saxophone or anything portable on your backseat or in your trunk, you don't want a bumper sticker or windshield decal to be an invitation for theft.

You can always be a bit more subtle if you still want to exhibit your craft on the highways. We once saw a vanity license plate that read EBGDAE, the tuning notes on a six-string guitar. At least that musician wanted to be robbed by someone who had a fundamental understanding of the merchandise.

MAKING THE MOST OF LOCAL MEDIA

To really get your message to the public, take advantage of the electronic and print media. We're not suggesting you take out a sixty-second spot during halftime of the Super Bowl, but with some careful research and legwork you may be able to take advantage of some relatively inexpensive advertising or free media services that are available in your community.

Newspapers and Magazines

Almost every community, regardless of size or location, has daily, weekly and monthly publications that reach a large section of the population. If you are in search of new students, we strongly recommend that you search out the best deal for the widest possible exposure through these publications. Most include a classified ad section listing items and services from used automobiles to chimney repair. Most classifieds have an "instruction" section that may include bartending classes, dance lessons and, most important, musical instruction. Most newspaper and magazine readers are adults, so tailor these ads to a mature population.

Daily newspapers in your area have the greatest circulation (especially the Sunday edition) but they are probably the most costly places to run an ad. We suggest running your ad more than once and checking into lower rates for repeating the ad. If you can only afford a one-time spot then you certainly want to consider the Sunday paper as your first choice. Sundays are the one time during the week when many families (especially those with school-age children) can afford the leisure time to kick back and read the newspaper. Therefore, someone is more likely to happen upon or search out your ad on a Sunday than any other day of the week and to be just relaxed enough to think they can fit a weekly music lesson into their schedule.

Since many people who buy or subscribe to a daily newspaper use the paper for a source of news and information but do not use it as commonly to search out information about services, it's often more economical and efficient to search out a different type of newspaper. Most daily newspapers are located in a big city surrounded by smaller communities and suburbs. Smaller communities often publish a weekly newspaper with more local sports, politics, community activities, etc. Since the classified sections of these papers are also geared more to the individual community, citizens of these communities are more apt to look for services in their weekly paper first, before referring to the larger daily paper. Many of the smaller papers work within a network of communities so your classified ad may also run in four or five other neighboring communities through their weekly papers. Because the cost is significantly less, you may be able to run an ad for an entire month or longer for the cost of one Sunday ad in the daily paper.

Consider running a display ad or reproduction of your business card in the local newspapers. This removes you from the classified section so you increase your visibility by placing an ad in a popular section like the local news or sports. However, the cost is greatly increased by this move and you may miss those people who look specifically for musical instruction in the classified section.

Larger markets may have a daily newspaper *and* a monthly magazine. These magazines are usually more upscale and geared to the business community and working white-collar crowd. They sometimes offer a classified section in the back of the magazine.

Your city's chamber of commerce may also offer a directory of businesses in the community. Consider including a business ad or reproduction of your business card in this publication, designing your ad for the type of reader you expect from each market.

VOICE LESSONS. Caring instructor with over fifteen years' teaching experience. Accepting students of all levels. Specializing in acoustic folk styles. Low rates. References available. Call days 555-5555.

FRUSTRATED by go-nowhere guitar lessons? Try my innovative approach to music. Lessons designed with your goals in mind. Call now. First lesson free. 555-5555.

Always Dream of taking music lessons? Here's your chance. Learn piano in the comfort of your own home. Experienced teacher. New to area. Now accepting students. Specializing in beginners and children. Leave message 555-5555.

Example 4-7. Newspaper Classified Ads That Appeal to a Variety of Readers

Local Cable Television

Most larger population areas have at least one local television broadcasting station. Smaller communities may have very small independent stations and a local access cable channel. While running an ad on the network or independent stations may be prohibitively expensive, there are numerous opportunities on much smaller levels through cable that you can take advantage of.

Your local cable company may run a separate station that carries printed information such as time of day, temperature, etc. It may also flash the number and address of the cable company in case you have questions. Our cable company offers a community marketplace where businesses can advertise their services. For a very affordable price an ad runs more than 130 times a week at regular intervals during the day. Many people flip to these types of stations for a few minutes each day to find out about community goings-on.

You can also consider producing a thirty-second or sixty-second television spot to run during a local break on a sports or movie channel received by subscribers. This type of advertising is directed to the market in your specific area and can be very economical in contrast to an ad on a network station.

Local access cable television basically allows anyone in the community to put on their own programming. This affords you two possibilities. First, you might be able to gain an interview, guest spot or feature on an established program. If you are just establishing yourself as a music teacher, it may be difficult to get someone to interview or spotlight you as an expert music teacher, so you may find it necessary to feature some other aspect of your career. Maybe the station has a program featuring local artists and you can showcase special instruments or a particular style of music.

Second, if you are truly ambitious, you can use the local access channel to produce your own show. You may have to take a course in production to familiarize yourself with the workings of the television studio. Courses in video production may be offered through the station or may be available from a local university or community college. You can learn to produce any type of show you want. Perhaps you can interview area artists and musicians and feature their work on your show. If you have a band, you can produce a series of shows featuring your band with guest musicians from the area. Our station has a show produced by a dance instructor featuring a class of young children. The same format can be used for young musicians. Perhaps you can organize several student recitals or group lessons to produce as a series. This is a great way to advertise your teaching style and abilities. You can even try developing a course in musical instruction to be broadcast weekly, then use the tapes from the series as promotional and/or lesson material.

Radio Advertising

Like television, local radio provides you many opportunities to get your name out to the public at an affordable cost. Community announcements are made on most stations, so you can publicize any performances or public events that you are presenting. Like cable television, radio may have special interest programming on which you can make a special appearance or be interviewed. For instance, if you specialize in teaching jazz trumpet, advertise your skill during their evening jazz programming.

Most college stations have programs that feature local artists. Some even have the facilities to do live broadcasts of bands. We know of many bands that have done live radio broadcast and received high quality, affordable recordings from the station. The broadcast often features interviews with the musicians, which affords you a great opportunity to promote your career as a teacher.

Community Calendars

Although it would be ideal to have an endless supply of advertising throughout your area, financial constraints inevitably rule in the end. You may place several ads in the daily papers or on the local cable channel and invest a modest amount of business capital up front. If you gain several students from your ads then it proves a good investment. You may place your ad, however, and several weeks later have nothing but a few crank phone calls to show for it. At this point you may have to rethink your market or try *using* the media without making the initial capital investment.

Most media sources have a community bulletin board listing happenings for the week. Concerts, clinics, recitals and workshops are all things that can be included in a calendar of events. Although this doesn't directly advertise your services as a music instructor, the benefits from the publicity you receive indirectly affect your referrals greatly.

Begin to create a list of media sources that publish or broadcast events of interest in the community. Be sure to include student newspapers from the area schools. If you have access to a personal computer, you can purchase a mailing label software program. Print a sheet of mailing labels for all media sources you have compiled (see Example 4-8). Then, when you have an upcoming event, you can quickly send a press release to each media source. Be sure that each time you compose a press release you include your experience as a private music instructor and a way to contact you. If the press release is published with the information about your teaching experience, you have successfully managed to receive some very valuable publicity *and* advertising for the cost of a postage stamp. If you use this system of press releases often and have an extensive list of media sources, you may want to consider investigating the bulk mail rate available through the U.S. Postal Service (see Example 4-9).

Community Calendar Coordinator
WWDD TV-50
Sunshine Lane
Anytown, USA 99999

Community Calendar Coordinator
Little Newspaper, Inc.
123 Elm Street
Anytown, USA 99999

Community Calendar Bulletin Board
Northern Cable Co.
Industrial Park Place
Anytown, USA 99999

Mark Starr
Arts&Leisure
New London Times
2999 Main Street
Anytown, USA 99999

Rachel Greiner
WNL Radio
Broadcast Lane
Anytown, USA 99999

Community Calendar Coordinator
WELD Broadcasting
PO Box 1334
Anytown, USA 99999

Example 4-8. Media Mailing List

****** **PRESS RELEASE** ******* **PRESS RELEASE** ********

Local musician David Smith will perform an evening of solo piano music on Friday, June 12, at 8:00 P.M. at the Union Public Library. The public is invited to attend. Admission to the concert is free.

Mr. Smith, a Union resident, is a well-known private music instructor in the area.

For further information about Friday's concert call 555-5555.

Example 4-9. Press Release

USING THE YELLOW PAGES

A one-time effort that can gain you many referrals is an ad placed in the yellow pages of your local telephone directory. It may be a comment on the power of advertising in our culture but think how often we use the yellow pages as our first source when deciding on a service.

The advantage of a yellow pages ad is the year-long exposure you receive. A chamber of commerce business directory or an issue of the town magazine is likely to be tossed in the bottom of the magazine rack or waste can, never to surface again. The yellow pages are at every prospective student's fingertips for twelve months a year. The disadvantages are that only students who are *looking* for music instruction find you and the cost of an ad in the yellow pages is quite high. To make it more affordable, most phone companies will divide the

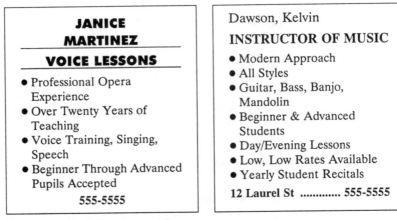

Example 4-10. Yellow Pages Ads

cost of the ad and bill it as an additional cost on your monthly phone statement. Unfortunately, if your yellow pages ad proves ineffective, you must continue monthly payments until the next issue of the phone book is published and you figure out what went wrong.

BUSINESS CARDS: FROM DRAB TO FAB

By now you should be getting the idea that self-promotion is the cornerstone of building an extensive base of students. Your very first investment should be in a good set of business cards. Luckily, this is a very affordable investment. It shouldn't be long before you get to the stage when you can't pass a bulletin board or shake hands with someone without reaching for a business card. Cards stay in a person's wallet or on a bulletin board indefinitely until someone needs a teacher and your name comes immediately to mind.

During any conversation in which the subject of music or music lessons arises be sure to offer your card and let the person know of your career as a music instructor. Even if the person you are speaking with has no interest in music lessons, at some point in a future conversation the subject may arise and this person can be a source for a referral. Without being pushy or rude, you can offer several cards for multiple referrals. Say "Take two, they're very small." Since business cards cost pennies apiece, you can readily afford to give them away to practically anyone.

Because you have so little space on a business card, be sparing with the information. However, don't make your card too drab because people might connect a boring business card with an uninspired music teacher (see Example 4-11). Make sure you state what your business is because your name and phone number are of little value if the person doesn't have any information about your occupation.

The tendency usually is to go in the other direction and try to include too much information on one card. You want your card to attract someone's eye, not to give them a headache trying to figure out just what it is you do (see Example 4-12). Also, some people are legitimately suspicious of those who claim they can do a million things well. Most of us have to be content with having a specialty. If you are a Jill-of-all-trades, consider having several different business cards for the various things you do. You may want separate cards to advertise your performing and studio abilities; your arranging, composing and music copying service; and your teaching business. Besides eliminating the clutter of too many services, this allows you the option of designing cards for each specific market (see Examples 4-13, 4-14, 4-15).

There are advantages to having several different business cards but there are also disadvantages to be aware of. You have to be organized enough to keep a supply of your various cards with you at all times — a stack in your car, some at the studio or store, some in your wallet. It may be impossible to keep things straight so you hand people the correct card. Someone who wants lessons may be completely confused if they get home and look at a card offering lawn care instead. One solution to the organizational (and cost) concerns of having multiple business cards is to have one generalized business card for everything you do. Don't make it too general but use it to attract people's attention and get them interested in what you really do offer them. The business card David has used for nearly a decade is shown in Example 4-16.

Making your business card attractive and eye-catching is important. Use color background paper in most cases. Remember that certain colors and certain typefaces connote specific images. Tan or ecru card stock with fancy lettering suggests an "uppercrust air" that's good for classical players and for cards given to parents. Bold colors, such as black, white, bright red and fuschia, and block print suggest a more modern approach. White is cheaper but color is much more interesting. Consider using color print as well, perhaps black lettering with color highlighting or graphics. Adding a design, logo or photo greatly enhances the appearance of your card.

Being able to hand a professionally designed business card to a

Jackie Steward

555-5555

Example 4-11.
*Too simple. Who
is this person? Is
she a hairdresser?
Is he a race car
driver? What does
this person do?
Where do they
live? Is there an
area code?*

GUITAR BASS DRUMS KEYBOARDS
* plus a variety of additional instruments *

JIM MORRISEY

Weddings, Club Dates, Private Parties,
Studio Work, Private and Group Instruction

Home: Work: M-F 9-5
(999) 555-5555   (999) 555-9999

Example 4-12.
*Too busy. Is there
anything this guy
can't do?*

Woodwinds

Alvin Bailey
performances, studio sessions

**Los Angeles
(999) 555-5555**

Example 4-13.
*Jazzy. For
musician-to-
musican contacts,
possible gigs.*

Woodwinds

Alvin Bailey
music copying, arranging, film scoring

Los Angeles
(999) 555-5555

Example 4-14.
*Business referrals.
Networking with
executives.*

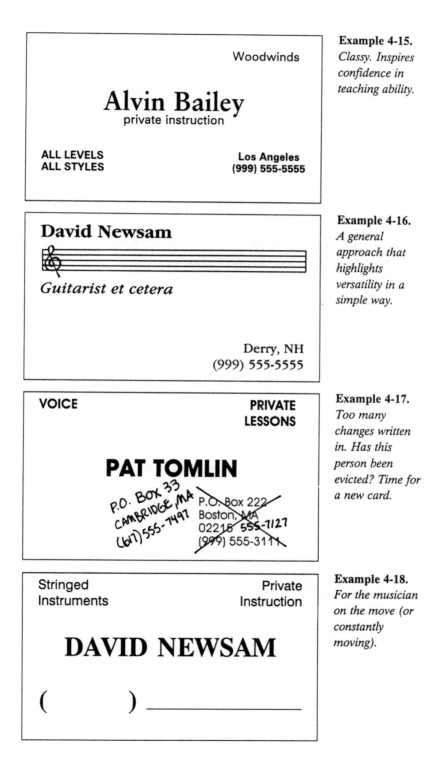

Example 4-15.
Classy. Inspires confidence in teaching ability.

Example 4-16.
A general approach that highlights versatility in a simple way.

Example 4-17.
Too many changes written in. Has this person been evicted? Time for a new card.

Example 4-18.
For the musician on the move (or constantly moving).

prospective student, a parent or a colleague enhances the important first impression you make. When someone wants to contact you about lessons, you don't want to have to ask the waiter for a pen and a paper napkin to write down your phone number. Your image is also greatly damaged if the card you hand out has three phone numbers scratched out and your latest written in (see Example 4-17). If you are the transient type, one option is to leave a blank space on your card so a number can be written in or typed in later (see Example 4-18). This way if you are forced into a move on short notice you don't have 450 useless business cards. You can keep a supply of a few dozen on hand and type in numbers as you go along.

CREATING A POSITIVE NETWORK FOR TEACHER-TO-TEACHER REFERRAL

Of all the methods of receiving student referrals, none is more valuable and rewarding than referrals you get from your colleagues. When you are in competition for students, it's easy to fall into the trap of feeling adversarial toward other teachers, but you should resist this temptation mightily. Other teachers can eventually become your strongest allies.

Networking with fellow teachers in your community is an important public relations move. Take time to hang out at the local music store and possibly meet up with a fellow teacher. If it is someone you don't know, stick out your hand and introduce yourself. Find out something about this person and let them know something about you. If the opportunity seems right, exchange business cards. These contacts can lead to important long-term relationships that can benefit you with many future referrals. You may even consider starting a teacher organization, newsletter or networking "club" or hosting a one-time "get-to-know-each-other" event.

Many successful teachers not only have a full teaching load but also have a waiting list of those wishing to study with them as soon as an opening is available. Certain students may wish to begin lessons immediately. Beginning students usually want to jump into lessons the minute they make the decision to take up a musical instrument. Most teachers with waiting lists have several colleagues to whom they refer potential students.

As you begin to establish contacts with your colleagues you may feel a sense of competition. If you teach drums and there is only one other drum teacher in town you may feel a conflict of interest in establishing a relationship with someone who could conceivably take away some of your business. But competition is healthy. It can push you to be more aggressive or ingenious in recruiting your students and in advertising or promoting your skills. It can also inspire you to become a better teacher. To attract students, you want to develop a method and a style that students can identify with you.

Another feeling that might restrict your networking abilities is simple inhibition. If you're embarrassed or insecure about introducing yourself to a fellow teacher, you may miss an important opportunity to develop a relationship with a colleague. Don't wait around and hope the other person will initiate the meeting. If you feel insecure, one of the easiest ways to introduce yourself is to say, "I hear great things about you. I'm really glad to finally get to meet you." Starting a relationship with a compliment always smooths the way.

While being timid may be a detriment to meeting other teachers, being overly aggressive can be a disaster. If you greet someone and start soliciting them for business before you even get their name, you will probably turn them off for good. And if they have an established network of colleagues, you may jeopardize any future contacts with them as well. Be aggressive in meeting teachers but avoid pushing people or making them feel used.

The best teacher contact may be your own former instructor. Who better to judge your abilities and character than someone who has worked with you and shaped you and your playing style in their own way? Many teachers refer work to former or current students they know to be capable, responsible individuals. Take time to contact your former teachers and let them know of your plans to begin teaching. Ask for their suggestions in developing certain methods. Share any difficulties you have encountered with new students, and share your feelings of fear or insecurity. Most teachers are very generous in sharing their knowledge and experience. We find it rewarding to refer work to former students and to see music become a more and more important part of their lives.

ENCOURAGING REFERRALS FROM YOUR STUDENTS

There is clearly no better advertisement for your work as a teacher than the knowledge you have imparted to your private students. As often as performing musicians are asked, "Do you teach lessons?" performing musicians are asked, "Are you taking lessons with someone?" What better way to get the word out than for your own students to refer their peers to you? (For a related discussion of student performances see chapter eight.)

One way to encourage referrals from your private students is to offer a bonus to anyone who refers a student to you. Print a coupon advertising a free lesson for each referral you receive. Perhaps you can have a contest in which the person referring the most students receives a month of free lessons. You can also offer musical merchandise, copies of your recordings, or anything that would encourage your students to talk to their peers about your incredible abilities as a music instructor. Remember that younger students, especially teenagers, often "hang" in musical circles. If a student is involved in music, his friends probably are too. Each of your private students can potentially provide referrals to you.

INCREASING YOUR VISIBILITY IN THE COMMUNITY

It should be fairly obvious by now that most of your advertising involves getting your name out into the public. This is definitely more involved than just taking out an ad in the daily newspaper and waiting for the students to start signing up for lessons. Besides advertising directly for students, a lot of your exposure comes from networking, referrals, and gaining visibility in the community.

Finding students requires continuous effort to get your name out there to the people who are currently or might someday be interested in studying with you. Surprisingly, the business of attracting students sometimes has little to do with music. You rarely hear a student say, "Mr. Jones can really play the french horn. That's why I like him." You are much more likely to hear, "My french horn teacher, Mr. Jones, is a really cool guy. He's nice and I've learned a lot with him in a short time." Finding students means being a diplomat, an active and visible member of your community, and a champion for music and the things "music people" believe in. You must be friendly and reliable, the type of person parents trust with their child.

The Financial Wisdom of Volunteering

The numerous opportunities in the community for volunteering, both musical and not, pay off in the long run. Musicians striving to perfect their craft spend many hours in practice rooms and rehearsal halls. Unfortunately, not a lot of networking takes place in these locations. You need to get out into the community just to meet other residents of your area. One way is to volunteer your time with a charitable or church organization. The people you meet may be the friends, relatives or co-workers of your future music students.

Volunteer to perform in churches and synagogues. We've gained numerous referrals by actively performing in our church. In addition, we have sung in choir, served on committees, and assisted in the maintenance of the church as a way of being more involved with the citizens of our community. The more people who know you, the greater the likelihood that they will be engaged in a conversation with someone about music lessons, and that your name will come up, not only as a terrific teacher, but as a nice person as well.

Nursing homes and hospitals are also wonderful places to share your abilities and spend time with people who may need strength and encouragement. What better way to do this than to perform for an appreciative audience.

In networking with the music educators in your area, offer your services as a guest lecturer in their schools. Make yourself available to augment a band or orchestra should they be short a player or need a "ringer" for a more difficult work they may present. Above all, become active in the parents' organization at school because that is where you come face to face with the providers of your bread and butter. Most libraries have a community room available free for nonprofit events. You can give a recital or a lecture on a musical topic at no cost to the participants.

Get involved in the community and in the lives of your students. Make them feel like they are more than just a source of income in your life. Attend their school performances, organize recitals, volunteer them (with their permission, of course) for community events, take them into nursing homes and hospitals. Give them a taste of how fortunate you feel to be involved with music and what a career in music might be like (see chapter eight).

FINDING A JOB

As most performing musicians and songwriters know, it is essential to have a carefully organized and professional-looking promotional package to offer potential employers. As you venture into the music teaching business, a similar kind of promotion package may serve you well as you apply to schools, summer camps, and even as you approach prospective parents.

The Promo Package

Each promotional package you put together should feature a resume listing your experience and education, a list of personal references and sometimes a photo. Include a demonstration tape, showcasing your performance abilities. Each package should include a cover letter composed for and directed to the specific individual or committee reviewing the material.

Photo. If you choose to include a photo, a simple black-and-white, glossy 8″ × 10″ should be sufficient for your package. It should be a head shot and you should appear relaxed and comfortable. Bear in mind that a photo can sometimes hurt your application rather than support it, so use your judgment. When applying for a teaching position at a private academy, it's a good idea *not* to include a full-bodied color photo of your glam-rock band in full pose. In most cases you should lean toward the conservative. Remember that first impressions are crucial in the business world.

Having a black-and-white photo can also be useful for publicizing events in the local newspapers. Most newspaper editors are more likely to publish a story about a player or combo if it is accompanied by a picture. If you are hired at a school, they may want a photo to include in their newsletter or faculty directory.

If you are simply creating a brochure that details your teaching experience, a small picture of yourself printed in the pamphlet may be sufficient. Parents, especially, like to get a glimpse of who will be teaching their youngster so they know whom to let in the door.

Resume. The dictionary defines "resume" as "*n.* a summary of one's personal history, background, work and education." For someone applying for a teaching position, a good resume can make the difference in getting that interview and being hired for the job.

If you have a word processor, designing a professional-looking resume is easy. If you have access to a laser printer, the quality definitely enhances your presentation. If not, consider consulting a professional so your resume best represents you. Don't use a typewriter to do your resume.

One advantage to having a word processor is that you can update your resume constantly. In addition, you can have several different resumes on file. If you apply for a job at a community college, your resume should highlight your education and classroom teaching experience. If a prospective student is reading your resume, more of your private teaching and performance experience should be highlighted.

Try to personalize each resume to the particular situation. Make your resume fit on one page if possible. Highlight only the important, pertinent information. You can go into greater detail during a personal interview, so leave the resume powerful but sparse (see Examples 4-19 and 4-20).

Like the photo to be included in your package, the resume should be neat, attractive and somewhat conservative. Printing a resume on neon orange may catch someone's attention, but what does it say about your ability to represent Stiff Upper Lip University?

Personal references. Each promotional package should include either several personal references or a statement saying "references available upon request." You may choose not to release the names and addresses of your references until you are being considered for the position available.

If you choose to list them, include three to six different references. Try to get a cross section of references to highlight different aspects of your abilities and interests. References from your profession are important, but personal references who can attest to your outstanding human nature are important as well (see Example 4-21). A politician, respected businessperson, doctor or community leader listed among your references helps round out your package. Don't include your mother or your best friend from high school as personal references, since there are legitimate questions about their objectivity.

For each reference include the person's title or position as well as address and phone number. Be sure to check that each reference person is comfortable speaking on your behalf and doesn't mind being contacted. Include a business phone and/or address for anyone who prefers not to be contacted at home.

It goes without saying that when choosing individuals for your reference list you should only consider people you feel are strong allies. Don't list the name of your ex-boss because she is a prominent politician in town if she just fired you from your last job, or if your position was so obscure that she won't remember you. Find people who have seen you in your best light and who can convey that impression to a potential employer. Most employers do call at least one or two references.

Demonstration tape. If this is your first time testing the job market, you may not have a very extensive or impressive resume. How do you demonstrate experience if this is your first shot at teaching? You can't. Teaching musicians who are just starting out must try to showcase

Shirley Foudy-Lewis
212 Long Street
Union, TN 99999
(999) 555-5555

TEACHING EXPERIENCE

Community Music School, Instructor, Music Faculty, 1989-Present
• Teach 25-30 private lessons and five performance ensembles weekly
• Serve on proficiency and placement examination juries
• Design original curriculum for private lessons and ensembles
• Serve as member of faculty Substance Abuse Awareness Committee
• Teach additional five-week specialized adult summer program

Northfield Guitar Workshop, Instructor, Faculty, 1990-Present
• Teach core classes in contemporary rock, blues, fusion and jazz styles
• Teach elective classes in improvisation, ear training and theory
• Direct student ensembles for weekly performances and perform in faculty concerts
• Wrote currently used textbook for advanced rock course

Brown Academy, Director of Music, 1993-94
• Taught five sections of music courses each semester
• Designed curriculum for music appreciation and innovative guitar course
• Directed student band and chorus, provided direction for seasonal concerts and musicals
• Coached boys' junior varsity soccer and girls' junior varsity basketball

Private Instruction, 1988-Present
• Teach students of all levels and ages, interested in a variety of styles
• Maintain extensive library of supplemental teaching materials for students
• Incorporate computer technology and MIDI into private lessons
• Prepare college-bound music students for admission and audition requirements

EDUCATION

Community College of Music, Union, Tennessee
• **Bachelor of Arts** in Music Performance; 1987
Graduated Cum Laude

VOLUNTEER AND COMMUNITY WORK

Community Jazz Ensemble, Director, Union, Tennessee, 1992-Present
• Initiative sponsored by the Girl Scouts of America for outstanding youth ages 14-20
• Performances include Palace Theater, Union; Union Memorial Auditorium
• Annual recording sessions at Sound Tracks Studios in Union, Tennessee

PERSONAL

Born 7/25/63. Excellent health. Married. One child. Baseball enthusiast.

Example 4-19. One-Page Resume

Shirley Foudy-Lewis
212 Long Street
Union, TN 99999
(999) 555-5555

TEACHING EXPERIENCE

Community Music School, Instructor, Music Faculty, 1989-Present
• Teach 25-30 private lessons and five performance ensembles weekly
• Serve on proficiency and placement examination juries
• Design original curriculum for private lessons and ensembles
• Serve as member of faculty Substance Abuse Awareness Committee
• Selected to teach additional five-week specialized adult summer program

Northfield Guitar Workshop, Instructor, Faculty, 1990-Present
• Teach core classes in contemporary rock, blues, fusion and jazz styles
• Teach elective classes in improvisation, ear training and theory
• Direct student ensembles for weekly performances and perform in faculty concerts
• Wrote currently used textbook for advanced rock course

Brown Academy, Director of Music, 1993-94
• Taught five sections of music courses each semester
• Designed curriculum for music appreciation and innovative guitar course
• Directed student band and chorus, provided direction for seasonal concerts and musicals
• Coached boys' junior varsity soccer and girls' junior varsity basketball

Private Instruction, 1988-Present
• Teach students of all levels and ages, interested in a variety of styles
• Maintain extensive library of supplemental teaching materials for students
• Incorporate computer technology and MIDI into private lessons
• Prepare college-bound music students for admission and audition requirements

EDUCATION

University of Tennessee — Union, Union, Tennessee
• Coursework in Master of Education Program; 1992-present

Community College of Music, Union, Tennessee
• **Bachelor of Arts** in Music Performance; 1987
Graduated Cum Laude

-1-

Example 4-20. Two-Page Resume

Shirley Foudy-Lewis
212 Long Street
Union, TN 99999
(999) 555-5555

PERFORMING EXPERIENCE

Union Chamber Players, 1990-Present
Contemporary chamber works by local composers
Performances include Palace Theater, Union Memorial Auditorium
CD entitled "New World Works" on Earthworks label; released 1993

Community Arts School Faculty Quintet, 1989-Present
Faculty Ensemble performing in a variety of styles and settings

Solo Guitarist, 1986-Present
Solo performances; classical and jazz guitar

Jonathan Skyles — Storyteller, 1986-1989
Accompanist for children's storyteller

VOLUNTEER AND COMMUNITY WORK

Community Jazz Ensemble, Director, Union, Tennessee 1992-Present
• Initiative sponsored by the Girl Scouts of America for outstanding
youth, ages 14-20
• Performances include Palace Theater, Union; Union Memorial
Auditorium
• Annual recording sessions at Sound Tracks Recording Studio, Union

Unitarian Church of Union, Music Director, 1994-present
• Organize weekly music program for church service
• Select music, rehearse choral group
• Book local and national performing arts groups for annual concert
series

PERSONAL

Born 7/25/63. Excellent health. Married. One child. Baseball enthusiast.

REFERENCES

Leonard Balley
Music Department Chairman
Community College of Music
140 Elm Street
Bolton, Massachusetts 99999
(999) 555-5555

Mary Hebert
Sounds Good Music
Main Street
Winchester, New Hampshire 99999
(999) 555-5555

Michael Anton
12 Abbey Street
Conval, New Hampshire 99999
(999) 555-5555

Lisa Cole
Office of Admissions
Community College of Music
140 Elm Street
Bolton, Massachusetts 99999
(999) 555-5555

William Smith, Headmaster
Brown Academy
Southwood, New Hampshire 99999
(999) 555-5555

David Smoltz, Director
Northfield Guitar Workshop
Box 1234
Northfield, New Hampshire 99999
(999) 555-5555

Example 4-21. List of References

another aspect of their talents. For many people it's their performance abilities. For someone with a doctorate from Yale, the highlight is their education. For someone who has taught private lessons for three decades, it is their work history.

Although we strongly recommend that you make private teaching a career decision and not a last resort, many of us started out in the field of music as players. Only after many years did the decision to teach become an option in our lives. Being a brilliant performer does not guarantee success in the role of teacher. However, having a wide variety of performing experiences and interests gives you much to draw on as you embark on your new career in teaching. A demonstration tape in your promo package might be just the thing to get the attention of that prospective client or employer.

As with your resume and cover letter, be flexible with your demo tape. Rather than recording and packaging one tape for every situation, have several options for each opportunity that arises. If you have just released a new compact disc with your band, you may be tempted to include a copy of the CD as a demo tape of your playing. It may be wiser to photocopy the album cover and any positive reviews you've received and use sections of the recording as part of your demo. Most people who are considering you as a potential employee or private teacher are not about to listen to a sixty-minute recording, especially if you are one of several candidates for the position.

Make your tape short—five to ten minutes should be sufficient. Tailor your demo to meet the interests or expectations of the people hearing the tape. If you are applying for a job as violin instructor at a classical string camp, is it wise to include a selection from your bluegrass band? It may help exemplify your versatility, but perhaps you want to include a sample of your work with a string quartet instead. And include a variety of selections that feature you prominently. Don't include a five-minute recording that only has you playing an eight-measure solo. Record the solo only and use the other four and a half minutes for other examples.

Be sure to include music that has been recorded professionally. Don't flip on your Walkman and start jammin'. When packaging your demo use high-quality cassette tapes and print a cover with your name clearly marked. Make sure you listen to the tape before sending it out to verify the quality. Sometimes recordings are duplicated on the wrong speed, for instance, and your oboe could sound like a piccolo. Cue the tape to the beginning of your selections.

Cover letter. While your promo package may change slightly from situation to situation, it should essentially be comprised of the same basic materials: resume, references, photo, demo and a cover letter. In highly competitive situations, some potential employers look no further than the cover letter and discard any with typos or misspellings. Be sure your cover letter is *perfect.*

Include your address and the name, title and address of the person receiving the materials. If you have spoken to this person previously, refer to that meeting or conversation in the cover letter. State clearly and precisely why you are sending the package to this person. You may be responding to an advertised position, be new to the area and in search of work, or following up on someone's referral of you for a position.

In a concise and simple way, state why you are qualified for this position and what you have to offer this employer or client. Instead of "I think I'd be a good teacher, and I don't mind teenagers so much," try " My extensive teaching and performing experience will . . ." Avoid weak language like, "I feel I could do a good job," in favor of "I will be a positive addition to your world-renowned faculty."

If you are a poor speller or have trouble with grammar or punctuation, use your computer's spell-checker and/or grammar-checker and ask someone else to proofread for you. Having someone else look over the letter is a good idea even if you think it's perfect. It is just human nature that we often overlook our own mistakes.

Conclude your cover letter with an expectation of an interview or further discussion and offer a phone number where you can be reached. "I look forward to meeting with you to discuss my qualifications. Should you have any questions please feel free to contact me at (999) 555-5555." Many good books are available through your public library or local bookstore on writing strong and effective cover letters.

Promotional Pamphlets/Brochures

Many music agencies offer prospective clients a brochure about the agency and the bands it represents. These brochures tend to be very glitzy, detailing the myriad ensembles available through the agency. Instead of sending a package of promotional materials, you may want to consolidate your resources and produce a brochure highlighting your many talents and abilities. You can choose a format that highlights only your teaching abilities, or create a more comprehensive brochure describing the many tasks you feel qualified to undertake.

JOE STANTON

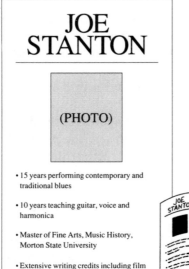

(PHOTO)

- 15 years performing contemporary and traditional blues

- 10 years teaching guitar, voice and harmonica

- Master of Fine Arts, Music History, Morton State University

- Extensive writing credits including film scores for two major studio releases

Front Panel

TEACHING

"I've studied for years with other teachers, but after several months with Joe, I'm playing things I only dreamed of before."
Tony Sumbury
age 23

"Joe Stanton is a caring, patient instructor with tremendous insight into the blues masters."
Linda Sprague
age 39

- Carefully designed program of instruction geared to the level, style and pace of the individual student

- Students of all ages and levels will benefit from this unique teaching approach

"Mr. Stanton is a neat guy, and his lessons are cool."
Todd Lyon
age 12

Back Panel

PERFORMANCE

"...a masterful mix of early roots blues, and screaming electric funk."
Steve Bouchard
Blues Line magazine

- **Smokin' Joe & the Fine Line**
National tours as opening act for blues legends, Elmore Jones, Johnny Summers and Ruth Greene

Appearances at:
- Chicago Blues Festival
- Isle of Lucy Blues Festival
- First Night Chicago

"Smokin' Joe & the Fine Line warmed up a cold Chicago New Year's Eve."
Robert Blaschke
Director
First Night Chicago

WRITING/FILM SCORING

"...the film's 1930s setting is made even more realistic with the presence of the bluesy soundtrack composed by Joe Stanton."
Steve Berman
Chicago Times

- Composed 12 original songs included on solo album released on Blue Times label

- Composed and orchestrated soundtrack for two Parastudio feature-length films, *The Guardhouse* and *Times of Trouble*.

"Joe's music gave the film the perfect edge..."
Lisa Cassandra
Director,
Times of Trouble

Inside Spread

Example 4-22. Brochure

Begin the brochure with a photo and biography, highlighting education, work and performance experience as you would in your resume. Use a more "reader-friendly" format, such as bullet lists, to highlight certain aspects of your experience. The brochure continues, describing each of your areas of expertise, section by section. You may have sections on performing, songwriting, film scoring, arranging, music copying and private teaching. Each section should list specific experience and work history (see Example 4-22).

The promotional pamphlet is ideal for the person diversified enough to advertise many musical talents. However, if you specialize in only one or two areas of expertise or are applying for one specific opportunity, such as a teaching position, it is preferable to use a package with resume and references. If you have the finances to design a package *and* a brochure then do so. However, the package is much more flexible for promoting yourself in a variety of situations.

SOME FINAL WORDS ABOUT MARKETING YOURSELF

We can't emphasize enough the importance of getting your name out into the public in a positive light. Promoting yourself requires confidence, perseverance and ingenuity. If you apply yourself to the task and let your creativity guide you, you are sure to enjoy name recognition, the respect of your musical colleagues, and a schedule full of eager students.

CHAPTER FIVE

TEACHING PRIVATE LESSONS TO YOUNG CHILDREN

The key to successful lessons is to tailor your teaching style to each population you encounter. Never is this truer than when you teach children from ages three to twelve. Using the same techniques and materials that you rely on for adults simply won't work with children. This chapter is designed to help you with teaching young children, so they remain interested and you feel effective dealing with them. Not only can working with children be enchanting, children are by far your most important client base, because if they stay with the instrument, you have created a customer for life.

There are two distinct aspects of working with small children to consider. Obviously, the most important is understanding children's needs and designing materials and methods that are within their capabilities and that spark and foster their lifelong interest in music. The other side of dealing with children is accepting the fact that while the child is your student, his or her parents are your paying customers. Dealing with that reality is almost always a feat of considerable patience and diplomacy.

RECOGNIZING AND DEALING WITH DIFFERENT PARENTING STYLES

The more comfortable and diplomatic you are with parents, the more success you can achieve with their children. Identifying particular parenting styles gives you insight into how to deal with each individual parent. Developing a successful relationship with each parent is crucial because the parent then becomes your ally in working with the child. When working with children, you welcome any assistance you can get.

A teacher encounters all types of parents. Remember that many times the two parents of a child fall into different categories, so don't assume that mom and dad are always on the same wavelength. Often they are at polar extremes. Also remember that a great number of parents are divorced or separated and may not always be communicating. The instructions or information you give one parent may never reach the other. (The same is true for some married couples.)

The Gusher

One parenting style we encounter gushes, "We're so *glad* he likes playing the drums." Then there's a nervous giggle and a knowing glance. "But we really want him to pursue a *real* career." This attitude is particularly prevalent in parents of teenagers.

Some parents seem to sit around waiting for their child to tire of this music thing. (And sometimes, it's a short wait!) They are often the type of parents who seemingly want to give their children the opportunity to pursue a talent in which they show any interest. Yet, when you get right down to it, the parents think they know exactly what is best for the child and becoming too serious about music certainly could interfere with the child's chances for real opportunity in life. Parents like these may not want to become as involved in assisting your instruction. Because they look forward to the day when that trumpet gets sold at the garage sale, they don't work as hard or as effectively in encouraging their child's musical growth.

Dealing with this type of parent is particularly difficult when you are faced with an extremely talented and/or motivated student. It is easier with a "traditional" instrument and style of music, of course, and more challenging with a rock-and-roller. When you identify this parent type, attempt to gradually involve the parent in the child's lesson. Show the parent that this child is more than casually interested in music. If you are very smooth, you may even be able to win the parent over by "playing both sides," convincing the parent that you are working hard to make your student aware of the rigors of a musical life. Meanwhile, in lessons, you are doing just that, and reassuring the student that he or she has what it takes to make it. The emotion to avoid here is anger. Parents don't always realize that it is insulting to musicians to assume that pursuing music as a career is a foolish idea. They just don't know what they don't know and you may be the only person who can enlighten them, gently.

The Pushy Parent

Another distinct parenting style we encounter looks like this: The parent arrives at the door, pushes the child through and talks about him as if he isn't even there. "Meet our son Ralph (age three). He's a genius. At the mall, he played the organ for an hour. Will you be done by four? His chess club meets then." Such parents often have a long list of activities that they believe are necessary for their child to become well rounded. You get the sense that they may already be preparing him for acceptance at that renowned private school or university (you are clued in by the sweatshirt). Musical aptitude will certainly look good on the application when little Ralph applies to Harvard. The child's other activities might include athletics, drama or public speaking, speaking a foreign language, and the list goes on. There may be undue pressure on the student to excel.

Obviously, some young children are musically gifted and should be given every opportunity for advancement. And you recognize the extraordinary talent in these students fairly soon after meeting them. The majority of your students, however, are not prodigies, and for them the pressure to succeed can be very discouraging. You need real diplomacy to calm the overanxious query: "Is he really talented, I mean *really* talented?" We have learned in these cases to keep the lessons fun, sometimes humorous, and never unreasonable. The parents who push their children to overachieve may need to learn this lesson most of all.

The Ideal Parent

The parenting style most appreciated by music teachers looks like this: "Jenny is really enjoying her lessons. How much do I owe you?" If this parent then adds, "How can I help Jenny practice her assignments more effectively?" you should count your blessings. Work with this parent, involve the parent with the lessons, and watch the child grow in self-esteem and enjoy making music. Parents who initially come to you in the other parenting styles may be "trained" into this attitude if you have the calmness and confidence to direct them.

Winning Parents' Trust

The most important aspect of your relationship with parents is to win their trust. If the parents are uncomfortable with you as a person, they will not feel comfortable with you as their child's instructor either. Therefore, it is imperative for you to project a professional image at all times.

Your first contact with parents is frequently made over the phone. "Speaking the part" is the first step in developing trust. Be courteous, confident (without sounding conceited) and reassuring at all times during phone conversations. Speaking to a parent and interrupting your conversation to reprimand your own children instills doubts from the start. Be attentive to the parents' concerns and try to satisfy them in every manner possible. Let them know that it's understandable to be cautious and that they can be present during all lessons or may sit nearby in a waiting area.

When you meet parents in person, back up your professional "phone voice" by dressing the part. Dress as conservatively and respectably as you can tolerate, especially for an initial meeting with parents. After establishing yourself as a teacher and having won parents' respect you can loosen your tie a bit.

Involving Parents in the Learning Process

Your main function as an instructor is to educate, but you often do much more. Part of a teacher's role is to motivate students to achieve greater goals. Motivating students to achieve and to *practice* is an important element in teaching music. With most adolescents and adults you do this directly with the student in a one-to-one situation. With younger children you need to concentrate much of your efforts on the student's parents.

Inviting parents to observe and participate in the lesson goes a long way toward achieving success with young children. In most cases the parent needs to know what the child is learning in order to monitor practice sessions throughout the week. If mom drops Junior off at your doorstep and waits in the car to pick him up, your ability to communicate what was covered in the lesson is greatly diminished. Even if you write out assignments for the student, the parent may not understand the important details without having observed them firsthand. Encourage parents to participate in the weekly lessons. At first you may be self-conscious about having observers, but remember that you know more about your instrument than they do; if you didn't, they'd be teaching their kids themselves.

Parents in today's society are certainly active and may spend much of their time taking children from one activity to the next with little time in between. The parent, while giving the child the best opportunities available, may not actually have any spare time to spend alone together with their child. By including parents as active participants in the music lesson, you give them the opportunity to spend some tremendous quality time with their child *and* help them understand the lesson material more fully. This inevitably allows parents to better motivate and guide their child's musical growth.

Be sure your studio can comfortably accommodate an additional body (see chapter three for suggestions). Allow the parent to become involved in the lesson and ask questions. If the parent is learning the lesson material, have the parent and child play together in class. This stimulates them to recreate the scenario at home during practice sessions. Most young children are happy to have an activity to do with their parents. We are certain that most parents benefit as well.

Even if the parent is not taking an active role in the lesson, his or her presence can contribute to your teaching effectiveness. The parent can help you to keep their child focused if the student starts to fidget or squirm. Perhaps the parent's mere presence will keep the child attentive. Be aware that this can backfire on you also. Sometimes the parent-child relationship dictates that the parent stay outside the studio during lesson times, especially as the child grows older.

You need to determine what works best in each situation. Try to avoid locking yourself into one approach that might be uncomfortable to alter. If mom has taken part in Jason's lessons since he was three, it may be difficult to ask her to leave when he turns twelve. Develop a system of inviting parents in on alternating weeks or for the last part of each lesson. This way the parent is involved and can receive assignment information without inhibiting the student for each and every lesson. This is a difficult area, so tread lightly. You must try to balance the student's and the parent's needs while finding the best environment for learning.

Written Communication

Whether parents are present in lessons or not, you need to find a system of communication to inform them of the student's progress and of weekly assignments. A parent information sheet is an effective tool for disseminating information.

On the following pages are several types of information sheets. The first is a general introduction letter that includes personal information and information about the studio in which you teach. The information may include your personal history and references, as well as parking and payment policies for the studio (see Example 5-1 on page 107). The information sheet can also include practice information. Suggested practice times and length of practice sessions are useful information for most parents (see Example 5-2 on page 108). A weekly

Dear (parent's name),

Welcome to the world of music at Oakdale Music Studio. My name is David Newsam and I will be (child's name)'s guitar instructor.

I am a graduate of the Hartt School of Music and hold a Bachelor of Music and Master of Music in music performance. I have been a professional educator for fifteen years and have been associated with Oakdale Music since 1990.

Our first lesson together is scheduled for (day　month　date) at (time). Lessons will meet each week at this time. Payment for the first month's lessons will be due at this time. See the payment schedule in the Oakdale pamphlet.

Parking for students at Oakdale Music Studio is located one block north of the studio at the intersection of Main Street and Webster Street. Parking is free.

I teach in studio #3. There is a waiting area just outside my studio. If you wait in this area I will meet you at the scheduled lesson time.

I will assign a method book at our first lesson, so please be prepared to purchase the book at that time. The average cost of the method books that I use is $12.00.

I look forward to meeting you and (child's name). Should you have any questions before our first meeting, don't hesitate to call me at 555-5555 (home) or 555-9999 (studio).

Sincerely,

Example 5-1. Introductory Letter to Parents of Young Children

Dear (parent's name),

The beginning of music lessons is an exciting time for both parents and children, and it is important to develop positive practice routines.

Here are a few reminders about practice:

- Daily practice of lesson material is essential for your child's musical growth.

- Each day should include at least one practice session.

- Several short sessions are preferable to one long session. Fatigue and lack of concentration tend to set in if sessions are too long.

- Schedule sessions at various times of the day (early morning, afternoon, evening).

- Review lesson material at each session.

- Keep sessions fun and engaging. If your child begins losing focus, return at a later time.

- Encourage your child to perform for you, your family and friends.

- Be sure to fill in and sign the weekly practice log.

Thank you for your support and encouragement. Your participation and involvement in the lessons will go a long way toward making lessons fun, enjoyable and rewarding for your child.

Sincerely,

Example 5-2. Letter to Parents With Suggested Practice Time/Routine

information sheet also keeps parents up-to-date on weekly assignments, schedule changes and recital information (see Example 5-3 on page 110). Have these basic materials typed, printed up and ready to give to parents. It sure beats writing out lesson information on the back of a used envelope.

A parent-student contract is an effective way to motivate both parent and child to set aside time for learning. It is simply a fact that lesson material must be practiced for progress to be made. Most young children don't practice without encouragement from parents. A contract can get both parties involved and puts responsibility on both sides (see Example 5-4 on page 111). A teacher-student contract is another alternative for motivating students and keeping you involved!

Be certain to talk to parents about their child's music lessons. Check with them about practice time and material. Since it's impossible to be with a student seven days a week, you need to make an ally of the child's parents. Involve them in every way imaginable. At the same time, give students room to grow without their parents' constant hovering. Allow students time to experiment. Don't allow parent-child relationships to become so regimented that the kids no longer have fun with music. If it isn't fun, most kids lose interest quickly.

UNDERSTANDING CHILDREN'S NEEDS IN PRIVATE LESSONS

Teaching music to young children has many wonderful rewards. Watching as the student grows to love music, progresses and reaches new heights is inspiring to even the most cynical teacher. Teaching young children can also be difficult and frustrating. However, if you prepare yourself with the proper materials and methods, cultivate just the right temperament, and become aware of all the developmental concerns involved with teaching children, then you can provide the musical foundation for tomorrow's professional musicians.

Reminders of Young Children's Developmental Abilities

Physical development is extremely important for each instrument. Asking a five-year-old to attempt to play the French horn is unreasonable. Strength, dexterity and denture are primary concerns when deciding if a student should begin a particular instrument. Each instrument carries its own concerns or recommendations for beginners, so even if a student has achieved the physical abilities to begin an instru-

Dear (<u>parent's name</u>),

Thank you so much for your support and participation in last week's student recital at St. Joseph's Church Hall. The event was a tremendous success and would not have been possible without your help. (<u>child's name</u>)'s performance was wonderful. Although (his/her) nervousness was apparent, the performance was strong and musical. The many hours of practice certainly paid off.

Just a reminder that next week's lessons will be cancelled due to the Thanksgiving holiday. We will meet in two weeks at our regularly scheduled time.

(<u>child's name</u>) has begun work on the pieces for next month's Christmas Concert at school. The new material is found in the back of (his/her) music folder.

My next student recital will take place on Saturday evening, March 12, at the South Road Elementary School. We will begin working on several new pieces for this recital after the Christmas Concert is concluded.

Thanks again for helping make last week's event such a success. Best wishes for a wonderful holiday next week. See you on (<u> date / time </u>).

Sincerely,

Example 5-3. Letter to Parents of Young Children—Weekly Updates

---

I, (Parent's Name), agree to:

• Take student to and from each week's music lesson.

• Provide student with instrument, supplies, method books and materials.

• Support my son/daughter by helping and encouraging him/her to practice.

_____

Parent's Signature

I, (Student's Name), agree to:

• Prepare for and attend each week's lesson.

• Practice all lesson material daily.

• Listen to, play and enjoy music each and every day.

_____

Student's Signature

Example 5-4. Parent-Student Contract

ment, elements such as attention span must be considered.

Young children can begin on piano as soon as they can comfortably reach the keyboard. Eight- to ten-year-old children can usually achieve success on such instruments as guitar, strings and percussion. Students may have to wait until ten years of age or more to begin instruments that require mature denture, large lung capacity, a strong back or tremendous finger dexterity (woodwinds, brass, larger stringed instruments). Success or failure depends on too many factors to be listed on these few pages. The only way to be certain for yourself is to test students personally. But be realistic. If you are teaching children for the first time, gain some confidence first before pushing the extreme range of age with beginners. Know in your heart that you can achieve success with someone ten years of age before attempting to instruct a five-year-old child.

Short Fingers and Attention Spans

The most important thing to remember when teaching young children is that their attention spans are much shorter than adults'. You may want to push the limits of their ability to concentrate, but you do not want to become angry about things they simply cannot control. It is unreasonable, for instance, to expect a typical six-year-old to sit still for an hour on a piano bench. A child that young gets uncomfortable and your patience wanes as the student begins to squirm. For that reason alone, lessons for most children under twelve should be a half hour.

Because children need more activity and variety, try breaking up the lesson into three or four distinct parts, including reading music, practicing rhythms, listening to recordings, singing (or humming) along, playing the instrument alone, accompanying you, working singly, playing simple duets, etc. Vary the style of the pieces you present. Set realistic goals for yourself, realizing, for instance, that if you can get a six-year-old to concentrate for half of a half-hour lesson, you've accomplished something. The more proficient a student is on an instrument, the easier it is for that student to concentrate.

Most of all, try not to be intimidating. Young children gravitate to music when it is fun and exciting for them. When weekly lessons are rigid and fraught with expectations, they join doctor and dentist appointments as anxiety-provoking duties.

Remember, too, that playing an instrument can be physically uncomfortable for little people at first. Let children know that it might make their fingers, lips, neck, etc., sore at first, but as they get used to holding the instrument it will eventually feel better. Think about "finger span" when assigning pieces early on, and pass along any tips you have to minimize discomfort. While you want to stretch abilities, you want students to feel good about their accomplishments. Children may need pillows on a piano bench (and help getting up onto them) or a footstool when playing guitar. You want children to put all their energy into being dexterous on the instrument rather than on staying balanced on the edge of a chair. Having these things ready and waiting in your studio lets parents and children know that you have anticipated their needs.

Quarter-size, half-size and three-quarter-size models of most instruments are available for beginners through local music stores. These are usually medium-quality instruments designed for children and can be a good initial investment for parents.

Counting exercises and games. Developing a student's ability to understand and keep time in music is a key ingredient to musical growth. Young children who start their musical careers with good counting habits have a much greater chance of being successful musicians later on in their lives. Including counting exercises and games in your lessons is not only important musically but helps liven up each lesson as well. The more activities you include in each lesson, the greater the chance for maintaining students' attention.

There are several distinct approaches to counting exercises. You certainly want students to count while trying to execute all lesson material. If they use their fingers to play the instrument, have them sing along and count out each measure as they play. For students who use their mouths to play (horns, woodwinds or voice), have them count out measures while you play the music. As you begin to work on more difficult rhythms or time signatures, have students sing the rhythms to understand the timing involved.

Besides counting while playing musical examples, you can work on counting away from the instrument. Develop exercises or games that focus on the concept of time, time signatures and rhythm. Games that involve clapping out rhythms can be simple but effective. Use recordings to emphasize difficult or unusual rhythms.

Using the metronome. Like counting, using a metronome can become part of regular practice, as well as a separate activity. It is the simplest, most effective and most overlooked method for developing a strong time feel. Encourage students to use a metronome at all times when practicing. Students who do not practice with a metronome think they are playing in time, but the metronome doesn't lie. Students who rush or drag tempos to account for difficult passages or inadequate technique should be especially encouraged to work with a metronome.

A metronome is a great tool for working on counting and time away from the instrument. Use one that accents different time signatures and have students guess which one you are in. Have students clap along with a metronome at various tempo settings. Challenge students to clap with the metronome so they cannot hear the click. (If they can accomplish this task you know you are getting somewhere!) Have students work on setting the metronome themselves to various tempos you give them. Remember that you accomplish two things by filling your lessons with this type of activity: You provide education as well as entertainment.

Listening exercises and games. Musicians and music students spend a large part of their time in isolation, practicing and perfecting their craft. When the opportunity to perform with other musicians presents itself, music students often have no idea how to listen to the other musicians around them. Teaching students the art of listening early on is an educational and entertaining activity for lessons.

Put on a recording and have students identify characteristics of the performance. Work at the child's level. What kind of instrument plays the melody? What time signature is this piece in? Was the beginning louder or softer than the end? How many times through the song did the singer sing? These are all simple but effective analytical questions for developing strong listening skills. This seemingly insignificant activity helps students understand such things as dynamics, orchestration, time and form.

Pitch exercises and games. Another important element of a good music education is solid ear-training skills. Encourage these skills in fun ways during your lessons. Have students play back simple melodic passages that you play for them. If this is too advanced, have them play back single notes. You can then progress to working with intervals, chords and phrases. Have students identify which note of an interval is higher or lower (or the same). Begin to develop dictation skills and have students write the melodies you play. Begin slowly and work to more advanced material. Ask students to play familiar melodies by ear. Have them start in different keys or different octaves, or use different fingerings. If they can execute the melody, see if they can identify the harmony as well. The more advanced their ear-training abilities become, the more readily they can learn other material. Strong ear-training skills help students memorize more easily later on.

Voice exercises and games. Ear training begins with the voice, so have students learn the connection between what they are hearing and their voice (and, in turn, their instrument). Do the unusual and unexpected. Have students imitate an ambulance siren. Try imitating sounds like engines, animals, rushing water. Ask them to imitate different instruments with their voice. Get them to sing low and sing high. This gives them a sense of their vocal range. (Make a note of their range when you begin working on voice exercises. You can refer to this when developing their ear-training abilities.) Have students match pitches with their voices. Get them to sing intervals and begin to understand the distances between pitches. Have them sing simple melodies and familiar songs. Try using patriotic, folk or holiday themes for starters. Be sure to pick a key within their vocal range.

Make the activities fun. A simple game of call and response is a valuable learning method that is very amusing for small children. You can even sing nonsense syllables instead of lyrics to add to the humorous nature of this activity. For example, singing along to the old Cab Calloway record "Singin' Hi Di Ho!!" can combine listening and vocal skills.

Using the piano (regardless of the instrument you are teaching). The piano is a fun place to work with young students. The technique required to sound the keys is minimal, so anyone can play. (Our six-month-old daughter plays every day!) It is a wonderful way to develop ear-training skills. In addition to matching pitches with voice and instrument, do it at the keyboard. The notes are directly in front of you in full view so students get a much better sense of how music works. Theoretical explanations of scales, chords and intervals make more sense to students when they can see them on the piano. Many instruments, such as the guitar, pose teaching challenges because the notes are so difficult to visualize. Starting students at the piano gives them more insight into the intricacies of music theory.

For young students struggling with the physical nature of their own instrument, the piano is a wonderful way to maintain musical momentum in lessons without causing students to become frustrated because of their struggles with technique. If you're not strictly a piano teacher, be careful or you may make some converts and lose business!

Increasing dexterity. Developing exercises and games for increasing dexterity is a fun way to encourage what is often painful and tedious practice. Repetition is an important part of developing dexterity, but it can also be boring. Develop games of repetition using timers, stopwatches or challenges. "How long can you play this passage without making a mistake?" "Let's play this together and see who messes up first." Similar games can be employed with technical considerations like range or tempos. "Let's see how fast we can play this passage" or "Let's see if we can hit this high note before we finish today's lesson." Remember that students may want to push too quickly too soon so be careful not to encourage students to play beyond their abilities. Young musicians constantly challenge themselves and you can help them with fun and exciting methods.

g Incentives for Practicing

.o single category of student is more motivated by incentives than ung children. You can use incentives not only to increase practice time, but also for achieving goals. You don't want to treat children like pets and wave biscuits in their faces to get them to play. But any method that stimulates learning and motivates students to play more and to be more goal-oriented is something of which you should take full advantage.

Most elementary school teachers use some system of grading students on assignments, projects and exams. As a music instructor dealing with young students, it's a good idea to initiate a weekly system to motivate students (and keep parents involved). Each week, issue students assignment sheets that clearly state the goals and objectives for the week. An assignment sheet should include pieces to be practiced, page numbers from method books, tempo markings, etc. Include a log of practice times as part of the assignment sheet or as a separate form. It is important to monitor weekly assignments in conjunction with practice times.

Again, it is a good idea to have parents involved with daily practice. Have them sign the practice log to verify times the students play. Ask them to check over the assignment sheet to see that all material is being covered during the week. When the student returns for the next lesson, go over the assignment sheet and the practice log. Comment on the practice times logged each week. Tell the student whether to increase the length of daily practice. Ask about their week if the practice schedule seems lighter than usual. Try not to hound students, but do remind them of the importance of practice.

Go over weekly assignments with students. Have them play each exercise or song. Help them with trouble spots and assign review material if required. After checking the assignment and the practice log, grade the student for the week. Give the student a check for logging sufficient practice time for the week. Give a check-plus if the student exceeded expectations. Place a star or sticker on the assignment sheet or in the method book for material that is successfully performed. This type of reward is essential for the young music student. If all you do is emphasize the negative, pointing out the many deficiencies and the need for more practice then you may never motivate children to excel. With praise, respect and nurturing you can turn these youngsters into eager and excited young musicians.

Young students also need to be motivated over longer periods. The

REBECCA								WED. 3:30	
Student's Name								Lesson Day/Time	

Week of: 5/9 - 5/15		Assignment: PG. 14, 15 VOL .1 FINGER STUDY #3							Grade: ✓+
Mon. 45 MIN.	Tues. 1 HR.	Wed. ½ HR.	Thur. —	Fri. 1 HR.	Sat. 15 MIN.	Sun. 1 HR.	Total 4½ HR.	Parent Signature *Mrs. L. James*	
Week of: 5/16- 5/22		Assignment: PG.16-18 VOL. 1 FINGER STUDY #4							Grade:
Mon.	Tues.	Wed.	Thur.	Fri.	Sat.	Sun.	Total	Parent Signature	
Week of:		Assignment:							Grade:
Mon.	Tues.	Wed.	Thur.	Fri.	Sat.	Sun.	Total	Parent Signature	
Week of:		Assignment:							Grade:
Mon.	Tues.	Wed.	Thur.	Fri.	Sat.	Sun.	Total	Parent Signature	
Week of:		Assignment:							Grade:
Mon.	Tues.	Wed.	Thur.	Fri.	Sat.	Sun.	Total	Parent Signature	
Week of:		Assignment:							Grade:
Mon.	Tues.	Wed.	Thur.	Fri.	Sat.	Sun.	Total	Parent Signature	
Week of:		Assignment:							Grade:
Mon.	Tues.	Wed.	Thur.	Fri.	Sat.	Sun.	Total	Parent Signature	
Week of:		Assignment:							Grade:
Mon.	Tues.	Wed.	Thur.	Fri.	Sat.	Sun.	Total	Parent Signature	

Example 5-5. Combined Assignment Sheet/Practice Log

week-to-week monotony sets in quickly without greater rewards for greater achievement. Certificates of achievement are another incentive you can use. Completing graded material or a method book serves as a landmark of graduation to the next level. Many method books include a certificate of completion to be presented when reaching the end. Certificates can also be purchased through school catalogs and stationery stores or they can be designed for your specific purposes. A computer drawing program can serve your needs adequately. Ask your local printing shop for assistance if you are without computer software or if you want to design something even more impressive.

Incorporating a system of ascending levels is another excellent way to motivate students to new heights. Use a large poster with a ladder or staircase with each rung or stair representing a new level of achievement. Each level can represent a period of time, amount of practice logged, a method book completed or new pieces performed. Initiating a system of rewards for achieving each new level serves as a further incentive for your students. Rewards for reaching new levels can be small gifts, gift certificates, or something fun and simple like an ice cream cone at the end of the lesson (with the parent's permission, of course).

A system of ascending levels can be particularly successful if you include your entire student population on the chart. There is nothing like peer competition to motivate students to achieve greater goals. Little Rachel may work just a little bit harder next week if she sees that her buddy Craig is already two levels above her on the chart. Be sure to keep all this competition in perspective with students. Rachel should not be too upset if Craig has had two more years of lessons than she has. Borrowing from swimming lessons (i.e. guppies, sharks, etc.) and karate (white belt, yellow belt, etc.), you can create a system in which levels are identified by names. Be creative and come up with names that correspond to your instrument.

Remember that there is one incentive that works every time, with students of all ages: Nothing is more effective than good old-fashioned praise. It's easy to become so wrapped up in systems and motivating that you forget that you're dealing with little human beings. And little human beings often respond best to warm, fuzzy forms of praise. It may cost part of your gross income to purchase gift certificates and ice cream cones. But it costs nothing to turn to your students and tell them in plain language that you think they are doing a great job. And more often than not, this type of incentive is most rewarding for the student.

Younger students often look up to you in ways you may forget. They may look to you to fill a void left by overworked or otherwise distracted parents. You may be like a big brother or sister to them. Hopefully they look to you as a good friend that they like to be with. The best rewards, words or otherwise, are those given from the heart. Treat your students with respect and watch them blossom under your guidance.

TROUBLESHOOTING PROBLEMS WITH YOUNG CHILDREN

Careful preparation and experience should ensure smooth lessons week in and week out. However, even the most seasoned veterans encounter problems when teaching young children. In most cases, involving the parents in the learning process is the key ingredient to establishing momentum in the child's studies. The parent can work with you to establish consistency, enforce rules, and encourage the student to achieve new goals each week. You may find, though, that in some cases it's the parents who create roadblocks to learning.

Dealing With Overzealous Parents

Some parents are so interested in assisting you in your efforts that they try to take over your role as teacher. Parents who have some musical knowledge or experience are sometimes worse than those without a shred of training or interest. (A little knowledge is a dangerous thing!) In situations with this overbearing type, involving the parent in the learning process can further complicate matters. Remember, you are the teacher! Parents can complement your teaching but they cannot become the instructor. You must establish that where musical instruction is concerned, you are in charge. Otherwise the overbearing parent can sabotage your relationship with the child. Remain in control at all times when dealing with parents of this type. Choose your words carefully and never let your temper get the best of you. Let them know that you are a professional with much experience and your system will prove successful if given a fair chance. Undue interference on their part could undermine the progress you have already made and make additional goals hard to reach.

Another type of parent that interferes with learning is the one who pushes children to achieve beyond their possible abilities. Such parents may force a child to practice unreasonable hours and expect unrealistic results. They may suggest advanced performance pieces that even you would have difficulty playing. They may be disappointed when their child fails to reach the level of proficiency they expected or shows a lack of enthusiasm for practice. Children in this situation usually attempt to please their parents with a genuine effort at first. But if these children fail and receive only negative feedback, they are most likely to become frustrated and lose interest in the instrument. At this point your job becomes monumental (or impossible). Troubleshooting this problem certainly requires some diplomacy. Show the parents that while their intentions may be sincere, their expectations are out of proportion. Demonstrate a realistic level of ability, perhaps in a recital of children of similar ages and/or abilities. If you have ever attended a Little League game and seen the screaming parents, you may think that this recital idea will not work either. You may be right; some parents are just plain unreasonable in putting pressure on their children.

If you feel a child is truly being affected by the parent's attitude then you should approach the parent directly. Work from the assumption that the parent wants the child to succeed and reassure the parent that the child can succeed *more* if the pressure is completely off. Confront this parent gently and then let the chips fall where they may. In some cases the direct approach is successful and you can return to positively challenging the student.

Handling the Student Who Never Practices

Dealing with students who don't practice is something all music teachers encounter with all levels and ages of music students. It is a particularly difficult situation when dealing with young children. Because most young children practice only if encouraged, you must instill the importance of practice in the student *and* the parents.

Establishing a strong parent-teacher relationship right from the start lets you constantly reinforce the importance of practice. From the first phone conversation, to the parent information sheet, to the student-parent contract, to weekly meetings at the lesson, parents should be reminded over and over about the importance of practice and the role they play in of their child's progress. You do not want to create an overbearing parent by forcing them to hound the child into practice sessions, but you do need them to encourage daily quality practice routines. Remind parents that students need a time and a quiet place to practice. They need a music stand and/or a metronome and supplies specific to their instrument. They need time away from their siblings and friends and encouragement and praise when they practice.

Children must also see the importance of practice, and using incentives is a good way of accomplishing that goal. Talk to students about your own routines for practice. Relate to them how you practiced when you were their age. Do not hesitate to tell them about any frustrations or negative feelings you may have had when you were younger. Children may feel as if they cannot share their feelings with you if you expect them to love to practice every day. Most people who play instruments have trouble getting excited to play on certain days. If you tell students that this is natural but they must persevere nonetheless, they'll feel better about themselves and may be more accepting of daily practice regiments. All musicians have to practice every day to become better musicians and ultimately have more fun. Whatever story or analogy you use to encourage practice, remember to stay positive about it even when talking about negative feelings toward it.

Handling the Student Who Practices but Does Not Improve

Sometimes you encounter students who do practice on a regular schedule, perhaps logging several hours of practice each week, without showing any signs of improvement. Worse yet, they may actually digress from previous weeks. This is where you earn your money as a teacher. You must look at just what and how the student is practicing and find a solution to the problem.

Your first concern should be whether or not the student is actually practicing for the time recorded on the log sheets. Perhaps the student is filling in the times and forging the parent's signature. Ask the parents about the log. Is the student playing during these times or just in the music room? If a student sits at the piano and reads comic books, that isn't considered a practice session.

If you determine that the student has been practicing as indicated then you must analyze the student's routine to see if he or she could be practicing more efficiently. Sometimes students practice their mistakes over and over again (and get better and better at making those mistakes). If this is the case, look for ways to show the student how to correct mistakes before proceeding to repetitive practice. The idea is to play slowly at first, increasing the tempo gradually after achieving success at each level. Playing at tempos that are too quick is one way to perpetuate mistakes. It may be helpful to record the correct way to play pieces so students have a tape to listen to once they have left the studio.

Be certain that the student is practicing the lesson material. Maybe that material is too advanced. Ask the parent if the child is playing the instrument but not practicing lesson material at all. Experimenting on the instrument is an important aspect of musicianship but it is just one of many. If the student sits down and just plays, making up music as he goes, then the results are predictable.

Check that the student is using correct technique when practicing. You can correct their technique in the lesson, but at home students may slip into bad habits and develop inconsistencies that hinder progress. Demonstrate ways to remain aware of technique during practice. Practicing in the mirror and using a technique checklist are two types of reminders for students (see Example 5-6).

In a few instances you may encounter a student who does everything correctly, practices daily, and still does not improve. It's possible that this child is stuck in a stagnant period and will emerge from it shortly. Do not get too impatient with young children. The student may just need some time to come up to speed developmentally.

In rare instances you may encounter a student who has no aptitude for music whatever. In these cases you may want to suggest very diplomatically to the parent that they terminate lessons for the time being. If the student shows any passion at all toward music, however, do not discourage them from playing the instrument. Be patient and continue to find ways to teach the student that prove successful. Not every student you teach will end up with the London Philharmonic Orchestra, but the ones who love music should be given every opportunity to continue their studies and find their niche in the musical world around them.

Occasionally, a student's lack of growth or progress is directly related to a learning disability. If this is a known situation then you need to work with parents and professionals to find the proper method for teaching the student. If this is only a possibility or a feeling, then you can ask the parent whether the student has any trouble in school subjects. Sometimes parents of children with learning disabilities need corroborating information from various areas of the child's life to get a sense of the disability.

Dealing With Learning-Disabled, Hyperactive or Handicapped Students

In a best case scenario the parents inform you of a student's learning disability before the first lesson. This gives you and the parent time to

TECHNIQUE CHECKLIST — GUITAR

1. Tuning the Guitar — Using a pitch pipe, tuning fork or piano, tune the **Low E String**.

- Press the **6th** string at the **5th** fret to tune the open **5th** string
- Press the **5th** string at the **5th** fret to tune the open **4th** string
- Press the **4th** string at the **5th** fret to tune the open **3rd** string
- Press the **3rd** string at the **4th** fret to tune the open **2nd** string
- Press the **2nd** string at the **5th** fret to tune the open **1st** string

2. Posture — Sit on chair with back straight
- Place left foot on footstool
- Place guitar on left leg
- Elevate guitar neck so head is at eye level
- Keep guitar close to body
- Right forearm should rest on outer edge of guitar only
- Rotate arm so right wrist is over sound hole
- Both arms and wrists should remain relaxed and in line
- Left and right shoulders should remain level
- Left-hand thumb should be placed on the back of neck
- Left-hand fingers should be directly over strings
- Fret the notes with tips of fingers only

* Be sure to check posture by practicing in front of a wall mirror. Be sure to check several angles (straight on, left side) to observe all possible techniques. *Remain relaxed at all times.*

3. Practice Reminders

Always practice with the metronome. This includes all warm-ups, exercises, scales and pieces.

Counting is an important aspect of time. Be sure to count out all passages as you play them.

Start each practice session with warm-up routine. Improper warm-up could result in serious injury.

Take plenty of rests during extended practice. Do not overpractice and risk injury. If you feel any tension in your body, take a break. If you experience pain regularly, be sure to mention it to me at your next lesson.

Have fun! Remember that the more you practice, the better musician you'll become. The better you get, the more enjoyment you receive from music.

Example 5-6. Technique Checklist

sit down and discuss the important concerns you both may have. Allow the parent time to explain the child's disability and the ways it affects learning.

Find out what type of counseling the child has received and what testing has been done. You may want to speak briefly with the child's teacher, school counselor, psychologist or therapist. Try to determine the ways in which the student learns best and what things to avoid. Be sure to explain the ways that you generally teach and troubleshoot any particular areas that may pose difficulties with the student.

Give the parents an opportunity to voice any concerns they may have or to offer suggestions for teaching their child. If the child has difficulty focusing on one subject for long periods of time then you can plan shorter, more varied subjects during each lesson. Spend five minutes on technique, five minutes on reading, five minutes on ear training, five minutes on rhythm training, and ten minutes on weekly assignments. Perhaps the opposite situation is true and the student cannot retain a wide variety of subjects, in which case you may focus on one particular area during each lesson.

Many students with learning disabilities have a difficult time retaining information from one week to the next. This can be very frustrating for you and the student. Use innovative ways for the child to remember information, perhaps with a simple song or poem, a funny phrase or a joke. The following is sung to the tune of "Three Blind Mice":

The first string is E, the first string is E.
The second string is B, the second string is B.
The third string starts on the note of G,
The fourth string starts on the note of D,
The fifth string starts on the note of A,
The low note is E, the low note is E.

These methods relieve a great deal of tension and are effective techniques for students to learn.

Hyperactive students or those diagnosed with attention deficit disorder (ADD or ADHD) can present particularly difficult problems, since they have difficulty concentrating and sitting still. These students require the utmost attention, patience and understanding.

Students with physical handicaps may seem to present an insurmountable challenge. However, these individuals have usually spent their entire lives learning to overcome their handicap and to function in society. They may not even view themselves as handicapped. Look beyond the physical disability; in most cases there are real workable solutions to what at first glance appears to be an impossibility. There are many role models in today's society, individuals who have overcome the greatest odds to achieve their goals. If a student possesses the determination and the will to succeed, it is your job to help him or her to realize that dream. If the student's attitude seems to say "I cannot fail," then success should just be a matter of putting the pieces in place.

If you have little or no experience dealing with students who have disabilities of any type, help is available. Both parents and professionals have years of dealing with the child's behavioral patterns. Seek advice and assistance from others when dealing with these sensitive and difficult areas.

Don't feel you must be doing things wrong if you are having poor results. In some cases a decision may have to be made that music lessons are beyond the reach of the student at this particular time. Don't throw in the towel after one or two lessons, though. Give it your best shot, seek the advice and assistance of others, try various methods and techniques for learning.

Remember that music is difficult to master for even the most blessed individuals. A learning disability or other mental or physical handicap can seriously limit the chances for learning music. With the proper methods, careful planning and a coordinated effort, however, many of these students not only learn the rudiments of music, but excel in a caring, individualized setting. It may require extra effort on your part but we guarantee the rewards are even greater than you imagine when you see the joy of music in the lives of these special children. In some unique instances, this is the activity that begins to open up new worlds and new possibilities of communicating with the world for these students.

Dealing With Gifted Children

Another challenge you may face is dealing with exceptionally bright students. Occasionally a student astounds you with raw talent and quick comprehension. Keeping up with this student can be exhausting. And remember that the student is an *exception*: Don't compare your other students to this student's progress.

Provide gifted children with lesson material of increasing difficulty. But, just because they are talented and can handle more complex pieces, do not forget to cover the fundamentals. A math genius still needs to memorize multiplication tables.

It's important to remember that gifted children are still children. While their comprehension may be light-years ahead of their chronological age, their social development may be right on schedule. Because they seem so advanced, it's easy to forget that they need reassurance, praise and comfort like any child. Most gifted eight-year-olds are still frightened before a recital and need a pat on the back after a job well done.

SOME FINAL WORDS ABOUT CHILDREN

It is easy to lose focus when you are dealing with small children in music lessons. When you are thinking philosophically about the merits of teaching, inspiring young, bright-eyed musicians seems the ultimate privilege. Yet, when you are confronted by the chaotic bundle of words, energy and perpetual motion that is a child, it is easy to lose inspiration and think, "How can I get this kid out of my studio?" "Did she wash her hands?" "How can I use up this time?" We encourage you to take a step back and remember why you are doing this. Teaching children is teaching them to love music. That is *your* assignment.

CHAPTER SIX

TEACHING PRIVATE LESSONS TO TEENAGERS AND YOUNG ADULTS

For some music teachers, the thought of a one-on-one encounter with a student in the throes of puberty is like a scene out of a Stephen King horror novel. Given the frightful prospect of having to deal with this bundle of walking hormones you might wish to teach only adults or children younger than thirteen. On the other hand, many teachers, especially those teaching guitar, bass and drums, end up with a teaching schedule comprised almost entirely of teenagers and young adults. It is essential for teachers to understand adolescent learners and their specific needs.

UNDERSTANDING TEENAGERS' NEEDS IN PRIVATE LESSONS

You're backstage at the local community theater about to present your students in recital. As you head onstage to welcome a roomful of proud parents and relatives, you overhear two of your students saying, "Like, Mozart's music is so geeky. Plus, his hair was bogus. Yo, Mozart! Didja ever hear of a barbershop?"

Such is the strange contradiction inherent in most teenagers. They are often tireless workers, multitalented, humorous and energetic beyond belief. At the same time they can be close-minded, cliquish and depressive. Most of them are also extremely moody, which means they can act one way one week and behave in a totally different manner the next week. It becomes the serious music teacher's challenge to wade through these treacherous waters and find the positive mix of talent, energy and sense of humor present in each teenage student.

The most glaring personality trait found in most teenagers is rebellion. In these years the individual finds the courage and manner to make the transition from dependent child to independent adult. It is a most difficult transition (as we can all remember) and often a painful process for everyone involved. Those most closely involved are the student's parents, and they generally suffer the brunt of the teenager's rebellion.

Many teenagers carry these feelings of rebellion into the community and spread it around to everyone with whom they come in contact. They may even experience a sort of transference and express their feelings toward their parents onto other adults. And what other adults come into contact with rebellious teenagers? Teachers! Staying one step ahead of that rebelliousness and *not taking it personally* are the keys to working peacefully with young people.

Avoid confrontation when possible. Try using a sense of humor without employing humiliation. If things become serious then do whatever is necessary to diffuse the situation. But realize that in most cases teenagers act up to receive attention, and if you can give them positive attention then you may avoid ugly situations.

Keeping Your Expectations Realistic

Recent studies show that an overwhelming percentage of young Americans have part-time or even full-time jobs while attending high school. When asked why they must work so many hours many students respond by saying, "So I can pay for my car." When asked why they must have a car, the response is often, "So I can get to work." The reasons may be more varied and serious than that. While we may have grown up in a time when one income could support an entire household, today's economy may require not only two parents to work but children may have to pitch in as well. The astronomical cost of higher education requires serious students considering college to begin dealing with the finances involved with education at a very early age. Whatever the reasons, the facts clearly indicate that more and more teenagers are entering the workforce.

In an effort to make their kids "well rounded," parents of younger children may encourage them to try more and more extracurricular activities—sports, music, various and sundry hobbies—and schedule their lives from dawn to dusk. As they enter the work force, however, many of the kids' extracurricular activities must be sacrificed.

Some students' passion for music cannot be deterred by a work schedule or a demanding store manager. But for a student to work and study music at the same time, something is sacrificed and usually that something is practice time. So, for students who either work or are active in several other activities, the time available to spend in the practice rooms is minimal. As a teacher, you must stress the essential relationship between studying music and an intense daily practice routine. At the same time, you have to accept the increased responsibilities of teenagers today and keep your expectations realistic. Being realistic means not getting all bent out of shape when a student calls and tells you that her manager scheduled her to work for the night of her lesson and she'll have to switch. You also must not become discouraged because students are not spending twenty hours per week practicing.

Be flexible. Each student's situation is different. If you have a student who doesn't work and isn't involved in any activities except music, you can be slightly more demanding in terms of practice schedule. If you are teaching the class president and soccer goalkeeper who works twenty hours a week at Burger World, however, then your expectations for practice and preparation must be lower. If this student is serious about music and hopes to enroll in college as a music major, then a confrontation regarding priorities may be in order. If, on the other hand, this student plans on studying another field in college but would like to play in the school's pep band, then you can be encouraging without being overdemanding. Expecting too much from a student may force a decision to forgo music studies altogether. You are then out one student for the time being and that young person may be without the gift of music for a lifetime.

USING APPROPRIATE MATERIALS AND METHODS

Relating to the teenage music student may be the biggest challenge facing some of us aging, conservative teachers. (That's any of you out there over the age of twenty.) If ever there was an age group that remains inclusive and nearly completely unresponsive to outside members, it is teenagers. By trying to be "one of them" you can come off as immature or unrealistic or just downright stupid. A better approach is to let them know that you understand them and their feelings while instilling in them a sense of respect for your experience, expertise and authority. The first step is to capture their attention.

Using Contemporary Music in Lessons

As a teacher you must know what you are capable of teaching, what you enjoy teaching, and what works for you as a teacher. For some, teaching contemporary popular music to teenagers is the selling point when attracting students. Perhaps you are a member of an original rock group or cover band and are constantly researching the most contemporary players and styles. For others, though, your knowledge of, passion for and patience of rock music has long since departed. Whether you fall into one category or the other or find yourself somewhere in between, using contemporary music in lessons is a surefire way to capture the attention of and motivate teenage musicians.

The teacher specializing in contemporary music probably doesn't need to be told of the importance of including music from the latest groups and instrumentalists as part of the lesson curriculum. Many students find this to be the ultimate learning experience: to be shown how to play songs or solos just like those on the recordings they listen to. You can use this music very sparingly if you wish, but it does get the teenager's attention.

For those teachers who have no interest in or desire to learn contemporary music, this approach won't work. But, without too much effort you can incorporate ideas into your lessons that help reinforce your established, traditional teaching methods or techniques. The easiest approach is name-dropping. Just being aware of a new group or younger performer can win the attention and respect of your teenage students, as they look past your bifocals into a new dimension of respect. To effectively appear "hip" you must do more than just pick up and read a magazine cover or album jacket. Some research is involved, but it can be simple and painless enough that even the most reluctant teacher joins the fun.

Researching contemporary music. One way to research new players and music is simply to turn on the radio or television. Check the listings and find a station that features the most contemporary music. Cable television should have at least two or three music channels that feature music twenty-four hours a day. Usually, the later you tune in, the more "alternative" sounding the music gets. College radio stations also feature many "new" bands and music and often have a show reserved for local music, which could be particularly useful for you to be aware of. Familiarize yourself with names of players, groups and songs.

If you are very serious about incorporating contemporary music into your lessons, you have to do more than just drop a name here and there. In addition to listening to broadcasts of new music, hook up a tape recorder and get down to learning the music. This doesn't mean transcribing hours of contemporary songs from musicians you wouldn't let into your house. Pick out a song here, a lick there, an intro or ending to a popular song, and work it into a lesson. The idea is to use this information to supplement what you already teach. You may discover that many contemporary players have roots in more traditional music, music that you have a much deeper understanding of than your students. Make students aware of how modern music has been influenced by traditional genres. You don't have to be teaching a heavy metal intro to comment to a student, "That new song out by (name of band) uses a (musical term) a lot like the one found in this movement." By pointing out these influences and relationships, you can build the foundation for many meaningful discussions of these influences and the concepts or techniques involved in playing them.

Reading contemporary music magazines can be very useful for deriving material to use in your lessons. One way is through name recognition, as mentioned earlier. Another is to use quotes from players to reinforce certain concepts. Ideas you describe are often brushed aside as insignificant until they are defined as important by someone's favorite musician. Elton John once said, "If I miss a day of practice, I notice it. If I miss two days, other people notice." (Elton John has significantly more clout than we do.) You can make handouts or include such quotes at the top or in the margins of the materials you disseminate. It is truly motivating for your students to see these quotes included in the lesson material.

Contemporary music magazines often include written transcriptions of songs, solos and concepts. You need not learn every transcription note for note. Be selective and find things that complement what you already teach. If you have been discussing odd time signatures, then look for a piece that incorporates this concept. If you have been working on a particular technique, find a solo that demonstrates that technique.

Whether you teach all contemporary music or none, you may want to look into the other camp for a moment. You can find great success in modernizing your approach to teaching. You can also encounter negative results from teaching entirely by rote. Students who learn nothing but songs or licks often get to a point where they need some explanation of what it is they are playing. Imagine learning the lyrics to a song phonetically without ever understanding the meaning of the words. After a while, the frustration of not comprehending the meaning of the music becomes evident. Therefore, while it is important to include contemporary music in the lesson, it is most beneficial to use this approach in a way that reinforces traditional musical concepts, theories and techniques. As a teacher you must relate to students but also give them valuable information that helps them become knowledgeable, freethinking and open-minded musicians.

Teaching More Advanced Theory

Treat music theory as a science of mathematics and you may expose your students to a whole new language that will provide them with a lifetime full of challenges. A person interested in numbers could spend a lifetime working equations, probabilities and word problems. Exposing music students to the theories of music provides them endless possibilities *and* an increasing understanding of the language of music. If you present theory as musical drudgery, you deny your students the opportunity to become excited about it.

Teenagers may have developed an attitude toward learning theory. "Man, I don't think when I play, I just let it happen." This may have worked up to now, but as they move toward more advanced and difficult music, that attitude needs some refining. Try using the analogy of music as a language. What if the student were to travel overseas as part of a foreign exchange program. Wouldn't they be concerned if they arrived and could not speak, read or write the language? After a few days of playing charades, the need for a more effective means of communication would become evident. This analogy should point out the importance of communicating the language of music. To converse fluently, you must dive in and speak the words, starting with the first lesson.

Analyzing a song or composition from the student's favorite artist is an easy way to emphasize the concepts of music theory. Simple questions such as, "What key is this song in?" or "What is the highest melody note?" or "What scale is the soloist using?" are effective ways to demonstrate a practical application of music theory. Keep giving the student real music examples and avoid getting too technical or theoretical. High school students are constantly being asked to learn material and memorize data bereft of any evident practical use. The more you do to make theory real, the quicker students begin to speak this new language.

Encouraging Composition

Because teenagers are trying to carve out an identity for themselves, encouraging students to compose their own music is an effective tool to use in lessons. It can become the basis of discussions of form, style, meter and many other aspects that might be overlooked during the course of a normal lesson.

Encourage students to imitate a composer or songwriter and try their own hand at writing music. Remember that when any student plays an original composition, the first words out of your mouth should be something like "That's terrific" or "That's a really creative piece. I especially like the part where. . . ." Avoid starting out with, "OK, let's work on that intro a little bit." You can get so caught up in listening for ways a composition can be improved that you forget the student has probably worked long and hard at this and is anxious about getting· your unconditional approval.

You need not introduce all aspects of theory before encouraging students to compose. It may be more effective to encourage students to experiment by relying on instinct and intuition. Then make them aware of the things that they have done after analyzing the composition. It is the first step in developing a unique, individual voice on their musical instrument.

Finding Incentives for Practice

When dealing with teenagers, use the power of positive example as an incentive. (Gold stars seem to lose their effectiveness around age twelve.) Students who look to you as a source of inspiration want to emulate you. If you finish playing an example for your student and notice his or her mouth hanging open in awe, then you can be reasonably assured that this student admires you and your abilities. Share with your student how you achieved your current level of proficiency. For most of us earthly humans that has been through years of study and endless hours of practice. Let students know what your practice routine was like when you were their age.

Using contemporary players as role models is also very helpful when trying to inspire teenagers to develop a practice routine. Use magazine articles, interviews and videotapes to gather quotes about effective practice methods. A student who hears about an idol who practiced fifteen hours a day as a teenager is more likely to take heed.

When discussing practice with typical teenagers, avoid statements such as "You'd better practice five hours a day or you'll never play like me." Their response (under their breath, naturally) might be something like, "Who would want to play like you?" Or they may accept it as a challenge not to practice at all: "I could practice five minutes a day and learn to play better than you." Chances are you won't elicit a positive response.

Try starting the lesson with a question. "What did you practice yesterday?" You will find great success in that line. It gives you a great topic for discussion during the lesson. Students, knowing that you are going to ask that question, prepare for it. But be aware that what they practiced may not be what you assigned last week.

Teenage students have many other musical interests that they would never think of discussing during the private lesson. They may belong to the jazz band at school that's preparing for a concert. They may play in a garage band rehearsing for their first gig next weekend. Perhaps they just wrote a song or riff that they have recorded on a 4-track. You ask what they played *yesterday* and if the student plays something new, you can use this opportunity to guide the student back to music fundamentals. The member of the jazz band may need some work on reading, phrasing or chord voicings. The garage band member may need work on time and dynamics. The composer needs further understanding of harmony or modes. This approach is especially useful if you have had difficulty getting consistent practice out of a student. Why continue to beat home a topic they refuse to work on? This new approach may inspire them to spend some serious practice time with an area that truly interests them.

Starting the lesson with "What did you practice?" also gives you a chance to emphasize the principle of a daily practice routine. The simple way in which you ask the question implies that it is a neccesary and essential part of learning music. If the reaction you get to the question is complete stupor or confusion, then you have a slight problem on your hands. If it is obvious that the student didn't practice anything yesterday, try naming the days of the week and see if that elicits any response. If you realize that a week has passed without anything touching the student's instrument except dust then you have a more serious problem to deal with.

We have a colleague who was giving private lessons to the daughter of a prominent politician. It was months before our colleague met the girl's father because of his busy political schedule. When they finally met after the daughter's piano lesson, His Honor asked how the lessons were going. Our colleague responded positively. The man then asked, "Is she advanced enough that she should begin practicing at home now?"

Every student, regardless of natural abilities, must practice to reach a higher level of accomplishment. Your responsibility as an instructor is to find a method that works for each student and continually reinforce this concept.

While a daily practice record is a great idea for younger music students, its results with teenage students may be mixed. For the serious academically oriented student, a daily practice log may be a useful tool for keeping the student focused on particular concepts (see Example 6-1). For the students who are socially active or involved in many extracurricular activities the log may simply be a painful reminder of their dwindling practice time and turn them off completely. Use your judgment.

Use positive peer pressure. There is no denying the sense of competitiveness among teenagers. You can make use of positive peer pressure to encourage students to practice. In chapter eight we discuss ways to showcase your students in concerts and recitals. Whether you do it as a formal concert or an informal jam session, getting your students to play and perform together is a great way for them to become part of a musical community. At the same time, they may find themselves at the bottom of the heap in terms of musical ability. This may be just the incentive they need to commit to an intensive practice schedule. We've heard endless stories of musicians who made a lifelong commitment to their studies after being fed a dose of this type of humility.

Another way to use peer pressure is to publicize the activities of your students. You can post flyers of student performances in your studio or classroom or you might develop a newsletter (see chapter eight) that includes a special section on student information. Perhaps a student is giving a recital at school or performing on cable television. Maybe a student band has an upcoming gig or has recorded a cassette album. Hearing what other students are doing can motivate students whose commitment has been somewhat lacking.

You can organize a concert for your students and bring in an accomplished group of young musicians. Seeing the level of musicianship of a group of their peers can truly give students some perspective on their own talent. It may motivate them to work much harder and may knock their egos down to size.

If you work near a college or university, schedule a field trip with several students. Contact the school and arrange to meet with faculty and students or take a tour of the music facilities. Coordinate your visit so you can attend a concert, preferably a student performance.

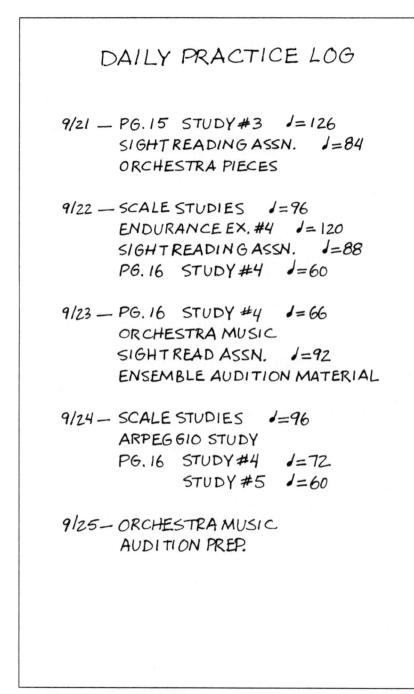

DAILY PRACTICE LOG

9/21 — PG. 15 STUDY #3 ♩=126
       SIGHT READING ASSN. ♩=84
       ORCHESTRA PIECES

9/22 — SCALE STUDIES ♩=96
       ENDURANCE EX. #4 ♩=120
       SIGHT READING ASSN. ♩=88
       PG. 16 STUDY #4 ♩=60

9/23 — PG. 16 STUDY #4 ♩=66
       ORCHESTRA MUSIC
       SIGHT READ ASSN. ♩=92
       ENSEMBLE AUDITION MATERIAL

9/24 — SCALE STUDIES ♩=96
       ARPEGGIO STUDY
       PG. 16 STUDY #4 ♩=72
              STUDY #5 ♩=60

9/25 — ORCHESTRA MUSIC
       AUDITION PREP.

Example 6-1. Daily Practice Log

This gives your students some long-range goals and challenges them to reach for that next level of competence.

Remember, you don't want to intimidate or humiliate your students. Try to make competition friendly. If you have exceptionally talented students involved in actual competitions, they are already aware of the commitment necessary to excel. These recommendations for using peer pressure are to encourage average students to practice. Remember you are dealing with a very emotional age group. Too much pressure may discourage. You want students to keep coming back, but to come back with a bit more ability week after week.

HELPING TEENAGE MUSICIANS WITH MUSICAL GOALS

Teenagers become involved in music for a number of reasons, and their interest spans the spectrum from hobbyist to college- or conservatory-bound to professional. Some students have played since elementary school and others just start because their best friend happens to play. You may encounter one student who can play Paganini caprices and one who wants to strum John Denver songs. Some students see themselves on a lifelong journey while others aren't able to see music beyond the week-to-week lesson.

From hobbyist to aspiring professional, students come to you looking for a way to make music a part of their lives. Your job as an instructor is to find out what priority music has for each individual and to fashion lessons around that level of commitment.

Accommodating Hobbyists

The biggest challenge for teachers of teenagers is to keep expectations realistic and in line with each student's commitment to music. If you just completed a lesson with a college-track student who has mastered the week's material, composed a two-part invention, and still had time left over to work on sight-reading and ear-training examples, then it's difficult to switch gears and deal with a hobbyist who only practiced once during the entire week. Avoid the tendency to carry your expectations over from one student to the next, and remember that the paying student is the consumer, buying your services as a lesson provider. For the hobbyist, fitting in one two-hour practice session in a week might be a great accomplishment, and should be commended. Encourage more practice time, but work at accepting situations for what they are. Whereas a serious student might learn a piece in one week, it might take a hobbyist ten weeks, piecing it together a bit at a time.

It's easy to become frustrated with a student. The tendency is to challenge the student to either work harder or to quit. In the case where a more serious student has set a specific agenda or goal, a confrontation *will* be necessary and important, especially if the student is looking to you for motivation. In the case of the hobbyist, however, you may want to delay any confrontation until you are one hundred percent certain that the student is getting nothing from the lessons. You may be surprised to find that because their expectations/goals are lower than yours (and they are also not comparing their progress to anyone else's) that they are reaping great rewards from studying music. We have seen students struggle for years to achieve a minimal level of proficiency. We have also seen these very same students make the leap to the next level and become quite capable musicians *in their own time*.

Remember that many teenagers are simply trying to establish their own identities. For some, an important part of that identity is the fact that they are aspiring musicians. At this time in their lives the aspiration is important and for some, that can carry them for a long while until they make the transition to becoming more serious students.

Encourage all of your students to become better musicians. At the same time, recognize the role music plays in the various lives of each student and adjust your expectations accordingly. Your reward should be to help hobbyists reach new goals and continue to enrich their lives by encouraging their music.

Helping High School Students Prepare for the College Track

For students who are serious about pursuing music as a college major or profession, you may become the most influential person in their lives. Some students will decide to further their study of music as a direct result of the relationship the two of you develop and the inspiration you provide them. No matter how a student has decided to study music in college, your responsibility as instructor becomes more clearly defined.

Assisting in the decision-making process. Your first responsibility is to paint an honest picture of how a college music curriculum would benefit your student. For some students this is obvious, for others it is somewhat questionable. If you have a student who has been on a track to college music studies and has been involved in the high school music program, your role may be simply to prepare the student for college expectations and requirements. For other students you must help them put their prospects for a career in music into perspective and see how an education fits into that plan. Some students simply are not proficient enough to be considering music as a major, and you may have to be the one to deliver the wake-up call. On the other hand, an insecure and humble teenager might not recognize his or her tremendous musical capability. With your constant reassurance and pep talks, this student might realize his or her inherent talent and go on to do great things musically. Your responsibility is to evaluate students' potential based on their performance, work habits, knowledge, experience and desire to excel.

Understanding state, private and conservatory requirements. You need to become familiar with the possible options for students wishing to study music in college. This means being aware of potential places to study your particular instrument, the benefits and drawbacks of each program, and the acceptance requirements and costs of the various institutions that offer music degrees or certificates.

Contact each school or university in your area as well as those across the country that specialize in your instrument, and request a catalog. Be sure to specify your interest in the music department and your particular instrument, since some schools have a separate catalog or brochure for each department or instrumental program. Familiarize yourself with each program, its faculty, facilities, and what it has to offer your students.

If you have difficulty obtaining a catalog from a school or need some immediate information, check with your local library or the guidance department of your area high school. It may help to contact the guidance department and talk to the counselors dealing with your individual students, especially those considering a career in music.

Getting to know college admission staff. Visit the schools in your area to get a more personalized view of each institution and what their music departments have to offer. Glitzy catalogs and brochures often paint unrealistic pictures of the programs they describe. Drop a note to the admissions office, letting them know you would like to see the music facilities. Being there in person, you can get a "feeling" about how the program operates.

You can also use this opportunity to meet with the faculty or department chair to discuss the program in more detail. Be sure to set up an appointment, since many college professors have extremely busy schedules. Meeting these individuals makes them aware of the role you play in their musical community. You gain a certain amount of name recognition that could benefit your students if you write them a letter of recommendation. It could also benefit you should the college need to refer a student to a teacher in your area.

If you are unable to schedule a meeting with someone from the department, see about meeting with someone from the admissions staff. They usually have scheduled tours and can answer specific questions you may have. Higher education is very competitive nowadays and admissions personnel are pleased to show off their programs.

Be certain to familiarize yourself with the faculty members of each school, especially those teaching your instrument. An average or below average program may still be attractive to your students if the school employs an exceptional teacher. On the other hand, a great facility is not worthwhile if the instructors are not suited to your student.

Entrance requirements: letters of recommendation. Pay particular attention to entrance requirements. All schools require scholastic records and test scores, musical background information, and several letters of recommendation. The student's high school takes care of all academic transcripts but the musical reference could be the determining factor for acceptance. Your difficult task is to give the student the most realistic yet positive reference you can.

Being asked to write a letter of recommendation for a student can be very flattering. Unfortunately, with all but the most exceptional students, your feeling of uniqueness and importance wears off quickly if you have several students waiting for letters to secure their acceptance. If you teach a predominately teenage population, you could have a dozen letters of recommendation to write at any one time.

Having struggled for years with a backlog of letters to write and little time or patience to devote to them, we have settled on a practical and timesaving method. Using the word processor, we created several master letters of recommendation that allow us to plug in information without having to compose a different letter each time. Because you are required to write letters for students of varying skill levels and potential, you need several different form letters: a polite but not-so-supportive letter, an average letter, and a glowing, positive letter. The form letters can include how long the student has been with you and in what capacity, the type of lesson material you teach, and any student recitals or concerts you have presented. When you add specific information about each student, you have a complete and personalized letter without having spent hours writing. Of course, you will have the occasional student for whom no form letter suffices, and you will have to come up with something totally unique. Happily, absolutely unequivocal and glowing letters of recommendation come fairly easily and are a joy to write.

In addition to developing letters of recommendation for your regular students, you may want to develop specialized letters for particular workshops or programs you have taught. If you teach each summer at an arts program or band camp, for example, you may encounter hundreds of students each year. Every one of these students is a potential candidate for a college music program who may need a letter of recommendation from you at some later date (often long after you can put a name to a face!). A form letter containing specific information about your teaching experiences at the workshop or camp greatly benefits you if you get dozens of requests for letters of recommendation. Include courses or lessons each student received and all special events and performances that each student participated in. This letter can be much more general than one written for your full-time students.

Helping students with audition tapes and audition preparation. Most colleges require a personal audition or submitted cassette in addition to letters of recommendation and academic records. As instructor, your job is to best prepare students for the audition process, helping them showcase their very best performances while keeping them somewhat calm.

Learn the exact requirements for each school. Some schools only conduct live auditions while others accept recorded audition tapes for students who live a great distance from the campus. Schools that hold personal auditions may conduct them at the school only, as a way to encourage the student to visit the campus. Other schools hold regional auditions throughout the country and overseas, using music faculty or regional alumni as audition judges. Certain schools audition music students only after they have been accepted to the general college. Be sure to find out which type of audition is required for your student.

Once you know the type of audition, identify the specific material to be covered in the audition. Some schools have very general requirements: Include three selections of contrasting style and tempo. Other schools have much more particular requirements, including specific works to be performed, scales or chord voicings to be played, and additional selections left to the student's choice.

Encourage your students to give themselves plenty of preparation

212 Long Street
Union, TN 99999
August 1, 1995

Director of Admissions
Belmont University
1900 Smith Blvd.
Nashville, TN 99999-5555

Dear Mr. Mulloy,

I'm writing this letter to call your attention to a former student of mine at the Community Music School in Union. Steven Malone was a student of mine in both the ensemble program and as a private student.

The ensemble program involves group performance in a variety of styles including blues, jazz and rock. Steven completed two levels of ensemble and demonstrated strong knowledge of chord voicings, improvisation and group interplay. He also achieved a reasonable level of sight-reading ability.

In our private lessons together, Steven reached level 4 of the required exams and he maintained a high B average. His understanding of music theory and composition was strong. He had a creative mind and was always searching for ways to apply new concepts to his instrument. Steven always maintained a positive attitude and had a refreshing sense of humor.

It was a pleasure having the opportunity to work with Steven over the past two years. I'm certain that Steven's music will always be the most important part of his life. I have no reservations in recommending Steven Malone to you. He will be a positive addition to your department and to your university.

Sincerely,

Shirley Foudy-Lewis

Example 6-2. Letter of Recommendation

To whom it may concern:

This letter draws your attention to a talented young student, Lisa Santana. Lisa attended the Community College School of Music summer program where I instructed her in sight-reading.

Lisa attended five one-hour group lessons that focused on beginner-level sight-reading for electric guitar. Lisa also received group instruction in chords and private instruction in theory, improvisation and technique. Lisa attended classes that covered diverse subject areas including theory, composition, notation, ear training and musicianship.

Throughout the summer, Lisa demonstrated a positive attitude and an intense desire to learn. On several occasions we met to discuss her classwork and to answer questions about the curriculum.

Lisa Santana is a mature and dedicated student. I strongly recommend her for acceptance to your school.

If you have further questions please feel free to call me at (999) 555-5555.

Sincerely,

David R. Newsam

Example 6-3. Letter Detailing Teaching Experiences at a Workshop or Camp

time. (Months, not weeks!) Many teenagers specialize in procrastination, so begin audition preparations early. If your student is submitting an audition tape for the first time, he or she may be unaware of the painstaking process involved in recording a high-quality, flawless cassette tape. Students must not think of this as a one-day project but as something that could take weeks to complete properly. You should devote as much of the lesson time as possible to audition preparation. This may be difficult if other material needs to be covered, if the audition material is dull and uninspiring, or if the student is terrified and therefore avoiding the material. You may need to balance the lesson with outside material to maintain some sense of continuity. This doubles the importance of advanced preparation.

Make educated suggestions when assisting a student in choosing audition material. Recommend pieces the student already knows that might be appropriate for an audition. Because you are familiar with the student's strengths, you can also suggest selections the student could learn that would best demonstrate his or her playing abilities. Choose challenging pieces the student can accomplish in the time allowed for preparation. Do not pick selections that will expose any weaknesses but do encourage students to present the most challenging pieces they can perform well.

Scholarships. Like most young people, many music students face difficult decisions about their future. Even after making the difficult decision to study music they have many tough choices about where to continue their education. That choice is often determined by finances. A student may have to settle on a school that was a third or fourth choice because the first choice is financially unfeasible.

As the instructor, you can make your students aware of and encourage them to apply for scholarships available through local programs, through national competitions, and through the school itself. Contact the lending institutions in your area and investigate any scholarship or trust funds that your students may be eligible for. Guidance counselors and music faculty may also know about local groups or agencies that sponsor awards or grants. We find it useful to organize a packet of scholarship information for interested students that each one can complement with help from other sources.

Most colleges have financial aid and work-study programs for eligible students. Music programs also offer scholarships based on performance abilities. Ability is usually judged by audition or submitted tape, so the importance of creating a high-quality and expressive audition tape cannot be overemphasized. You may also be asked to write a letter of recommendation for scholarship applications, so be prepared to detail how your student will prove to be a worthwhile investment.

Alternatives to a College Music Education

Probably the most difficult decision any teenager has to make is whether or not to pursue music academically or professionally or both. Deciding on a music education can bring about a great deal of turmoil, so be prepared. You may be asked by a distraught parent what *you* think a particular student's chances are of making it in the music business.

Tread lightly when parents ask you to counsel their children about a career in music. Many parents come to you with their minds already made up. They want you to support *their* decision concerning the student's future. It may be extremely difficult to convince parents that you can actually make a living and be happy with a career in music. And you may have to resist the temptation to point out that they obviously don't know their own son or daughter very well when it is so clear that the love of music is a driving force in the youngster's life. Be honest about the insecurity and uncertainty involved with a music career, and emphasize the determination and hard work needed to achieve success. But if the student possesses talent and a desire to study music, then offer an honest appraisal of the benefits of a music education.

The uncertainty of a music career or the increased pressure from parents will convince some of your best students to forgo studying music in college. Though you may feel disappointed, you should suggest alternatives so the student's love of music and opportunities continue and their studies will be guaranteed. Find a school that allows students to minor in music. This eliminates private music colleges and conservatories, but many public universities and state colleges have excellent music programs that can be accessed through minor courses of study. Investigate these programs to be certain that they offer courses and instruction to non-music majors. Talk to students there, if possible, to gauge how feasible it is for non-music majors to take courses. Some programs talk up the availability in their catalogs, but the reality is that every semester the music courses are filled with waiting-listed music majors before registration begins. Many programs are closed to students outside the department, and others offer only a small number of courses. Instructors employed by the college may offer private instruction outside their daily school schedules; however, the cost of these lessons usually must be paid by the student. Sometimes these private lessons can be taken for credit, sometimes not.

Although it may seem like a concession at the time, suggesting a music minor may give a student time to make an intelligent decision about future studies. A student who has experienced university classes, both music and nonmusic, is in a better position to figure out how music will fit into his or her life. Then the student may be able to switch to a music major or transfer to a conservatory or music school.

For some students the decision about a college education comes down to a financial one. The desire, talent and drive are there but the tuition money is not. This need not deter the student from a continued music education. Encourage the student to maintain lessons under your tutelage. If the student feels this is the time to move on to another level or another approach, recommend another teacher for the student to study with. (You may have to make that suggestion yourself if the student doesn't recognize the need for this—see "When to pass a student on to another teacher" in chapter ten.) Most geographic areas have one or two teachers who have tremendous reputations for being exceptional teachers. Perhaps you are one of these teachers, but if you haven't gained this reputation, then it may be wise to let your student move on to that next level and study with a truly outstanding instructor. Be sure to check out the teacher's rates and availability (many in-demand teachers have long waiting lists).

Whether students go on to major in music at college, or continue their studies with you or someone else, the thing you must instill and encourage in them during each lesson you teach is the love of music and passion for knowledge. If all is working as it should, you benefit by gleaning some of that initial enthusiasm, love of music and drive that got you into teaching in the first place.

Helping Students Prepare for the Professional Music Track

Some of your teenage students look at music as a professional career goal. Some may already be working musicians who want to increase their knowledge as a way to advance their careers (see chapter seven). Most are at the inception of the journey into the field of music. As their instructor, you can play a major role in influencing their decision to become working musicians as you encourage and assist their first steps.

Encouraging students into the field. Like a blossom that blooms when given precisely the right amount of sunlight and water, a student can grow to great musical heights under your guidance and influence. For the student who comes to you with a strong interest in learning music but little or no formal instruction, you may serve as the catalyst for tremendous understanding and growth. You never know who will walk into that first lesson or what their musical potential is. Many students thrive on the care and attention given by a dedicated teacher and many talents are unearthed by a teacher willing and able to cultivate a student's gift.

When a student displays an obvious aptitude for music, your job is to "contact the authorities." For both young children and teenagers you should talk with the student's parents. Let them know that their child may possess an exceptional musical ability. Your job is to be excited about it and extremely selective. Not every student will be the next Mozart. Don't use this merely to win over a student or parent, because it will surely backfire.

If a student possesses enough humility, share your opinion with the student directly. Let students know when you think they have excelled beyond expectation. It is *always* important to give any student positive reinforcement through compliments and constructive criticism, but when you approach a truly gifted student, your tactics should be different. Be serious and let the student know you are entirely sincere. Make such students aware of the significance of their accomplishments. Because they have no basis for comparison (they are not music teachers!), they may not know that their abilities or progress are unique.

Once you have spoken to student and parents, suggest a track for continuing and increasing the student's musical growth. Private instruction should be number one on the list. If the student's growth is exceeding your knowledge or style as a teacher, however, don't hesitate to pass this student on to a more advanced or learned teacher. There is no shame in having planted the seed of learning in a talented musician. The shame enters the picture if you hang on to students as "yours" when they would continue to grow exponentially with another instructor.

An advance track toward professional goals can also include increased lesson time, perhaps from one hour to two hours per week. Investigate summer or intensive study programs that would benefit the student. Summer programs run anywhere from a few days to the entire summer. Do research on programs relating to your instrument and request brochures to have on hand. Summer band camp provides a great opportunity for talented students to hone their craft, network with like-minded individuals, and derive inspiration to achieve their career goals in music.

GIVING TEENAGE STUDENTS OPPORTUNITIES FOR PERFORMANCE

Chapter eight covers the importance of student performances and recitals. For most students this is their first stage experience. For gifted students this may be the first of many more important performing opportunities you help provide for them. One way to showcase their talent is to *feature* them during student recitals. Give them extra time in the spotlight to show off their talents.

While student concerts are an important part of their journey to professionalism, they are only a small part. For truly gifted individuals, you need to supplement those opportunities. One way is to include gifted students in your performances to help them get a feel for what performances are really like. Perhaps they could sell tickets at the door or help with equipment. If they enjoy technology, let them help run the sound or do lights. With advance notice to the other musicians involved, let the student sit with you while you play the opening night of *The Mikado* with the local summer theater group. This gives students an up close and personal view of what the music field is really all about. Many teenagers have a glossy and unreal image of what it means to be a professional musician. Experiencing a night or two out with you may drive home the message: No limos here, just long, hard hours for little pay.

Once you gain confidence in the abilities and maturity of gifted students, do not hesitate to refer jobs to them. Maybe you've been offered a gig that doesn't offer much money or that requires playing a style of music you feel uncomfortable or uncertain about. These instances can be perfect opportunities for you to offer a job to your student. Many of us got our first big break from a teacher who showed enough confidence in us to refer work to us.

Remembering that part of (or all of) your professional career involves teaching music, don't hesitate to encourage your students into the field of teaching. If your student exhibits patience, knowledge and initiative, and if you have a waiting list, why not give that star student several beginners? Putting a student in the teacher's role may help redefine his or her own goals and be a springboard for a future as a professional musician.

TROUBLESHOOTING PROBLEMS WITH TEENAGE LEARNERS

The fact that you are dealing with individuals entering the most crucial period of their lives is troubling enough. Add career choices, personal identity crises, physical changes, and overprotective parents to the mixture and you spell trouble with a capital T (right here in Teacher City).

Remember that the rewards you reap from your relationships with teenage musicians outweigh the difficulties. Here are several problems that may confront you and some suggestions for dealing with them.

Parents With Misgivings About Musical Careers

Most parents shudder at the thought of their babies throwing their lives away to become musicians. We've even met some music educators who discourage students from considering a career in the music field.

The way parents share their concerns with you is often very rude and insulting. Imagine parents approaching a restaurant owner to discuss their daughter who is a waitress. "Mr. Owner, we want you to talk to our daughter. She's been working here for four years now and she loves her job. The problem is that she is thinking about becoming a restaurant owner and doing it for the rest of her life. You must help us. Is there anything you can do to discourage her from making such a terrible decision?" We have actually had parents approach us in this manner, concerned about their child entering the field of music. Their feeling is, "If only they would do something that would guarantee them a job." One student displayed remarkable musical and performing talents. He was a rather shy bassist who came to life when he got on stage. His parents had convinced him to study accounting and go into banking for the sake of job security. He graduated with his degree at the same time that more than half the banks in our state were in financial ruin.

There are no guarantees in life. If you have dreams, goals, and a passion for music, then you should go for it. There are few greater achievements in life than supporting yourself by doing what you love to do. There is no denying that opportunities are limited and that it requires hard work, persistence and luck to achieve these goals. But settling for less can only make you unhappy.

Your role as teacher is to walk that fine line between parent and student. You must reassure parent while encouraging student. If a student truly wants to make music a career then you need to support that decision. Be honest with the student about the path he or she has begun. If the student has an opportunity to study law at Harvard, then maybe you can suggest forming a band with lawyers as a side gig. Do not paint a rosy picture of a rocky road, but impress upon the student the joys you have encountered making a living as a professional musician.

Lack of Commitment

As a student enters the teen years, many changes take place. Teenagers experiment with many things, social, school, hobbies, etc., in an effort to form their identities. Perhaps they take on too much. Maybe they need to devote a great deal of time to a new project or activity. Whatever the case, many teenagers exhibit a lack of commitment to their musical studies. Your job is to try to uncover the reasons for this behavior and to assess its seriousness. Is the student going through a phase, a process of experimentation, a search? Has the student demonstrated enough commitment in the past to justify letting things slide until the phase passes? Or is this the beginning of letting go of music completely?

As in many relationships it is often difficult to break ties. Perhaps you have taught a student for a long while and the student feels that quitting would be letting you down. Maybe the student is simply unaware and cannot see his or her dedication diminishing.

Confronting a teenager about lack of commitment is a delicate matter. Jumping in and accusing students can immediately put them on the defensive. Instead talk to the student. Ask about practice time or interest, and try to get the student to see what you have seen. Once it is out in the open it may be very easy to work out a solution. You can suggest that the student take some time off to assess commitment. You could suggest trying a different teacher. Maybe just bringing up the subject will help the student recommit to studying and get back to better ways. Avoid waiting too long to broach the subject; doing so could cause you to get frustrated and snap at the student. Remember that teenagers are young adults and need to be treated that way. Scolding or shaming them has negative consequences. It is an emotional time for these youngsters and you can be a friend to them rather than an enemy.

Recognizing When a Student Is Using You as a Therapist

Because teenagers' lives are often filled with turmoil and difficult decisions, many students use the music lesson as an opportunity to share their problems with their teacher. You may act as a guidance counselor, a career advisor, a college admissions liaison, or a close personal friend. When your role begins to take on too personal a nature, you may end up becoming a sort of therapist as well. Many students feel uncomfortable or refuse to discuss issues with their parents or school counselors. You may be the one adult the student feels at home with sharing personal information. You must decide when that information is pertinent to the music lesson and when it is outside the realm of your position. When a student crosses that line, you are responsible for stopping it and directing the lesson back to music. Most teenagers have some situation arise that they need to share with someone. You must be aware that your position ends with being a music instructor; refer the student to a qualified counselor or therapist, if need be.

Lack of Communication With Parents

Because teenagers tend to withdraw from their parents, you may have very little contact with a teenage student's parents. Teenagers with their own transportation usually travel to lessons alone. Those parents who do drop off and pick up their students may do so without making any real contact with you. It is a good idea to stay in contact or initiate contact with parents whenever possible. Avoid waiting for a stressful time, such as a crisis or college decision-making, to contact parents. Let parents know periodically how their child is progressing in lessons, but make sure you tell your teenage students that you're going to call so they don't feel conspired against. Sponsoring events like recitals and open houses (see chapter eight) are wonderful ways to encourage meetings with parents and showcase your work with students. Be sure to welcome parents into the lesson at any time and encourage your students to involve their parents in their progress as musicians.

SOME FINAL WORDS ABOUT TEENAGERS

Teenagers are a category unique in every respect. Dealings with teenage students run the gamut from fun to frustrating, from rewarding to depressing. One thing is certain: Emotionally, there is nothing like a teenager. If you can overcome the obstacles that teenagers put in your path and connect with these young musicians, your role as a mentor can be life-changing. For students who possess drive, determination and talent, those qualities are defined during this period. Students who are to move to the next level and become adult (professional) musicians evolve during their teenage years. As their instructor, your responsibility is to guide, inspire and challenge these students to reach their goals and to set new ones. Those who reach that next level will look back at your influence with gratitude. For teachers, there is no greater reward than having set another individual on a lifelong path. It may be difficult to remember this when your teenage students are acting rebellious. But if you hang on to this thought during those hard times, in the years ahead you'll bask in the satisfaction of a job well done.

CHAPTER SEVEN

TEACHING PRIVATE LESSONS TO ADULTS

W hen you begin teaching music lessons or classes to adults, you see similarities between adults and younger students. After a while, however, you discover the uniqueness of the adult student and the importance of learning to deal with adult learners on a different level than younger students to keep them interested in sticking with lessons, and with you.

While the diversity among adult students may remind you of that found in teenagers, the parameters are much different. It is important to develop an understanding of the different types of adult learners and their specific needs in private lessons. The professional adult player may have immediate goals to troubleshoot, the hobbyist may be harder to motivate, and the entire population of adult learners generally has many more outside commitments that can interfere with music studies.

TEACHING ADULT HOBBYISTS

Most adults have responsibilities that include work, family, community and much more. For adults under a great deal of pressure, the goal in taking up a hobby is to relieve some of the stress of daily life. Adults who come to you for music lessons are generally looking for one important thing: a diversion from their daily lives that will provide relaxation and enjoyment.

For these adults, the lesson itself is a big part of their musical experience. They're more concerned with having fun during the lesson than the result of each lesson. Making the lesson informative but entertaining, inspirational yet relaxed helps achieve this balance. The challenge to teachers of adult hobbyists is to inspire, instruct and entertain simultaneously.

The Teacher-Student Relationship

The relationship you develop with the adult learner should take on several characteristics. Whenever possible, the relationship should be friend-to-friend as well as teacher-student. You are also a fellow member of the community. With younger students, it is important to present yourself as the authority figure. When teaching adults, it is still important to be in control, but try to relate to the adult learner as a peer as well.

As with other age groups, you need to maintain an air of professionalism, and at times you may need to strongly encourage practice or understanding of certain concepts. But the greatest success comes from making the adult students feel as if they are a part of the music field or profession. The fact that you possess the skills necessary to support yourself through music lends credence to your stature as an instructor.

You don't need to spend every minute of the lesson *teaching* the instrument. Discuss your career or performing experiences. Tell about the big gig you had opening for a well-known musician. Share some of the horror or humorous stories from your teaching and performing career. Show an interest in students' lives as well. Ask about the student's spouse or children and events they may be involved in. Know the student's work or business history and try to maintain a knowledge of their week-to-week commitments. It helps adult learners feel appreciated if you can comment, "It's a wonder you got to practice this week since your kids were on school vacation. Now there's some real dedication for you!"

Of course you should avoid spending *too* much time on the personal aspect of the lesson, so you won't come off as an egomaniac who would rather talk than teach. Not every student wants to hear about your career and/or personal stories. Even those who are interested in some personal conversation feel cheated if they leave the lesson thinking they have not been taught something. Look for the right balance between personal and professional dialogue in each lesson.

As with younger students, every adult reacts differently to your personal approach. You must work to recognize what each student is looking for in their lessons and which approach will benefit their learning the most. In most cases, adult students have a pretty good idea of what they want out of lessons and can communicate that to you if you are willing to listen.

Expanding Horizons and Fulfilling Dreams

Many adults say, "Oh, I took music lessons when I was a kid but I quit. I wish I had stuck with it." Our response to that is, "You can always try again!" Other adults say they wish they had taken music lessons as a child, but they couldn't afford it, or their parents told them they were tone-deaf, or the only instrument left in the band was tuba and they wanted to take accordion lessons. Naturally our response is, "Why not do it now?" It is never too late to start a new hobby.

For many adults the lack of a creative outlet is a frustration in their lives. Some once had a creative outlet that gave way to the mundane tasks of everyday life, and others have always felt that something was missing for them. There may be a void that only some artistic endeavor can satisfy. That is why many adults turn to creative activities such as quilting, woodworking, sculpture or *music*.

Some adults have had a lifelong yearning to study music and never had the opportunity to purchase an instrument and take private lessons. Many adults decide to study music after all those years of waiting and wanting. The adult pool of prospective students is an often overlooked category.

Their Expectations and Yours

Although younger students might be drawn to "picking up" an instrument on their own, most adults who decide to take music lessons want formal instruction to help them take that first step. You have an eager, open-minded student coming to you for private study. Adults are generally more patient and realistic in the expectations they bring to private lessons, but they may be more self-conscious about plunking or wheezing out a version of "The Streets of Laredo." While younger musicians want to see immediate results, adults are more apt to realize the commitment involved in studying music and the necessity for practice in order to achieve positive results.

Remember that for many adults the music lesson is there to relieve, not create, pressure. Expecting a complete commitment from adult students could threaten them. As with teen hobbyists, you may have to slow down the pace to keep students involved without making them feel overworked or inadequate. It can be difficult at times to remember that an adult beginner is no different than a child beginner. In fact, in many ways it is more difficult to learn a new skill as an adult. A child has no ego, no attitude, no hang-ups to get in the way of the learning process. For an adult it's often difficult to get beyond those barriers.

He or she may be nervous and embarrassed playing in front of you, so make the student feel at home and comfortable during the lesson. Exhibit as much or more patience when teaching adult beginners than you do with children. They may need more time to get involved in the routine of studying, but once they begin to see results, they should be well on their way.

Using Appropriate Materials and Methods

Many adults can be set in their ways, and that may extend to the types of music or the artists they listen to (or won't listen to). One sure way to grab an adult's attention is to make use of music from that student's youth.

During the first lesson, encourage students to improvise. No matter what age or ability they are, have them take a solo on a chord progression for a couple of minutes. This accomplishes many things. It helps students overcome the fear of playing in front of you. They may only play for a few seconds or just run up and down the scale several times. It does not matter. No matter what students do, the act of improvising a solo is very freeing. It encourages them to make things up on their own. It begins to remove the fear of making mistakes. It gives them some insight into music theory and constructing melodies.

When choosing chords for students to improvise over, use a progression you think the student will recognize. If they are interested in blues or blues-based rock, play a typical 12-bar blues. If they are interested in more contemporary rock or jazz, play a familiar progression from that style. If you feel inadequate or unfamiliar with a particular style then you may want to take advantage of computer technology or play-along tapes to provide a background for soloing. Even if students have no interest in soloing or improvising, use this technique to encourage them to begin to find a voice on their instrument and to relate that instrument to a style they are comfortable with.

To take full advantage of this approach to teaching, you must become fairly well-versed in a variety of styles and songs. One way to accomplish this is through transcriptions. Having written arrangements at your disposal is invaluable when dealing with the adult hobbyist. Many adults are perfectly comfortable working on different songs from week to week. As long as you have an inexhaustible resource (your personal library, preferably) for new materials, you can keep the student happy, challenged, and coming back week after week.

If you don't have written arrangements at hand but are fairly proficient at on-the-spot transcribing, you can aid your cause by collecting an eclectic and extensive library of recordings. This way you have some flexibility in choosing pieces to work on and present to your students. The simple process of building this collection exposes you to a wide variety of music and enhances your versatility and knowledge of popular music. So join that record club or visit that used CD store and start building new shelf space.

Think of yourself as a studio musician who needs to be prepared for any situation that arises. A good studio musician goes into a recording session ready to play anything. The better versed studio players are in many styles the better chance they have of doing the job and getting called back for the next one. As a studio teacher you should also prepare yourself for any student who walks in the door or calls on the telephone. So turn on that oldies station, dig out your old records (if you can find a record player to play them on), watch MTV occasionally, and build your repertoire so you can build your student roster.

Incorporating Practical Theory Into Lessons

While most adult hobbyists want to avoid intense discussions of theoretical rules and concepts, many students are very open to some discussion of the theory behind the music they are learning. Like children, most adults want to know why something works the way it does. Adults may want to know what forms the basis of the inner workings of a piece of music, a technique or a musical passage.

There are many useful and interesting ways to incorporate theory into your lesson plans. For example, suppose you want to introduce a scale. First, you can demonstrate what it is and its importance in a specific musical style (such as a blues scale). Then you can explain the theory behind building the scale. Once it is introduced, you can use it for building melodies and/or improvising. With an average student this whole process should only take a few minutes. Yet you have taught an approach that can help the student for years to come.

This is just one example of incorporating theory into your lessons. Demonstrate the importance of introducing the *why* as well as the *how* in music. Once this language is established, the student's understanding of music is infinitely more complete. Many students have struggled against learning theory for years, but often the introduction of these concepts is the freeing act in their musical understanding and expression.

Choosing Pieces Together

One sure way to discourage a student is to force-feed music that
the student cannot relate to. A child may have no difficulty playing
simple tunes that an adult considers obnoxious or boring. While learning simple material is essential to the growth process, an adult may
have little patience for practicing "This Old Man" for thirty minutes
every day. So while the importance of utilizing a beginning repertoire
is obvious, it is better to be more selective in choosing pieces for adults.

Develop your own library of materials for students of all ages. You
can customize each lesson to the particular student. For an adult student who is a sixties fan you can use a Janis Joplin melody. For a
Christian student you can use a hymn or other religious piece. In each
instance you can use the material to introduce a particular concept,
such as reading. By using diverse materials you encourage each student
in a positive way.

Adult hobbyists usually have specific ideas about material they want
to work on. They may know that the music is too difficult for a beginner, but they work toward that goal if it is reachable. If your new
student, who has never touched a piano, has always wanted to play
ragtime, you may have to delay working on that style until he or she
learns the basics. But, if your fledgling trombone player wants to learn
"When the Saints Go Marching In" right off the bat, why not? Making
an honest assessment of a student's potential for learning a specific
style or piece is part of your job. If students' goals are reasonable, let
them know that if they work on the fundamentals and certain techniques, they will reach those goals. If their goals are unreasonable,
however, be honest and practical and perhaps suggest an alternate
plan. Regardless of the approach you take or the goals of the student,
it's important to incorporate a personal approach to choosing lesson
materials. Allow the student to influence the choice of materials and,
when appropriate, to actually choose the songs to be worked on.

One way to learn a student's interests is to have the student record
some music for you on cassette. There are two types of tape you might
request. The first is a tape that catalogs the student's influences from
the time he or she began listening to music to the present. This gives
you tremendous insight into the musical path the student's life has
taken and helps you determine a direction for lessons. This approach
also helps students define how they have "grown up" musically and to
see where they have taken certain departures and where they have
"arrived." Because this assignment is personal and insight-oriented,

many adult learners get a lot of personal satisfaction from making such a tape. You can then use their recorded examples to reinforce theoretical or technical concepts.

A second approach is to have students tape specific music they would like to learn. You can transcribe the music and show students how to perform it. Be prepared to transcribe music of all sorts and of varying degrees of difficulty. If you are uncomfortable with, uninterested in or unprepared to do this transcription, then find an alternative method. Transcribing often takes time outside the lesson. Your lesson fee should cover the lesson time plus a minimal amount of preparation time. If you spend hours each week transcribing music for a half-hour lesson, you may want to work out a different arrangement or fee schedule.

Let adult students have a say in the material they work on, but be careful how you incorporate their ideas. If this happens randomly the lessons can seem haphazard. If student choice is integrated into an organized and systematic approach to teaching music, however, the results can be remarkable. Check over your existing lesson materials. Do you routinely use the same method book? Is this because it's really the best for every student or because you are familiar with the examples?

Finding the right mixture of appropriate materials and concepts is often difficult, but when that balance is achieved the end result is rarely negative. So work hard to incorporate student influence into your lesson plans while maintaining a steady course toward improvement. You must be prepared for adult learners who want to play classical piano, folk guitar, jazz bass, sing-along guitar, hymns on the organ, Dixieland, bluegrass mandolin or Jerry Lee Lewis with their feet. In other words, your personal library and repertoire must include music that covers the full spectrum of styles and tastes.

Coping With Family and Work Responsibilities

Each age group has its own "problem areas" to deal with. Adult learners are no different. The most common problem among adult learners is their tremendous responsibilities that diminish their commitment to seriously studying music.

As an instructor, you should be aware of the time constraints on your adult students. No matter how inspired they may be to learn and practice, there may be no way other than giving up sleep to invest the time needed to improve their skills. For some people time constraints may be a temporary or periodic problem. Holidays and school vacations bring additional pressure to be with family. Businesses have periods of increased activity that may put constraints on students at different times of the year. Motivated students can work themselves out of these "dark" periods in their playing and back into a regular routine. Others may have difficulties finding the routine again, and it becomes your job to encourage them back to a practice schedule.

Many beginners have no idea just how much time needs to be invested to learn an instrument. It's your responsibility to point out that progress is directly related to the amount of time invested in practice. In some cases you may have to suggest that a student take some time away from lessons to catch up on material or reassess their commitment to studying. After a "time-out" for a strictly periodical time constraint, the student may return to lessons refreshed and motivated for a new beginning. But if the student has no drive to really learn the instrument, then he or she may hang up lessons completely and write them off to experience.

Family Plans

One obvious advantage to teaching more than one member of a family is financial. Another advantage to teaching on the family plan is the reduced work in recruiting students. You can recruit two or more prospective students by exerting the same effort normally required for one student. This effort includes advertising costs, as well as general phone and paper work necessary for setting up and maintaining lessons for each student.

Although adult students have many family commitments that conflict with their own lessons and practice times, the priority can shift from a personal interest to a family one if music lessons become a family activity. Many families today are committed to finding "quality time." If dad and daughter both take music lessons, that becomes an important activity they develop together. Rather than dad playing guitar and daughter doing tap dancing as separate activities, music binds them together and builds their relationship. This holds true between spouses and partners as well. What better way for a committed relationship between adults to grow than through music.

The family teaching plan also offers built-in camaraderie and competition that are very useful for inspiring new students. Parents can monitor and regulate practice times. Children can help keep parents enthusiastic and energetic about their studies. Each side inspires the other, thereby keeping the music instruction fresh, exciting and fun.

Whenever possible, try to create a family plan from your existing students. Inquire about your adult students' children and whether they may have an interest in studying music also. Offer the parents of your younger students an opportunity to take lessons. Often parents "simply hadn't thought of taking lessons themselves" and are flattered and/or intrigued by the idea. Advertise special reduced rates for family plans. With convenient scheduling, you can give the second lesson in each family for half price. You may even consider offering two for the price of one for a group lesson. If parent and child or a couple take lessons together as beginners, eventually their rate of progress or musical interests could separate them, thus making two individual lessons a future possibility.

MEETING THE CHALLENGE OF TEACHING PROFESSIONAL MUSICIANS

Professional musicians who come to you for musical instruction offer a difficult and rewarding challenge. They want to be pushed to the limit of their abilities. They have specific areas they want to focus on and often expect immediate results. They may have gaps in their knowledge or weaknesses in their playing that you must troubleshoot. Remember that they must have identified the weakness or gap in knowledge themselves to have sought you out in the first place.

Working professional musicians offer insight into your own playing abilities. Inexperienced teachers can find this challenge a difficult one because all their insecurities are exposed. For the successful instructor, the adult professional gives more satisfaction than any other student. The professional musician demonstrates immediate and practical applications of the material you cover. Invested in the subject, the professional musician takes pains to prepare for each lesson and to investigate the material to its fullest. For the teacher ready to meet the challenge of instructing the professional musician, the rewards are lifelong and significant.

Understanding the Needs of Professional Musician Learners

As a professional musician, put yourself in the position of the person who is considering taking music lessons. It is often difficult and humbling to decide that music lessons are required. Many people see it as being a failure at their craft. It is similar to having to see a therapist or marriage counselor. Rather than seeing lessons (or therapy) as a way of improving themselves (or their relationships), people often use these tools as a last resort to salvage something or solve major problems. In addition, some may fear a societal attitude that those who seek help are failures. All these elements lead to a sensitive situation when a professional musician comes to you seeking lessons. The first thing you need to do is make the person feel at ease with the prospect of being a student again.

Once the decision to study music is made, the path is usually clear. Most professional musicians who decide to take music lessons want to focus on specific problem areas. Perhaps they have difficulty with time or rhythm. Maybe they lack theoretical knowledge or improvisational abilities. They may be unable to read the charts that the band leader is giving them. Perhaps a band that a musician works with is moving from swing into more rock classics or wants to play jazz sets, and this professional has little experience in the new area. Some people want to learn a specific style: The violin player wants to learn "fiddling," the bassist wants to learn funk slap. Whatever the case, the student usually wants a specific need met.

Build some initial confidence in these students, convincing each one that a.) I can teach this subject, and b.) you can learn this subject. Hopefully, your performing and/or teaching abilities drew the student to you. If the student is still uncertain about being in lessons, however, it is crucial that you grab that student's attention and instill confidence in your ability as a teacher.

The professional student with specific needs wants to address those needs right from the start. Such students cannot expect solutions overnight, but they want solutions set in motion right from the first lesson. The first lesson with any student is the most important one. It sets the tone for the relationship you develop for months to come. In the first lesson with a professional, you must demonstrate your abilities as a teacher and a player while starting the student toward solutions to his or her musical problems.

Some students may come to you without a specific need in mind. They may simply feel like the "weakest link" in some performance situation. You must identify what area or areas need work, then address those needs. In most cases these weaknesses are obvious. Usually after hearing someone play for several minutes, you can identify specific weaknesses in technique or form, such as technical deficiencies, time and phrasing problems, or a host of other areas. Try to convey your impressions to the student, to give a sense of what you feel needs work. Once the problems are verbalized, most students recognize them in their own playing and agree with your assessment.

Try to be very encouraging after hearing someone play for the first time. Avoid negative criticism of the student's playing. Do not overwhelm the person with dozens of problem areas you feel need work. While you may see the need for a long-term overhaul of a student's playing, it may be best to offer short-term solutions for the most glaring weaknesses and work from there. Once a working relationship has been established, it's much easier to refine other areas in a much more frank manner.

Filling Gaps in Knowledge

When a professional musician comes to you for lessons, do your best to fill in the gaps in their music knowledge. While the possible list of difficult areas is too extensive to list here, some obvious ones are sight-reading, time, rhythm, phrasing, technique, intonation, tone, theory and improvisation. Everyone has some weaknesses. As a teacher, you can help your students strengthen their overall musical knowledge and playing abilities and make them versatile and respected musicians.

Providing instruction to "fill in the gaps" often requires a complete change of approach in your teaching methods. You might be used to following a weekly lesson plan that includes checking weekly assignments, introducing new material, reviewing regular material, and occasionally venturing off into unknown waters. But to really get into areas like those mentioned above you may have to spend an entire lesson on one specific concept. If you are working on rhythm, you may need to play one riff or phrase over and over again until it starts to gel rhythmically. If sight-reading is the subject, it may take a whole lesson to plow through a new piece of music. If time is the problem, you may find yourself sitting and clapping with the metronome for an entire hour-long lesson.

This may seem like an unreasonable amount of time to spend in one area. But it is important to demonstrate this process to your student. You may say "You need to play this chord progression for thirty minutes before it will start to come together," and the student may nod his head and say yes while thinking that you really mean thirty seconds. If you walk the student through the process and play the progression together for that length of time, the experience takes on greater meaning and significance. The next time a problem arises perhaps the student will have the necessary perseverance and determination.

Don't use this method to intimidate students or make them feel inferior. A classical musician may have no insight into jazz improvisation or feel, so attempting to solo over the chord changes to "Giant Steps" by John Coltrane would be a fruitless exercise for that student. Rock players may have never read a note in their lives, so asking them to play Bach inventions is a waste of time. The idea of filling in the gaps in someone's knowledge does not mean jumping around from one subject to the other haphazardly without introducing, following up on or relating the subject to other material. Filling in the gaps is meant to develop well-rounded, versatile musicians. If the rock player can benefit from reading music by increasing chances for doing studio work or playing in rehearsal bands, then introduce the subject and systematically increase the difficulty of the material over time.

Filling in the gaps is something that every player needs to focus on at one time or another. When used effectively, it can be a great teaching tool and a great change of pace from the regular routine of weekly lesson plans.

"Exchange" Lessons for Professionals

Some professional musicians seek you out as their teacher because of one specific area of your playing or teaching ability. They may be accomplished professional musicians; they may even be more accomplished or well-known in the field than you. However, they may have a special need or deficiency in a certain area that they feel you can help them with. Perhaps it's the rock player who cannot read or the classical player who simply cannot swing. Maybe their theoretical or harmonic knowledge is lacking.

You can treat these individuals as you would any prospective student coming to you for lessons. Or you can capitalize on this unique opportunity and take advantage of this person's own area of expertise by exchanging lessons. Divide a one-hour lesson in half: You play the role of instructor for the first half and the student instructs for the remainder. This way each of you benefits from the other's knowledge and it costs neither of you any money for lessons. (See chapter nine for the tax implications of barter arrangements.)

If the person seeking instruction is younger or less skilled, with some knowledge to offer but not your professional equal, you may consider a three-fourths plan as an alternative. Offer the student half-price lessons in return for sharing some of their knowledge. Instead of switching roles for half the lesson, the student's share of the teaching time would be one-fourth of the lesson time. The student may offer you a chance to stay more "contemporary," maybe even providing you with transcriptions or techniques you can use in your teaching of younger students. At the same time, the student gets some hands-on teaching experience in a friendly and supportive environment. You may even give the student encouragement and confidence to begin teaching private lessons.

TEACHING COLLEGE STUDENTS: THE MUSIC MAJOR

Teaching college students can involve dealing with hobbyists and semi-professional musicians, but this section is devoted to that unique category of student, the college music major. College music majors are in musical purgatory. They are in transition from teenagers to adults. They may not be professional musicians at the present time but they are certainly headed toward that goal. You should treat them the way you would any adult professional musician, keeping a few things in mind.

The University Music Department

Teaching at a university or as an adjunct faculty member for a college music program can be a demanding role. Your students are learning *required* material and you must issue them a grade for their work during the term. Being in a position to influence the student's grade point average affords you a different level of respect. However, most college students look beyond the grading system. They look to you for inspiration, direction, opportunity, and hope for their future.

The biggest challenge you face in teaching the college music major is successfully integrating required and desired material. While music majors expect to spend most of their time perfecting their performing skills, many are overwhelmed by the outside work and requirements placed upon them. They may be finishing a portfolio (composition and arranging majors), preparing for a senior recital (performance majors), student teaching (music education majors), or working on other significant projects included as part of the graduation requirements.

Many times the required repertoire is very difficult, especially if the material is unfamiliar. Most of the lesson time may be spent preparing required materials or selected pieces for proficiencies or jury exams.

This leaves little or no time for exploring the students' real interests, leaving them unsatisfied. They may feel they're spending a great deal of time and money practicing material they may have no interest in and that they're neglecting what they came to school to learn.

As an instructor, you should first try to convey a sense of understanding. At the same time you need to demonstrate and illustrate the importance of the required material and its relationship to the student's area of interest. Making students feel that the required material is a waste of time only serves to further frustrate them and probably discourage them from properly preparing the material for the exam.

Try to weave the requirements into a student's area of interest when time permits. If the student is well prepared and/or motivated to work alone on the required material, then don't hesitate to branch into other musical areas that give the student more satisfaction. If you can successfully integrate required material into lessons and cover additional areas while motivating and challenging students, your reputation as a respected faculty member is certainly enhanced.

Stepping Into Adulthood

The first challenge most college students face is adjusting to the freedom and pressures of college life. Many students are away from home for the first time in their lives. They face new academic and social pressures. For some, you may be the only one-on-one contact they have during their stay in school. Although they may meet with a curriculum counselor or faculty member on occasion, your weekly meetings give them a sense of stability. Because of this, they may rely on you for suggestions and information concerning all aspects of their personal and academic choices. This personal aspect makes your role as college instructor even more difficult.

In your first lesson with a music major it is important to establish a working relationship and gain the student's respect. Find out if the student is registered for the proper courses and has acquired all the important materials needed for the semester's work. Find out how the student is coping with the transition to college life.

The rigid schedule of high school days is now replaced by an irregular college schedule. For some students this is a positive situation that they take full advantage of. Having large blocks of time in their schedule affords them the opportunity for periods of intense practice or study. For others, especially the less disciplined, this newfound freedom poses a challenge.

One solution for the less-disciplined student is to require that he keep a daily log of his practice routine (see page 136). This is a wonderful way for the student to monitor his practice time. It also serves as a good gauge for determining how much time and effort is being put forth in particular areas. The student may be practicing a great deal but without direction or neglecting the required material in favor of other interests. The daily log serves as a good guide for both you and the student. You may actually want to check the student's log on a regular basis, either weekly, quarterly or during exams.

Preparing for a Life of Performing

Students in a music school or program live in a rather artificial environment. The best practical experience that the college student can receive is performing experience. While you can't provide work for each of your students, you should try to provide students with as much practical experience as you can before they leave school. This could mean using a student as a sub for work you can't do or referring a student to others when you choose not to accept a performance opportunity.

You can help your students gain performing experience by organizing recitals, jam sessions and concerts. Despite the fact that most colleges provide each student with performing opportunities, there is always room for more. Students may be enrolled in ensembles, chamber groups, orchestras and shows. They may even be doing recording and band projects outside of classes. But the more performing experiences students get, the better prepared they are for the real world. It may take extra time for you outside your regular teaching schedule, but your students benefit in many ways. Most important, the extra attention you give to help organize a performance shows students that you are truly interested in their well-being outside the classroom.

You can organize various types of performances. You can schedule a jam session and secure a house band for people to drop by and play with. You can advertise an open concert and reserve a room for people to drop by and perform or listen. You can organize a formal recital and secure a performing hall on or off campus. Printed programs, lighting, sound, etc., all add to the professional atmosphere of the performance.

Don't underestimate the powerful impact these performances can have on students. They can spend hours and hours in the practice room in preparation for playing experiences, but it's impossible to duplicate that actual performance experience. Even the most confident student may feel a rush of anxiety and stage fright when actually placed in a performance situation. And the only way to overcome those conditions is through repeated exposure. If you act as the coordinator of these events and ask your students to nail down all the logistical details, they get experience in planning as well. The more experience they have, no matter how insignificant it seems, the better prepared your students will be for their performing careers ahead.

SOME FINAL WORDS ABOUT ADULTS

Adult learners are very often the most challenging students to teach. Whether it be the delicate ego of the insecure beginner or the insatiable quest of the professional musician, your job is a difficult one. However, meeting these challenges gives you a unique sense of accomplishment. You have succeeded in motivating and inspiring a fellow musician, a neighbor, a peer. And your success often results in lifelong friendships and rewarding relationships with those in your community and in your field.

CHAPTER EIGHT

STUDENT RELATIONS: KEEP THEM COMING BACK!

As for any good business, the Golden Rule should be your foundation for private lessons. Treat students the way you would like to be treated. Your relations with your customers, your students, determine the long-term success of your teaching business. To remain an in-demand teacher in your community, you must connect with students so they want to continue to study with you and refer their friends to you.

Part of establishing meaningful relationships with your students is making them feel special. Let students know they are progressing, and that their hard work is paying off. Showcase them in recitals, or connect them with other students to form bands or to "jam with" to give them important outlets for their musical expression. Involve them in your personal and performing life so they feel that you're more than just a teacher, but someone they can call a friend. Take an interest in their personal lives and help them achieve higher musical goals. All of these elements reinforce that sense of friendship and camaraderie, and help foster a positive learning environment for students to grow in. Your lessons together become an important aspect of their lives, one that they will want to continue for a long time to come.

NETWORKING TO HELP STUDENTS FEEL LIKE "PART OF A TEAM"

Students often fashion their personalities around the musical instrument they play or the music they are involved in. (This is especially true with young people.) What better way to let those personalities shine than to allow them to connect with other students with similar leanings? If you teach even a small number of students you have a tremendous resource for your individual students: each other.

Students of all ages can connect best with other like-minded people.

Not only can they benefit from meeting and befriending similar people, but, more important, as musicians they can meet and share music together. Getting together with other musicians helps them in more ways than one. Certainly the social aspect is an important one. Having a musical friend to practice with, jam with or hang out with helps the student grow musically. But the performing element is especially crucial to every student's growth. Performing with you during lessons is only a tiny fragment of the performing possibilities. Playing with school ensembles is an important outlet as well. Playing with peers should be an important part of that spectrum. Whether the students sit down to play classical duets, sight-read through pop tunes, or organize a garage band, playing music with each other not only supplements their music lessons, but also creates a new focus for them to investigate and set goals.

The easiest and least formal way to help students network with each other is simply to introduce them. Students may already know someone else who studies with you but feel uneasy about or unaware of the possibility of playing music together. Introduce students as they come in and out of your studio. Encourage them into dialogue by starting up a conversation between them. "Johnny this is Jason. He goes to the same school as you, maybe you've seen each other around the halls." Or, "Jane, this is Ellen. She will be entering the high school this fall. Who should she talk to about auditioning for band?" Initiating the conversation gives them permission to continue on their own. Perhaps the following week you can encourage them to exchange phone numbers or plan a meeting after lessons. If you feel they are musically compatible then suggest that they play together. You can provide them with some music that showcases their abilities.

Another method for making all your students aware of each other is to organize a list of everyone who studies with you. This list is something you already have in one form or another. You can simply organize a student list and include phone numbers and/or addresses of all your students. (Be sure to check with students and parents to be sure they don't mind having that information distributed among your student population.) Make copies of the list available and distribute it to each student. Update the list periodically to include newer students or new phone numbers and addresses. Once students receive the list they may recognize a name or see an address in their neighborhood, and you may have helped establish a connection that could benefit everyone involved. Even if a student does not recognize anyone on your list at first, they may eventually meet someone whose name sounds familiar and recognize that they both have you as a teacher.

Most students are shy or intimidated by the prospect of getting together with other students to play music. Rather than leaving it up to chance that students will connect, you can take a more aggressive tack such as purposeful introductions and/or a student roster creating networking among your students.

Creating Student Duos, Trios and Bands

To augment your students' musical studies, create opportunities for them to play in duo or group settings. One method of incorporating group playing into your curriculum is initiating an ensemble program and making it available as a service to your students. Set aside lesson times (at least an hour long for larger ensembles, one-half hour for duos or trios) for students interested in group playing. Categorize ensembles by style, age, level of ability, etc. You can even choose to select students for ensembles through an audition process.

You can choose to include this service as part of your basic lesson fee (knowing that it will attract and keep students) or charge an additional fee only to those who take part in the ensemble program. The fee for group lessons or ensembles can be much lower than an individual one-hour lesson, proportionate to the number of students involved. For example, if you charge thirty dollars per hour for lessons, then an ensemble with six students allows you to offer the service for only five dollars per student. This makes the idea very attractive to parents and students who cannot afford an additional outlay of cash. If more preparation is required, or if you have to rent an appropriate space, then a slightly higher fee is reasonable.

Network with other instructors in setting up an ensemble program. If you teach drum set, for instance, the likelihood of putting six students together in a room and having anything musical result is rather slim. However, putting a piano student together with a saxophone student, or adding a drummer to a guitar ensemble benefits everyone involved. Percussion ensembles, string quartets and brass quintets are all common musical formats for group playing. If you teach at a studio with other instrumental/vocal instructors then consider approaching them with the idea of initiating an ensemble program that incorporates all instruments. The program creates more teaching opportunities for everyone and gives the students a tremendous outlet for their musical talents.

If you have neither the time, facilities nor desire to initiate group instruction or ensembles with your students, then check your area to see if opportunities exist elsewhere in your community. Perhaps a community music school or adult education program offers group playing opportunities. Contact school band directors to see if they offer performing opportunities to members of the community (often they welcome players to fill missing positions in their ensembles). Contact your colleagues to see if they offer an ensemble program for their students and could use an accompanist or soloist. The simple referral of a student to an ensemble or group playing opportunity reflects well on your professionalism and your connection to the musical community in your area.

Encourage all your students to participate in an ensemble program of some type. Much of their time may be spent in solitude, practicing alone, or playing along with tapes, computers or recording machines. There is no substitute for playing with other musicians, no matter what the student's age, interest or level of ability. In many cases, the act of performing with other musicians, especially in front of a live audience, exposes the student to a new level of enthusiasm about music.

Combining Lessons to Bring Students Together
Another way to get students to play in duos is to invite them to play together during their lessons. The easiest way to initiate this method is to have students with back-to-back lessons combine their times. In other words, if James has a lesson from 2:00 to 3:00 and Bryan is scheduled from 3:00 to 3:30, then overlap their lesson times and encourage them to play together for you. If Bryan arrives early, ask him to come into the studio and have him and James play for ten or fifteen minutes together, going over into Bryan's time if necessary. If things work well, ask Bryan to arrive early each week and make it a regular part of their lessons. Having students play together, especially if they are musically like-minded, gives them a new feel for the music. Playing with you during lessons is not as good because you may be well advanced of the student's abilities or not tuned in to their particular interests. Playing with a fellow student, especially one who is similar in ability, is a more satisfying way to play.

While this scenario does not present itself often it should be taken advantage of when it does. Even if the two students have little in common musically or are not comparable in ability, positive things may result. If one student is well advanced of the other, it serves as inspiration to the other to excel. It also offers more advanced players insight into their own struggles or keys them into the role of the teacher for a few minutes.

In some instances you can purposely schedule two students back-to-back to create this opportunity. Perhaps you have some keen intuition that two students will hit it off, and this way they can meet each other and play together under your watchful eye and careful direction. Make sure you let your students know that playing with others and overlapping lesson times is something you think will benefit them musically, otherwise it may appear that you are just trying to consolidate your work.

ENCOURAGING STUDENTS TO PARTICIPATE IN RECITALS AND CONCERTS

Involving students with other students in social and musical ways is a generous service you can provide. It demonstrates your continued interest in their musical and personal growth. However, no one activity or event serves as better public relations for you and your business than student recitals. Recitals give your students that essential outlet for public performance. Student recitals also give you exposure to the community and, most important, an opportunity to show parents, friends and relatives the hard work that you and your students have put into making music.

Student recitals can take on many forms, from individual performances at the conclusion of a private lesson to a formal concert in a public hall or auditorium, complete with programs, ushers, sound, lights and popcorn. In fact, rather than deciding to do recitals one certain way, you can use many different approaches to showcase your students' talents.

Informal Recitals

The most informal recital is to ask a student to perform during the lesson time. Have the student prepare a new piece of music or have them review several recent works and allocate time during the lesson for the performance of the piece(s). You can have the student perform the music for you alone or you can invite in parents and/or friends to be the audience for the informal concert. Having an audience is a plus. It gives the student a sense of a real-life performance setting. It may even cause a mild case of performance anxiety, which is something most performers must deal with at one stage of their careers or another.

Try to make the recital seem as much like a performance as possible. Set up chairs for your "audience" in front of a "stage" for your performer. Make the event seem different from playing during the regular private lesson. If there is no audience then record or videotape the event to simulate a live audience. (This also affords you the chance to review the performance at a later time with the student.) Some teachers work on a fairly regular schedule and students know that, for instance, the third lesson of every month will include a short recital. Scheduling like this helps students budget their practice time to prepare pieces.

The act of performing, even in a setting that is usually reserved only for lessons, helps students strive for a new level. Instead of just learning the notes to a song or a new piece of music they must be able to take that music to a point nearing perfection.

Informal recitals are a good way to connect with parents also. Instead of leaving mom and dad in the waiting area week after week, recitals involve them in the musical progress their child is making. More important, informal recitals are something parents can organize on their own. Show them how easy it is to create the feeling of a concert by moving a few chairs and turning off a lamp or two. Encourage parents to have the child play for family friends or relatives at holiday gatherings, or parents can set up weekly times for children to play their weekly lesson material. After Sunday meal, Jimmy can give a five-minute recital for the entire family.

Organizing informal recitals at home helps parents become excited about music and helps them understand how to be supportive. Informal recitals should be a positive experience for students, not pressure situations that discourage playing. A child should never be forced to play against his or her will. The goal of the informal recital is to get the student more comfortable in preparation for larger, more formal events.

Semiformal Recitals

A second approach to presenting students in recital is to organize a small recital in your home or studio featuring several students. Parents and friends should be invited, so the number of students taking part in the recital is determined by the space you have available for students and their families. If you have more students than you can present at any one recital in your studio, plan to present several different recitals. You can organize each recital so that students of similar levels or interests perform together. You can organize the recital to include students that all have lessons on the same night (and schedule the recital on that lesson night).

Individual recitals in your studio and these small group recitals both tend to be somewhat informal. No special dress is required by you or students. They are in a setting that is very familiar to students and parents so the atmosphere should be relaxed. Some things you can incorporate make the event a bit more exciting. Using a personal computer, you can create a program listing the students and the pieces they will perform. Have copies for parents and extras for the students to keep for their scrapbooks. Have light refreshments before or after the performance. Invite prospective students and their parents so they can get a sense of your teaching abilities and the kind of effort you give to the students (and the kind of results they can expect!).

Formal Recitals

The final example of a student concert is an all-out affair. Instead of presenting your students in an informal setting, locate a hall you can reserve for the date of the concert. Perhaps the studio or school you work for has a facility for this purpose. If not, check with your local library, museums, schools or churches to inquire about reserving their hall for a student recital. You can also check any local organizations that have a building (Elks, Kiwanis, Masons, etc.). Sometimes private businesses, such as law firms, can be persuaded to let you use their facilities. Parents of your students may have connections to places, so check around. Many places are willing to donate their facility for nonprofit events. As long as you are not charging admission (which you probably shouldn't), shop around until you find a room that suits your needs and can be used for free. If you do have to pay a fee to rent a room or a piano, consider asking for donations from the audience to help defray your costs. If the amount is small, then skip the donation idea. Remember that these students are paying your rent and grocery bills, so don't nickel and dime them over what is a public relations event for you anyway. The benefit for your students and the publicity for you far outweighs the cost of renting a piano for one evening.

Plan your concert well in advance, for it requires some real effort to organize and present one in a professional manner. After dealing with this type of presentation several times you begin to develop a system of organization that allows for things to go smoothly. If this is your first time planning such an event, give yourself loads of up-front time and expect the unexpected. What may seem like a fairly simple event takes careful planning and a great deal of patience.

Once you have found a location for your event and have decided on a date, begin working on the concert immediately. There are two distinct areas of focus: the music to be presented, and the preparations necessary for organizing and publicizing the concert.

The musical preparations are similar to what you go through for an informal recital: choosing material, regular practice and review, memorizing and preparing the music so it's of concert quality. Because of the magnitude of the more formal concert, weeks, maybe months, of preparation and practice should be allowed to get this music ready for performance. Pay more attention to material that is most challenging. If ensemble playing is on the recital program, then additional time must be allocated for coordinating rehearsals.

Make sure you impress upon your students what is expected of them well in advance of recital time. Remind them that they should not only have the music down pat, but they should decide what to wear. Tell students to inform their friends and relatives so they can plan to attend. The last thing you want is for students to feel they've been caught up short and didn't understand the magnitude and importance of the concert performance.

After you reserve the hall and decide on the music, work on publicity. Contact local media outlets and provide them with a press release announcing the nature, date and location of your event. Include biographical information about yourself and perhaps some information about the students taking part in the concert (see Example 8-1). See chapter four for ideas about different media outlets that you should contact about your recital. Print fliers that advertise the event. You can distribute these to your students and also hang them in well-traveled areas. Be sure to post one in the location of the event (see Example 8-2).

As the date of the recital nears and the music for all students and ensembles has been decided upon, design a program for the concert. Include the names and composers of all the pieces and names of the performers/ensembles. You may want to include some information about yourself and your students in the program as well, such as what schools the students attend, how long they have studied music, etc. (see Example 8-3). Have the program professionally printed and be

---

****** **PRESS RELEASE** ******* **PRESS RELEASE** ********

Piano instructor, David Smith of State Street in Union, will present a recital of his students on Sunday, February 27, at 4:00 P.M. in the Gardner Auditorium at the Union Public Library. The event is free and open to the public.

Mr. Smith is a graduate of Hartt School of Music and holds a degree in music education. He has been involved in music education for more than twenty years. He is the former director of music at the Union Regional High School. Currently, Mr. Smith is on the staff at the Riverside Community Music School.

David Smith instructs more than forty piano students in the Union area. His current and former studetns have won numerous awards and scholarships for their musical achievements.

The recital will feature more than a dozen of Mr. Smith's piano students. Featured in the performace will be Jill Sinclair of 34 Jackson Terrace. Jill is a senior at Union Regional High School and has been awarded a full musical scholarship to attend the University of Miami. Jill will perform the works of Beethoven and Schumann.

For more information please call 555-5555.

###

Example 8-1. Press Release Announcing a Recital

certain to have enough copies for everyone who attends. Extra copies make nice mementos for students, so be sure that each student gets at least one copy.

Prior to the day of the event you should contact the facility to make sure all details are in order. Check on lighting, security alarms, heat, etc. Be sure you will have early access to the hall and allow for set-up time. Ask about seating. Will you have to set up or fold up chairs?

PIANO RECITAL
Sunday, February 27
4:00 P.M.
Gardner Auditorium
Union Public Library

FREE ADMISSION

**David Smith will present
a recital featuring more than a
dozen piano students.**

**Students will be performing the
works of Bach, Clementi, Beethoven,
Schumann and much, much more.**

**Please come out and support these
talented young musicians.**

For more information call 555-5555.

Example 8-2. Flier
Announcing a Recital

What about electricity? Is there a fuse box or trip switch in case you lose power? If it snows will you be responsible for clearing sidewalks? Plan for all possible disasters so if anything happens you are completely prepared.

If at all possible, plan a dress rehearsal to work out all the details. Students should have a chance to play the concert piano (if there is one), hear the acoustics, and practice walking on and off stage. Bring some masking tape and make a small *x* on the floor where you want students to take bows. Be sure everyone knows the order in which they'll perform.

On the day of the show be sure to give yourself plenty of preparation time. If you are planning a sound check with students or ensembles be certain that it is done well in advance of any audience arriving. Have the lighting and seating organized and have programs available as people enter. You may want to have someone handing out programs and assisting people to their seats. (Maybe a sibling or friend of one of your young musicians could serve as usher.) You may want to plan for a reception following the recital or ask parent volunteers to handle

---

Sunday, February 27, 4:00 P.M.
Gardner Auditorium
Union Public Library

**David Smith presents
a recital for solo piano**

Introduction by David Smith

Jessica Norman	**age 12**
The Merry Farmer	R. Schumann
John Williams	**age 10**
Minuet in G Major	L. Beethoven
Betsy Steinbeck	**age 15**
Fur Elise	L. Beethoven
Dana Stevens	**age 17**
Sonatina in C Major	M. Clementi
Billy Stevens	**age 15**
Prelude #1 in C Major	J.S. Bach
Jill Sinclair	**age 18**
Sonatina #1 in G Major	L. Beethoven
Wild Horseman	R. Schumann

Special thanks to Clair Smith, Jenny Sinclair, James Sinclair and Joe Stevens for their help with today's recital. Thanks also to all parents and friends for their support and encouragement. Most of all, thanks to all the performers for their hard work and dedication.

Refreshments will be served at the conclusion of the concert.

Example 8-3. Recital Program

---

this part. If you have food or coffee for later, make sure you have someone who can be responsible for that. If not, prepare everything beforehand so it is ready at the conclusion of the concert.

You will be the emcee of the evening's events. Make sure there is a microphone or that you can be heard by all audience members. Be sure to thank everyone for coming and supporting your students, and especially thank anyone who has helped with the preparations. Introduce each student and perhaps say a little bit about each one as they come on stage to perform. Prepare students backstage so they enter and leave the stage in an orderly fashion. Help them help each other: "OK, everyone check each other's ties. Everything on straight?" Some teachers choose to perform a piece or two at student recitals; others feel that this can upstage the students. Do what feels right to you.

Most students are nervous about performing in public so it is your responsibility to remain calm at all times (even if you feel panicked!). Help ease their tension with humor and keep the mood fun and relaxed. You probably went through similar recitals when you were a student. You are certainly familiar with those moments of panic or anxiety that your students may be experiencing. Let them know that you felt what they are feeling and survived. Discuss techniques for dealing with the stress of performing in public. Give them the confidence they need so their performances are the best they can give. While a public recital often produces a great deal of anxiety, learning to deal with nervousness is part of becoming a performing musician. If a student can overcome the pressure and the result is a positive performance experience, you may have a student for the long-term. Remember that while for you a recital might be a mundane, yearly event, for some students it is the highlight of their year. Join in their enthusiasm and make it as special as you can.

While a great deal of time, preparation and energy must be invested to produce a successful large-scale student recital, the rewards are well worth your effort. The positive experience for your students is invaluable. The interaction with other students and the exposure to public performing are important elements of encouraging lifelong musical goals. In addition, there is no better showcase for your teaching talents and the talents of your students. Guiding them through this musical experience gives you more respect than ever. You may find your students more dedicated to you and to their music than you ever imagined possible.

USING A NEWSLETTER

The teacher-student relationship is *the* most crucial element of your success as an educator. No matter how much talent, ability or knowledge you possess, if you are unable to relate to your students, then your chances of succeeding as a music instructor are limited.

An easy and effective way to stay connected to students is through a newsletter. You can use a newsletter to disseminate information, reminding students of important dates, assignments, recitals, holidays, makeups, etc., and to inform students about personal events. Announce any area performances you are giving, encouraging students to attend if possible. Let students know of recent events in your private life such as new teaching positions, awards you have received, a new child on the way. Certainly you could mention these things during lesson times but too much non-music-related information may give students the impression that they are not getting their money's worth. The social aspect of private lessons is important, but too much talk and not enough music can be dangerous and unfair. The student newsletter gives you a forum for getting out information without using up valuable teaching time.

The newsletter can be something you produce occasionally, whenever important information or "newsworthy" events take place, or it may become something you use more regularly, perhaps monthly or even weekly. If you use the newletter on a regular basis it can become an additional teaching tool that supplements regular lessons. Use it occasionally to talk about musical experiences or concepts. Include excerpts from magazine articles or inspirational quotes from famous musicians. Perhaps you can recommend good music books or recordings for students to check out. Including a good musician joke now and again might be funny. (You might have heard a few of those in your time!)

However you decide to use the newsletter format, it is a sensational way to keep in touch with students, both musically and personally. Using a personal computer or typewriter to produce the letter makes it simple to photocopy and distribute to students. You can even personalize the newsletter by using your computer to address it personally to each student, if you're into mail-merge or label programs. This allows you to include assignments or information specific to each individual student. Simply edit each newsletter to include the name and assignment for each student and print a copy. Be sure to save a copy of each newsletter to update or use again in the future or with new students.

You may want to develop a special newsletter for parents of younger students. The teacher-parent relationship is very important when you teach young children. Chapter five has sample letters to parents of young children. These ideas can be amended slightly and reworked into a newsletter format. Additional personal information can then be included. You may want to use a slightly more serious tone when distributing a newsletter to parents. Avoid the musician jokes! No need to perpetuate stereotypes about musicians. Try to remain professional in your letters and help to further build parents' confidence in your character and teaching abilities.

HELPING STUDENTS FEEL APPRECIATED

Within the teacher-student relationship exist many dynamics. You must be teacher, leader, mentor and friend. Students look to you for feedback about their playing. (Except when they forget to practice —

NEWSLETTER

I have included this letter with your lesson materials this week to make an important announcement and to remind you of some important dates that are fast approaching.

The big announcement is that we're moving! After many months deciding, saving and searching, my family has finally found a new home to live in. The bad news is that lessons will be interrupted for several weeks while we set up our new home. The good news is that we will have an incredible new studio in which to conduct lessons. One of the things that made the search for our new home difficult was finding a place with a suitable teaching room. Well, it was worth the wait because we stumbled upon the home of a doctor who had an office and a waiting area in his home. With the help of my handyman brother-in-law we should be able to convert it into a studio with a waiting room in no time at all. I'll inform you of the date we will be moving as soon as I get it. It should take at least two weeks to complete renovations from that date. Hopefully, one of those weeks will correspond with vacation week so we'll only miss one official lesson. I'll let you know for sure by next week.

Don't forget that the date for the spring recital is May 25. The concert will be at 7:00 P.M. in the junior high school auditorium. We will have a dress rehearsal on May 24 at 2:00 P.M. (in my new studio!). Final preparations on your music should begin at this time. Thanks for the effort you have put forth so far. I know this is going to be a fantastic event, one that you and your parents will surely be proud of.

Have a wonderful week and work hard on all your new music.

Take care,

David

Example 8-4. Occasional Newsletter Announcing Pertinent Information

Dave**NEWS**

Welcome to another installment in the ongoing "Life of Dave" series. The first word is that the house-hunting has ended and we're asking for donations in the form of cardboard boxes. Let the packing begin. Dr. Donigan's former home/office will now be Dr. Dave's new home/studio. We will probably be moving the last weekend of April. Anyone who would like to help with the move should let me know. We will be offering an hourly wage or lesson credit to those who assist in the move.

The May 24 dress rehearsal will be held at 2:00 P.M. in the new studio. The concert is May 25 at 7:00 P.M. Anyone who can assist in setting up chairs, organizing the reception area, etc., should sign up on the sheet in the waiting area of my studio. Please sign up to bring some type of refreshment also. We also need plates, cups, utensils. We will be arriving at 4:30 P.M. to begin set-up on the 25th.

I will be performing this weekend with the University Faculty Ensemble at the Performing Arts Center. The concert is Saturday night beginning at 7:30. A $5 donation will be accepted at the door. The university will also have a food bank set up to benefit the homeless shelter. Please bring along a nonperishable food item for a good cause.

Sunday aftenooon will be Jazz Jam Day at The Tavern. Come on down and enjoy a fun afternoon. Anyone who wants to sit in with the band is invited to bring their instrument along. The music begins at 3:00 P.M.

Have a great week and try to get your recital pieces together for next lesson. Keep working hard. I appreciate the effort you've made.

Take care,

David

Example 8-5. Newsletter

then they prefer not to hear your opinions.) They look to you to correct technique flaws and wrong melody notes, or for more general affirmation of their progress on the instrument.

Every student wonders, "Hey, how am I doing?" Few come right out and ask, and even fewer ask, "How am I doing in comparison to so-and-so?" You must find a way to instruct and motivate students while making them feel appreciated as human beings and letting them know that their hard work is also appreciated. Lack of praise can discourage students from continuing to work hard. "I give up. I work so hard to impress her and she never says anything to me." On the other hand, constant praise may serve as a cue not to continue working hard. "I didn't practice once this week and my teacher said I sounded like Pavarotti. I never have to practice. I just keep improving anyway." The balance between discipline and praise changes from student to student. However, you definitely need to give students feedback about their studies, both positive and negative.

Cards and Gifts

Students also need to feel appreciation from you beyond the weekly private lessons, particularly at holiday times. When social custom dictates that friends exchange cards and salutations on the occasion of holidays, teachers should consider extending that custom to their students. This shouldn't mean going out and buying twenty-dollar gift certificates for each of your students' birthdays. That is certainly an option, but it would be a huge financial investment for someone who teaches fifty students per week. However, if you so choose, giving out cards to students for birthdays, graduation, holidays or other special events is certainly within your reach. If you decide to present students with gifts, consider making them yourself. Baked goods or small crafts are a thoughtful, easy and affordable way to give gifts to students. Giving out cards and/or small gifts is usually greatly appreciated by students (and their parents). It casts you in the light of a caring friend, not just a music teacher.

Many times students present you with gifts at holidays and for special occasions such as a wedding or the birth of a child. Be sure to treat these gifts as you would ones from your own relatives. Record which student presented you with which gift and be certain to acknowledge these gifts with thank-you cards.

Keep records of important information about individual students. When a student meets with you for the first time, record information about his personal life to help facilitate this procedure later on. What is that student's birth date? What year does he graduate from school? Information such as this can be used in sending out cards to students for special occasions. You can check your records periodically (once a month for instance) and send cards to appropriate students for special occasions.

Keep a record of each student's address and parents' names so you can mail cards to students' families at holiday times. (Remember that nowadays students and their parents often have different last names!) A little organization goes a long way in this area. Some computer programs and personal data files remind you of important dates once you program them in. Whether you use a card file system or the latest high-tech software, the more organized you are the easier your business is to maintain and the more successful you will be.

Certificates

Use certificates of completion when students graduate from one level to the next, complete a method book, and move to the next volume or series, etc. Certificates are a source of pride for parents and students alike. They are a simple way to show students that their efforts are appreciated and that your involvement is meaningful.

Parties

Inviting students and their parents to your home for an open house or reception is another way to let students feel your appreciation. You can have a formal reception or make it an informal stopover at holiday times or any other occasion.

SOME FINAL WORDS ABOUT PUBLIC RELATIONS

Few teachers have the time or organization to incorporate all of the ideas in this chapter into their teaching. Start small, with a simple in-home recital and see how it goes. Produce one newsletter and see how your students respond. Hook two of your star students together to do a duet. Decide that you are going to send high school graduation cards to the four seniors you are teaching right now. Many people avoid doing anything new because they feel that they will be "locked in" to doing it that way forever. However, just because you do a large-scale recital this year doesn't mean that you have to do one every year.

We hope that you are in the business of teaching music because you love it. Part of remaining enthusiastic is building real relationships with those you teach. It is frighteningly easy to end up feeling that teaching has become drudgery. Incorporate some of these ideas into your teaching, get to know your students and get recharged. Not only does it improve your teaching, in small ways it improves your life.

CHAPTER NINE

FACING UP TO YOUR FINANCES

Making your living as a music teacher requires intestinal fortitude, perseverance, and a sense of humor. Never is this so apparent as when you have to manage the details of your financial life. Unfortunately, musicians have a reputation for living hand-to-mouth, on the financial edge, and while this may appeal to those of you with the starving-artist mentality, not all musicians are fated to live this way. You can build your teaching business, your musicianship and your confidence by taking command of your finances.

BUDGETING FOR AN INCONSISTENT INCOME

Like many other occupations, music teaching's yearly cycle is an inconsistent one, so budgeting and careful planning are requirements. Just as the construction industry is often seasonal, off during the winter months and on during fairer weather, the music teaching profession is seasonal too, but it seems to follow the opposite trend. Young student musicians, especially, seem to be more conscientious during the winter months while during the spring and summer their minds turn to anything but music lessons. Knowing this cycle ahead of time and planning for it promise peace in the house and peace of mind.

Scheduling Around School Calendars

More often than not, your schedule follows that of the schools your private students attend. If you teach elementary or high school children, you may have a difficult time maintaining a full schedule during the summer months. You may also find yourself forced to take an additional week off during Christmas and spring breaks to coincide with vacations. In school districts that have year-round schooling, you might have three weeks off at a stretch followed by a ten- or twelve-week term. Call your local superintendent's office and ask for a school calendar. If you draw students from several districts, you may have to make two or three calls, but this saves a lot of time and headaches in the long run. These calendars also make you aware of teacher workshop days, final exam dates and the like.

To teach ... or not to teach during school vacations. If you do decide to teach during school vacation periods, you can consolidate your schedule to avoid huge gaps of open time during your day due to absent students. Mid-morning slots may be easier to fill than your regular evening times because during vacations, many students, especially teenagers, like to go out at night.

Or you can decide that it isn't worth the hassle of rescheduling students, scheduling makeup lessons, etc. School vacations are the time to schedule your own vacation. If you're organized enough, popular enough and aggressive enough, it is possible to take a trip and perform while on your vacation. It may take some time to establish the right contacts, but perhaps you can schedule a working vacation for your family in a resort area.

Planning for Cash-Flow Problems

If you don't secure additional employment, these vacation weeks, as well as other gaps in your schedule, pose serious cash-flow problems. Cash-flow problems can be minimized, however, if you are prepared for them. Remember that in teaching, inconsistencies are a constant. If you earn $500 during the third week of September with a full lesson schedule, don't assume that you will earn $500 every week throughout the year. Fantasizing this way is tempting, but financially suicidal. What might seem like a $25,000-a-year lesson schedule could well be only half of that when you factor in all the off times during the year. You may eventually be teaching only thirty to forty weeks a year, which greatly affects your annual net income.

Planning for those rainy days, months and seasons! Someone famous (and rich) once said, "No one plans to fail, they fail to plan." "Planning" and "savings" are words that people think musicians are unfamiliar with, but that simply isn't true. Musicians are perfectly capable of planning and saving. Having lived through both the risky and the secure, we believe that living on the edge of financial security is far preferable to living on the edge of financial ruin. In keeping with this dull and conservative perspective, we recommend that you work out a budget of your expenses and projected income over the year.

This way you develop a good system of saving and planning for periods of additional expenses and diminished income.

Learn your financial rhythm and learn to save. For most teachers of music lessons, the period from the start of the school year in September to the December holidays is usually a pretty consistent one. Students generally have good motivation at the beginning of the school year and attend lessons regularly.

The holidays begin a more difficult time for many students to remain consistent in their attendance. They have family responsibilities, school pageants and concerts, inclement weather days, holiday shopping, colds and flus, and exams. At the same time, you may encounter additional fiscal responsibilities. Holiday gift purchases, travel to see loved ones, heating expenses and year-end investments all put additional strain on your wallet.

It therefore becomes essential during the fall months not to live week to week. For teaching musicians, this is a time to save, preferably putting a certain percentage of your earnings into an account that you won't touch. When the going is good, the temptation is to run out and purchase that new amp or car stereo, when what you really need to do is save for January's fuel bill or April's tax bill. Many people, musicians included, seem to spend when they have the money and struggle through leaner times. It's wiser to save when the going is good. Be careful during lean times not to load your credit cards or take out unnecessary loans; you only make good times lean by having to pay back all your debts.

One way we've saved is to put away 10 percent of everything we make during these better times. Every time you make a deposit at the bank, simply skim off ten or twenty percent into a savings account. It is a difficult habit to establish, but if you do this consistently, it becomes automatic and you simply don't think about the percentage being available to you. Then, when you really need it desperately, it's there. (We recommend putting savings into a money market account that makes it a little difficult, but not impossible, to get to the money.)

If you know you are headed toward extremely difficult times, increase the percentage you put away. If you or a partner makes regular income through a more traditional job, another way to save is to have a certain percentage of a paycheck directly deposited into a savings or money market account. If you make lesson or gig money in cash, you must be particularly diligent about depositing it into an account right away. Cash that lies around the house tends to be converted into take-out Chinese food and pizza rather quickly.

Another savings gimmick many musicians use is to deposit all money from lessons or gigs or a side job into one account to use during tough times. You can also consider giving up a bad habit (smoking, for instance) and accumulating the savings for future use.

We have also spent periods of our life on what we fondly call the "MSP," which stands for the "Maniacal Savings Plan." Before buying our first home we packed brown-bag lunches and went without any luxuries to work toward a greater end. Packaging our savings plan in a fun and humorous way made it a lot easier to eat all those grilled cheese sandwiches and to forgo concerts, new furniture and the latest CDs. The point is to trick yourself: Do whatever works to "pay yourself first" and help you save. You will thank yourself in the long run when you finally get out of debt, get that new instrument you've always wanted, or are able to buy a home or car.

Summer or Seasonal Opportunities

Because schedules during the summer can change so dramatically, consider making a major change in your teaching lineup. Some teachers reduce their schedules significantly during the summer and go to great lengths to accommodate the vacation plans of their students, while others forgo their summer teaching completely and resume a full schedule at the end of summer. This leaves these private lesson teachers open for a number of performing or additional employment opportunities.

Taking on performance work. One standard solution to the inconsistencies of the yearly teaching schedule is to take on additional, part-time work during off seasons. An obvious choice is performing. The connection between your performing career and your teaching profession should be an important one. The publicity and exposure from public performances certainly bolsters the respect you receive as a private teacher.

The difficulty in relying on your playing career as a part-time supplemental income is that performing has even more ups and downs than teaching. Performing in a wedding or function band on weekends is a great way to supplement your income. But your wedding band might be booked solid during the spring and fall and not work for months during the cold days of winter. Your German band may work every day in October but not get another gig till December. Your Irish band might work four jobs on a Saturday in March but take three months to total four gigs in the fall.

Give careful consideration to how your performing career can supplement your teaching. With the right planning and budgeting it can be the perfect way of becoming a full-time musician.

One way to increase opportunities for performance, if you can get away for the whole summer, is to travel to a tourist spot. Many resort areas come to life seasonally, and entertainment is needed nightly. If you are lucky enough to be located near a resort area you can maintain a light teaching schedule during off times and take advantage of the many performing opportunities available. Clubs look for specialty or contemporary bands, even for weeknights. Less lucrative but more interesting or uncommon gigs are a possibility, too. For instance, if you normally work in a traditional wedding band or "general business" band, you can work some jazz gigs into your summer schedule.

In busy resort areas, club owners sometimes want specialty "theme" bands for a Blues Night, Casino Night, Hawaiian Night, Fifties Night, Big Band Ballroom Dancing, Country and Western, etc. You can even suggest such a lineup to a restaurant or club owner who hadn't thought of it. Summer activities outdoors often call for Dixieland or bluegrass bands. You can put together a group of musicians to capitalize on these opportunities or, if you are really into the public-relations aspect of your teaching, you can fill these gigs with advanced-level students to provide them with performance opportunities.

Summer is the time to explore performing opportunities for yourself within your own community as well. If you work from 9 to 5 and then teach evenings and weekends at the local studio during the rest of the year, you probably find it impossible to maintain consistent rehearsal or performing schedules with your band, ensemble or duo. So summer is the right time to air out your rehearsal studio and contact the local club owners and booking agents. The night life heats up in the summer and local clubs may be persuaded to consider entertainment when they hadn't before.

If you can work singly, providing piano, guitar or flute music, for instance, think about playing in smaller restaurants or even exclusive shops or malls. While these are not necessarily glamorous gigs, some musicians consider them paid practice, since they are essentially providing background music for diners or shoppers.

You may like the idea of summer employment away from your basement studio but not want to spend it in smoky barrooms or restaurants.

Perhaps this is your opportunity to put down music completely for a few weeks. You could use many other occupations to maintain that steady income during those down times in your teaching schedule. We have worked in various capacities: alumni representative, substitute teacher, camp secretary. You could also do temporary work in any number of different fields.

If you enjoy being outdoors you could lifeguard at a pool or town beach, become a tour guide, or do landscaping or construction. Maybe you could spend spring break at a culinary course and put your studies to work during the summer by working in a restaurant. Perhaps you have a craft or trade and could open up a summer business or enter your crafts in the county fair circuit. The main thing is to maintain a steady income without the anxiety of a strained summer teaching schedule. As discussed in chapter one, many summer music camps and enrichment programs are offered throughout the country, and if you are able to travel, you may be able to stay involved with music while enjoying the great outdoors.

Combining Resources

An ideal living situation for a musician is to have a spouse or significant other with a steady income and benefits. This is true for both male and female teaching musicians. With this arrangement, you can rely on the steady income to meet your monthly financial obligations and use the income from your teaching for savings, investments, etc. Obviously, a great deal of personal commitment must be made to the relationship before this kind of arrangement can work smoothly. Both partners must be interested in the same outcomes and must be working toward a common end.

The greatest benefit of such an arrangement is that you can plan around a steady income, knowing exactly what is available for rent, car payments, etc. Mortgage companies usually require that you have some steady enterprise before they lend you a big chunk of cash. In our case, even though our music income is greater than our "regular" income, our mortgage company chose to ignore a large portion of music income because they felt it was not guaranteed.

A steady income from a spouse may also mean the opportunity to buy health, dental and life insurance benefits at affordable rates. Many health plans cover a spouse and children or allow for additional members of a family to buy into a health policy. As you know, the expense of health insurance is significant, and unfortunately many self-employed individuals go without health coverage because of the high costs.

One pitfall of this arrangement is seeing the steady income as the "meat" and regarding the music income as "gravy." It's very tempting to turn all the money made through music back into more musical equipment, and an inequality develops in who provides for the essentials and who provides the extras. So, if one partner makes a living through music and the other through a steadier enterprise, you may have to work on issues of balance, equity and shared vision.

BARTERING: A DIFFERENT KIND OF INCOME

Often a student wants to continue private lessons but is in a fiscal bind and unable to continue. One of the surest ways to maintain a full teaching load, especially during these tougher economic situations, is to learn the art of bartering.

High school students who are out of work can trade yard work, cleaning, snow shoveling or running errands for lesson time. Perhaps that college senior could baby-sit on the day of his lesson in exchange for lesson credit. Possibly the out-of-work hobbyist could do some maintenance work or house painting. Parents can trade computer time, financial planning or bookkeeping for lessons for their children. In some situations you may find a barter system more rewarding than a monetary system. How about finding a plumber who plays piano or a carpenter who wants to learn drums? Like music teachers, these tradespeople often work strange hours and may be able to fill those hard-to-fill lesson times. We've had days when one student was mowing the lawn, another was watching the baby, and a third was doing windows! Especially if you really enjoy giving lessons and want to keep your schedule full, this is a painless way to get the services you need. Be creative with what you need done and who can do it.

Some of the best barter arrangements we've made have been with colleagues. For instance, we have a mutually beneficial relationship with a musician who owns a recording studio. We spend one morning a week at his studio giving him lessons in theory and improvisation. The arrangement is convenient for him because he can still be at his studio and answer the phone if a call comes in or deliveries are made. In exchange for his lessons, we receive studio time. It's been a great way to get accustomed to the equipment, produce demo tapes and do studio projects without the pressure of paying a high hourly rate at an unfamiliar studio. Because we have an enjoyable business friendship with the owner of this studio, we have completed projects that might have been forgone had we not had easy access to a studio. Some of these projects have in turn produced lucrative gigs or appointments. We also enjoy this musician's expertise about recording and feel that we share a professional camaraderie.

It is important to note that the IRS treats most barter payment as income. Transactions done by barter may have to be reported as income just as if you received a check (see page 204).

INSURANCE: COVERING YOUR AXE, VIOLIN OR PIANO

Insurance is an area where, traditionally, all but the most serious musicians have buried their heads in the sand. Insurance seems too expensive, and some people believe they may not be able to secure insurance for their enterprise because it is only a part-time pursuit. Because income is often unpredictable in the music business, planning for insurance payments often takes a backseat to seemingly more pressing concerns. We avoided purchasing insurance for a long time because we were intimidated by the prospect of sitting down with an agent and explaining exactly what it is that we *do*. Also, we were convinced that insurance was too expensive for us. We were wrong on both accounts.

Insurance is simply that. Its purpose is to insure you against loss or theft or disaster. It may seem unnecessary until the moment you look through your broken back windshield to the trunk where your prized saxophone used to be. Insurance certainly helps family relations when your stout Aunt Ethel mistakes the harpsichord for a bench. It is also worth every penny in peace of mind when a student coming in for a lesson trips up your front steps and smashes her chin on the brickwork. Purchasing adequate coverage through a reputable salesperson is another part of taking control of your financial and professional life that pays for itself quickly in terms of serenity. We are not insurance professionals, and this section is meant simply to provide a framework for understanding the issues associated with insurance coverage for teaching musicians. Especially if you are giving lessons in your own home or rented apartment, we urge you to purchase basic insurance coverage to protect yourself and your business. In case of emergency, you will be glad you did.

When purchasing most insurance, it is wise to contact an independent insurance salesperson. Independent agents represent multiple companies, can "comparison shop," and, as a result, can find the best value for your money. They also may be able to consolidate several of your policies (home, auto, business, umbrella) and thereby save you some money. Ask colleagues to recommend an insurance agent, because agents who have experience working with teaching musicians already understand the many complexities of the business.

Home and Renter's Insurance

If you own your own home, you probably already have a homeowner's insurance policy that covers the house and its contents in case of fire, flood, theft, etc. Most basic homeowner's policies cover the building, contents, liabilities, and medical payments to others. Be sure to check your homeowner's policy to see if it extends to your home business. (Not all do—see page 198.) As a musician, you want to be sure your coverage provides for the *replacement* cost of the contents and the building. You may have paid $100 for that Martin guitar in your college days to someone who didn't know any better, but its replacement cost today is probably significantly higher. If you can only get back what you paid for it originally, you have essentially lost the instrument in case of accident or theft.

There are, of course, limits on what you can claim as "contents" of your house without adding an additional rider. Within "contents," a small amount is usually allowed for jewelry, clothing and furniture. A stereo system and VCR, for instance, are probably included as part of "contents" in the case of theft, but an extensive collection of valuable musical instruments is not usually covered unless it is scheduled onto a specific rider. If not scheduled onto a rider, the value of your collection of rare jazz LPs may be lost forever when the river rises to meet your basement. Most homeowner's policies contain a deductible portion that you negotiate with your salesperson, so you may be responsible for paying the first $250 or $500 of loss.

Renter's policies cover everything that a basic homeowner's policy covers with the exception of the building. Your landlord should carry insurance that covers your building. Homeowner's and renter's policies are basics for most people and can be purchased very affordably. For the musician who teaches mostly outside the home, a simple homeowner's or renter's policy may be adequate coverage, as long as instruments are covered under the "contents" section of the policy. Check with your insurance agent.

Using Riders for Special Situations

As an attachment to your homeowner's or renter's insurance, you can purchase additional coverage for a variety of situations. A musical instrument rider can be purchased for a collection of musical instruments, or for one or more specific instruments. You can also purchase riders to cover part-time business pursuits, computer equipment, recording equipment, lighting and sound equipment, and vehicles. If you carry separate business insurance, riders can be purchased as attachments to that basic coverage as well. When purchasing a rider, you are required to list the insured items by serial number or identification number, and you may be asked to photograph specific pieces for the insurance company.

Musical instrument riders. A musical instrument rider (sometimes called a "floater") protects the instrument from "any peril the item may sustain." That means that if you drop your Stradivarius off the balcony while serenading the neighborhood, the item would be covered, without a deductible. You incur no cost if your instrument is lost, damaged beyond repair or stolen. Musical instrument riders are very affordable and are a must for rare or priceless instruments and any instruments that you need to replace immediately if they are damaged or stolen. The cost of a rider is determined by the amount of the insured instrument's exposure, so if you cart your French horn into civic centers in large cities, thereby increasing the risk of theft, the premiums might be slightly higher. If, on the other hand, you are insuring a grand piano (slightly less portable for your average thief), the premium is likely to be less. If you use your instrument primarily for business and its exposure is significant, you may be charged commercial rates for coverage. Commercial rates are higher, and you may choose to provide coverage only for those instruments that would be difficult or impossible to replace without coverage. As with all insurance concerns, the amount you should buy depends on how much risk you are willing to live with.

To get a musical instrument rider, you have to have appraisals on your instruments or have the receipts from recently purchased instruments. You may already have an appraisal of an older or rare instrument if you took out a loan to purchase it, because your lender certainly had it appraised before loaning you the money. (We know of a violinist who has a *mortgage* on his $60,000 violin!) Appraisals are affordable and inherently worthwhile. You may find certain instruments you don't even need to insure and others whose value you had underestimated or overlooked. Look for a reputable appraiser who has been in the area for a while and who has expertise in musical instruments. If you are unsure, check with colleagues or call the music department at a local university for a referral.

The Musician's Union, Music Teachers National Association, American String Teachers Association and other organizations also provide affordable insurance coverage for members' musical instruments and equipment (see "Resources" at the back of this book).

Computer riders. Like the rest of the world, a lot of musicians have home computers to help with the basics of living: budgets, bills, personal and business correspondence, and record keeping. Some musicians use musical software to help them compose music, transpose songs, and create material for lessons. Computers are also sometimes used as integral parts of high-tech musical instruments. Like musical instrument riders, computer equipment riders can be attached to either homeowner's or business insurance coverage and tend to be extremely affordable. Computer equipment is usually covered under what is called an EDP (electronic data processing) rider. Check to see what your basic homeowner's policy covers without a rider. Because this coverage is so affordable, it is certainly reasonable to cover these items.

Incidental business pursuit. One question that teaching musicians often ask is, "If I teach lessons in my home, must I purchase business insurance or does my homeowner's policy cover me?" You can purchase an "incidental business pursuit" rider to your homeowner's or renter's policy to cover part-time work that is not your main business. For instance, if you work during the day at a music store (your main business pursuit) but give a few lessons at your home in the evening, you can purchase a rider that protects you against liability in case a student gets hurt while in your home or apartment taking lessons. A typical homeowner's policy covers guests who might hurt themselves, but not clients. Additional coverage provides you the means to cover any cost that might arise accidentally as a result of your business, especially in the case of a lawsuit. If you have something to lose (a house, a collection of instruments, etc.) it is very worth your while to look into this option. You may have to shop around and be persistent to find a company willing to insure you, but incidental business pursuit policies are available.

Mortgage Cancellation Insurance

If you own a home and pay a mortgage, look into mortgage cancellation insurance. As the name implies, if you die, the company pays off whatever is left on your mortgage so that neither your estate, your children nor your surviving partner is responsible for paying off the mortgage. The value of the coverage decreases so you are always covered for exactly the remaining portion of the mortgage. The premium usually remains constant and is based on your age and certain risk factors (whether you smoke or have a poor driving record, for instance) at the time you purchase the policy.

Mortgage cancellation insurance can be purchased through banks and through insurance companies. One thing to keep in mind, however, is that banks often list *themselves* as the beneficiaries of the payment. In other words, you pay the bank while you are alive, and if you die, they will gladly pay off the rest of your mortgage and then keep the house for themselves! You might have years and years of equity built up in the house, but because the bank makes the final lump sum payment, it becomes entitled to do whatever it wishes with the property. Insurance companies, on the other hand, usually allow you to name the beneficiary of the payment. In this case, the company pays your named beneficiary what is needed to pay off the remainder of the mortgage and then that person can live in the house without having to make mortgage payments, or can sell the house.

Business Insurance

Business insurance is for those who are fully employed as musicians. Like any small business, musicians are entitled to purchase a basic business owner's policy. Basic business coverage includes coverage for your building, if you have one, your office, office equipment, and liability for any customers using your business. Most coverage includes some protection of other people's things if they happen to be on your premises when they are damaged or stolen. For instance, if you take in a small number of instruments for repairs and they are damaged in an office flood, your costs could be covered. Similarly, if your band travels to a private home and the drum set gouges huge holes in the hardwood floor, your repair costs would probably be covered. Note, however, that these are not costs directly related to teaching music lessons.

Most musicians are in that gray area where they certainly *are* a business, but, unlike contractors or flower shop owners, few have a bona fide shop or much liability. Because of that, some insurance professionals advise you to purchase a general personal liability policy to protect yourself from lawsuit regardless of whether you are in a business or personal pursuit.

If you operate your vehicle more than 50 percent commercially, you may wish to purchase a business auto policy. While this policy covers you more completely than a personal auto policy, it is also significantly more expensive. You must clock at least 15,000 commercial miles per year to qualify for a business auto policy.

Disability Insurance

Musicians who rely heavily on their music income should seriously consider purchasing disability insurance. You may not be able to return to work immediately after a serious illness or accident, and therefore may not be able to keep up with mortgage, rent, car or student loan payments. A broken arm can significantly reduce a drum teacher's ability to give lessons. Unless you work full-time for a music store, high school, college or university or have a good "day job" with terrific benefits, you are probably running the risk that, if injured or sick and unable to make payments, you may lose some of your assets. Again, if you have anything to lose (a house or car) you may want to protect it by purchasing disability insurance. Also, if you have nowhere to go in case you couldn't come up with your monthly rent, you should consider buying disability insurance so that the worst-case scenario, ending up on the streets, does not happen to you.

Many car payment plans through dealerships and banks offer simple disability insurance as part of the plan so your car payment is taken care of for six months or a year if you are unable to pay due to disability. Call your financier if you currently have a payment plan to see if this is true for you. This option may get you through a short-term disability period. Some credit cards also carry this sort of insurance for the minimum credit card payment only.

Disability insurance replaces a portion of the income that you lose as a result of illness or injury. Bear in mind, however, that it is not intended to make anyone rich and that your lifestyle may be severely curtailed if you have to rely on your disability income alone in case of emergency (another reason for taking saving seriously!). Short-term disability insurance policies typically kick in after seven days of complete disablement and cover 100 percent of your salary for approximately twelve weeks, but the length of time and percentage of coverage vary by company and by policy. Long-term disability payments customarily kick in after this short-term period is finished, for up to an additional fourteen weeks at 100 percent of your former salary. After this period, disability payments are usually curtailed to 65 percent of your salary and can continue for as long as you are totally disabled or until retirement. Long-term disability insurance is a safeguard against real financial tragedy and should be considered part of your total financial plan.

Umbrella Policies

As the name suggests, an umbrella policy acts as a protector over all the other insurance you have in place. These policies fill gaps you might have in your existing coverage at very affordable rates. Because so much coverage can be purchased so economically in umbrella policies, they are a good addition to basic homeowner's, renter's and/or business owner's policies. Talk with an insurance professional about the possibility of adding an umbrella to your existing coverage.

Life Insurance

Both whole life and term insurance can be good investments for the teaching musician. Term insurance is generally more affordable in the short run while whole life insurance has some long-term benefits. In terms of life insurance, teaching musicians are no different from the rest of the folks out there. We all live with uncertainty, and life insurance is meant to provide for your family or estate in the case of your untimely death. Whole life insurance can also be used as a long-term investment or savings plan. You must evaluate your situation: the other people who depend on you and your income, the amount of debt you would leave behind, the amount of income you have coming in. Talk with an insurance professional about all your options.

RETIREMENT CONSIDERATIONS

Musicians often fall into the trap of avoiding retirement planning because they hope they never have to retire from doing what they love. While this is a luxurious position to be in, over the years your situation may change because of illness, injury or evolving interests, and you may wish that you had planned more seriously. For the teaching musician, retirement options are numerous, so it is extremely important to consult a financial planner to find a workable plan.

Using an SEP IRA

Because self-employed individuals cannot belong to a 401(k) plan or partake of the many benefits offered by corporate employment, the government makes a few concessions. One of them is the SEP IRA.

Self-employed persons can put away a relatively high percentage (15 percent in 1994) of their business profits to fund their own Self-Employment Individual Retirement Account. The amount contributed to the SEP IRA is tax deferred, meaning that you can take it right off the top of your income and pay taxes on it only when the time comes to use it, presumably when you are of retirement age. There are penalties for early withdrawal, of course, and so it is prudent to speak to a professional to make sure it this the best option for you.

Building Retirement Savings

Musicians have the same financial and retirement concerns that others have. You want to be able to send your children through school, pay your medical bills, and not be burdensome to others when you are no longer willing or able to earn your own living. Saving for this time may be the last thing on your mind when you are thirty or forty and enjoying the prime of your life. However, as the stability and security of programs like social security dwindle, we all must sit up and take notice.

To prepare for your retirement, consider stock and bond options, series EE savings bonds to pay for education, aggressive growth and more stable growth mutual funds, and life insurance options. You may have access to any number of savings options through a day job and may even be able to draw from a pension in certain circumstances. Our advice to you is that a solid financial planner can help you navigate this treacherous terrain, and the sooner you do it, the better. Simple mathematics can tell you that the earlier you start planning, the less painful it is.

TAXES: FACE YOUR FEARS AND FILE AN EARLY RETURN

For many music teachers, April 15 is the bane of their existence. As unbelievable as it might seem, with the proper organization, the right attitude, diligent record keeping and experienced professional assistance, taxes can become a necessary but nonstressful part of your daily, quarterly and yearly business. We encourage you to face your fears and file an early return!

Hire a Professional

For years we agonized over our own tax forms, got into loud fights over filing, and finally, on April 15, filed for an extension so we could

repeat the whole demoralizing process in August. We do not recommend this route for you. No matter how much income you make from
teaching or how you plan to file, the best advice we can give you is to get
professional help with your finances. Most CPAs and tax preparation
services are surprisingly affordable and well worth the small investment. (Consider the cost of the marriage or personal counseling that
you will avoid.) Every year the tax laws in this country are changed
or modified. Items that were deductible last year may no longer be
deductible this year. Limits on contributions to charitable organizations or individual retirement accounts are amended yearly. Unless
you are an aspiring accountant or self-proclaimed financial wizard, the
best way to deal with the ever-changing rules of the Internal Revenue
Service is to hire an experienced professional whose job it is to be
familiar with these changes. It is to your advantage to hire an accountant who is also somewhat familiar with the music industry. Another
reason to hire a tax professional is that if, as in your worst nightmare,
you are audited, your tax professional can guide you through the process.

Here are some ways to deal with your finances and organize your
records to help you better prepare for that April 15 date with the IRS.
This section is not intended to be a tax-preparation guide. Because of
the changing nature of the laws, it is best to consult your accountant
and develop a relationship and a system that works best with your
specific financial concerns.

Different Types of Income

Part of the complexity of most teaching musicians' finances is the
fact that their gross income generally contains money from a variety
of sources. The first source of income may be regular wage earnings
(reported from an employer on a W-2). Some musicians supplement
this income with performance or lessons that may be paid by check
and reported to the IRS on a 1099 form or that may be made in cash
with no official record of the transaction. If you claim any income as
a result of lessons or gigs, you have to file Schedule C, which lists
business profits and losses. Of course, you must report any interest
and dividends you may make on accounts, CDs, stocks and bonds, etc.
A few musicians may have royalty and rental income to report as well.
Almost without exception, a working musician and private teacher can
kiss the possibility of filing an EZ form goodbye. Accept this, and learn
the benefits of having income from multiple sources.

W-2 income. Your wage earnings are reported to you on a W-2 form from your employer, and usually federal, state, social security and perhaps local taxes are deducted from your total wage earnings. You are most likely to receive a W-2 from a school, a music store, or a nonmusic job. Usually at the beginning of a job and then again at specified times during the year, you are asked how many dependents you would like to claim on this income. For instance, if you are married with one child, you could claim up to three deductions for yourself, your partner and your child. The more dependents you claim, the less tax your employer withholds from your check.

For teaching musicians, the benefit of having W-2 income is that you may be able to have enough taxes withheld from your W-2 pay to cover the taxes on your consultant earnings. In the example mentioned earlier, you might want to claim only one dependent, or even none, so your employer withholds more and you don't get socked with a big tax bill in April. You may even get some back! Some argue that you are then relinquishing your control over your money and giving it to the IRS for those months when it could be earning interest in *your* account instead. This is true, of course. For a lot of us, though, we know that it wouldn't be in our accounts if we had it. (It would have been "invested" in concert tickets, a car payment, or a weekend on the coast.) So letting the IRS keep the money for you is just good business sense. There are, however, restrictions on the amount of taxes you can ask to be withheld to "cover" for your additional income. Consult your tax professional to ensure that you do not go over this limit, which of course is subject to change every year.

1099 or consultant income. Consultant or business income is reported to you on a 1099 form. This is income from which no taxes or social security is subtracted. You are most likely to earn this kind of income from such part-time work as gigs or giving lessons at a school, music store or other enterprise.

When you receive this sort of money, it is important to remember that you are responsible for paying taxes on it. The fact that you have a 1099 form means the enterprise that issued it also sent a copy to the IRS. If you received a $1,000 check from the Anytown Community Music School in November, and a 1099 form in January, it means that the IRS is keeping a lookout for you to report that $1,000 as income. If you don't report it, they will wonder what happened to the taxes due on that money, and chances are, they will come looking for them.

When you are a bandleader, or even if you lead an occasional gig, it is imperative that you keep a record of who you subcontract to. For instance, if you are paid $600 for a string quartet to play at a gallery opening, the gallery usually writes a check to you. You then split up the money the way you see fit and pay the three other members of the quartet. The gallery reports to the IRS that they have paid *you* (under your social security number) that $600. If you don't have a record of paying the other three members of the quartet, you are responsible for paying the taxes on that $600. This adds up quickly even if you lead only five or ten gigs a year. (In the example above, $3,000 to $6,000 additional income would be reported under *your* social security number.)

If you are a full-time leader, you will probably issue your own 1099 forms to your players, in which case you definitely need professional guidance in filing your return. 1099 forms *must* be filed for any individual who you've paid more than $600 in the past year. You must fill out a Form W-9 and have a federal tax ID number or social security number for each person to whom you send a 1099.

Cash, checks, and barter. If your music business mainly consists of private lessons, a great deal of your income is made in cash and in personal checks from students. The IRS requires that you report all cash, personal checks and barter income on your Schedule C.

Barter payment, trading service for service, is treated as income. If you trade your services as a private instructor with a massage therapist for weekly massage sessions, then you must claim the amount of your barter transaction as income. (In this case, each of you should claim the transaction.) The current exception to this general rule is if both parties claim each other's service as business expenses. For instance, if our teaching studio needs painting, we may trade lessons with a professional musician who also works as a painter. He may claim private lessons as a continuing education expense, which is deductible on his taxes. If we claim his services as a business expense as well, neither of us needs to report the transaction as income.

Making the Most of Deductions

Because you are self-employed as a teacher of music, you are able to take advantage of all tax laws available to a small business. Many of the expenses you have taken for granted for years are now considered business expenses and deductible, thereby lowering your tax liability. Besides obeying the law, the real benefit of filing income you make from lessons or gigs is that you can actually come out ahead of the game by reducing what you owe in taxes.

Driving to a student's home for a lesson, subscribing to a music magazine, and taking a prospective student out for lunch are all deductible under current tax laws. Any equipment or supplies you purchase, any lessons or workshops you attend, and any insurance that you carry for your business are all business expenses. Anything you do to continue your education, related to your musical pursuit, can be deducted on your taxes.

Mileage. A huge business expense each year is the mileage you travel to do business. Driving to accomplish any aspect of your business, whether it be teaching lessons or recruiting new students or traveling to buy or repair equipment, can be deducted on your Schedule C. You must keep a record of your business mileage, and the IRS decides how much you can deduct per mile. If you are a music hobbyist, these expenses cannot be deducted. Once you make your first dollar teaching lessons, you can use this tax break.

Using a home office or studio. You can deduct a percentage of your rent or mortgage as well as your utilities if you have a studio set up in your home or apartment. You can't teach in your bedroom or kitchen and deduct the space as an office. The office must be a place you use exclusively to earn income and must be your primary place of business. If you teach at a school or studio and not at home, then you can't claim your office even if it is used only for music because you are not earning your money there. Even if you practice, do lesson plans or do billing from your home office you can claim it as a deduction only if you earn income there.

To qualify for this deduction, you must use the space only as an office or a studio, and the IRS has become fairly picky about this recently. It is best to really plan for this and keep the area very specifically designed for teaching purposes. Our studio does not double as anything else; the furnishings and decor are all about the teaching of music, the books on the bookshelves are about music, the files are all music related. If anyone came into our house, they would have no doubt what we do there. We did the same thing in very small apartments by making very clear delineations between what was living space and what was teaching space. This helps you (and, in the worst case, the IRS) understand what part of your home is the studio, and it helps your professionalism. Students and their parents are infinitely more comfortable reading a music magazine in a tiny corner of your studio

MILEAGE RECORD

Date	Reading	Destination	Mileage
Monday,	75,372	Home	–
June 16	75,376	Sounds Good Music	4
	75,380	Home	4
	75,392	Jim Sweeney	12
	75,397	Tim Fiore	5
	75,401	Jane Sher	4
	75,409	Bill, Jon Reed	8
	75,425	Home	16
	75,427	Groceries	2
	75,429	Home	2
			57
Tuesday,	75,429	Home	–
June 17	75,481	Swing Street Studio	52
	75,533	Home	52
			104
Wednesday,	75,533	Home	–
June 18	75,585	Swing Street	52
	75,637	Home	52
			104
Thursday,	75,637	Home	–
June 19	75,649	Boys and Girls Center	12
	75,653	Cafe Italian	4
		(meeting – John Wilson)	
	75,662	Jason Thompson	9
	75,664	Rudy Rowles	2
	75,665	Tim Morrone	1
	75,669	Roberta Downey	4
	75,682	Al Anderson	13
	75,684	Beth, Tammy White	2
	75,689	David Austin	5
	75,690	Betty Thomas	1
	75,701	Home	11
			64
Friday,	75,701	Home	–
June 20	75,705	Sounds Good Music	4
	75,709	Home	4
			8

Example 9-1. Mileage Record

than they are sitting at your kitchen table reading the back of a cereal box.

If you are designing a room in your home to be used as an office/teaching studio, keep in mind that all expenses incurred are deductible. Everything from carpeting and soundproofing to curtains and wall hangings is considered a business expense if it is included in the space where you actually earn money. Chapter three speaks to the challenges of teaching at an in-home studio more specifically.

Charitable contributions. Personal charitable contributions, such as donations to a house of worship or established charitable organizations are not included on Schedule C; they are itemized deductions claimed on Schedule A. However, if your *business* donates to a charity—playing at a benefit, for instance—then you may be able to deduct this from your profits. We have donated lessons to various auctions and benefits.

Be careful to separate charitable contributions from advertising costs. A donation to a theater group for an ad included in their playbill is claimed as advertising, not as a charitable contribution.

Work with a tax professional to prepare your return. Shop around until you find a tax professional in whom you have complete confidence. Don't be intimidated by the process, and don't convince yourself that there's nothing a professional can help you with. If you assume certain things are business losses or deductions and they aren't, that is a red flag to an IRS agent and almost guarantees you will be audited. The cost of our tax professional is returned to us at least 300 percent by the deductions she finds for us and, truthfully speaking, if we had to put a price on the peace of mind the service buys for us, her fee would be the greatest bargain on earth.

Making Quarterly Payments

If you file a Schedule C and make most of your income as a self-employed individual, you are required to make quarterly payments to the IRS. This is a pay-as-you-go system that all businesses must deal with.

You set up quarterly payments based on 100 percent of the prior year's tax liability. For instance, if you paid four thousand dollars in taxes for the previous year, then you would be required to pay quarterly payments of one thousand dollars each. If your business did not make a profit in the previous year, you are not required to pay quarterly.

For example, if you made $1,000 in lesson income on top of your "day job" but deducted $1,200 in related expenses (supplies, mileage, repairs, continuing education, etc.), your business would actually offset your day job income by $200, thereby reducing your tax burden slightly. You would not be responsible for making quarterly payments. On the other hand, let's say that this year you quit your day job and begin teaching lessons full-time; if you expect to make a profit on lessons this year, you should make quarterly payments.

Saving for Your Tax Bill

Consider yourself an employee in your business. As a business owner, you are responsibile for withholding tax for each employee, including yourself. Consult your tax professional to estimate your tax liability and begin to *withhold* tax from your business income. Otherwise, you'll have a very unpleasant surprise at the end of the tax year. It may be a good idea to incorporate a system of savings so that, say, a certain percent of every dollar goes to savings designated for taxes. Some banks and credit unions even have special funds called "tax funds" you can set up at no additional cost. It may seem like a big bite out of your earnings, but if you've taken out too much it can be your own little tax refund. If you've prepared well and estimated accurately, then you may avoid the panic and the penalties that come with a huge tax bill.

As a business, you are required to pay any state tax as well as federal income tax and social security tax on your business profits. For many new small businesses, it is the social security tax that poses the real strain. At present the social security tax rate for self-employed individuals is up to 15 percent and it may climb higher.

Remember that if you are receiving W-2 income, for withholding purposes, you can claim fewer dependents than you actually have. This increases the amount deducted from your "regular" or "day job" wages, thus decreasing the amount of money you need to set aside for taxes from your Schedule C income.

The Daily Log

In talking to our tax preparer each year, the one piece of information that rings loud and clear is to maintain a daily log of every aspect of our business. You business log gives you the most peace of mind in everything from filing your yearly return to preparing for an IRS audit. It sometimes feels awkward or cumbersome to write down every little trip you take to the music store, or every CD you purchase, but the log gives you a true record to which you can refer at the end of the tax year. Keeping such a log is like aerobic exercise — it requires discipline.

The log is your daily record of each and every detail of your business transactions. In the log you record distances and locations of every place you travel. Note what you did when you got there, who was there, how much you spent and on what. If you buy a newspaper to check out prospects for teaching in the local school system, log it.

Keeping receipts is important, especially for any large purchases. A personal computer purchased for your business can be written off as a business expense (probably depreciated over a period of several years — talk to your tax preparer).

It is not necessary to have receipts for everything you purchase in order to deduct it as an expense, as long as you record the purchase, in detail, in the log. For instance, you may attend a workshop of music educators and attend a meeting to discuss business. While there you order out for food. One bill is presented and then divided among the members of the group. While you don't have a receipt for your portion of the meal, you may deduct the cost of your portion if you record it in your log. It may be useful to write in detail where you ate, with whom, and what business was discussed at the meeting. The more in depth your records are, the simpler it is to recall the event if you are audited several years down the road.

Saving Receipts

Save receipts even if you record transactions in your log. It may help to organize receipts according to how they are filed for tax purposes. We have separate filing folders or envelopes (we've used both over the years) for dozens of types of receipts including tolls, parking, clothing and cleaning, music supplies and more. We also have a large red basket into which we throw all unfiled receipts, just so none gets lost or thrown out in the inevitable shuffle.

At the end of each tax year, organize all receipts and any other records and store them with your tax return. Then you have everything together should you need to refer to your records to answer questions in the future.

Deposit Records

In the event of an IRS audit, you have to compare the income you claim against your bank records; therefore, keep records of all deposits you make and where they came from. This includes all cash deposits.

DAILY TAX LOG

6/16 — STRINGS 2 @ $5.99
        REPAIR GUITAR $50.00
        LUNCH @ DANNY'S $24.62
          W/ SUE BURNS (COLLEGE DECISIONS)
        DINNER @ BURGERWORLD $4.76
          (ON THE ROAD TEACHING)
                                    $91.36

6/17 — PICKS 5 FOR $1.00
        GUITAR WORLD MAGAZINE $3.95
        NEWSPAPERS (GLOBE/HERALD) $1.10
          (TEACHING VACANCIES)
        LUNCH @ DANNY'S $8.95
                                    $15.00

6/18 — CD'S $44.85
          (SONGS FOR WEDDING 6/21)
        VOICE LESSON $30.00
        DANCE CLASS $15.00
                                    $89.85

6/19 — DRY CLEANING $24.50
        LUNCH @ DANNY'S $17.42
          (W/ JOE DELANEY — NEW STUDENT)
        DOWNTOWN MAGAZINE $1.50
          (CLUB LISTINGS)
                                    $43.42

6/20 — NEW TUX $350.00
          (W/ ALTERATIONS)
        AMP REPAIR $60.00
                                    $410.00

6/21 — LUNCH @ SUBWORLD $5.50
                                    $5.50

                    WEEK TOTAL $655.13

Example 9-2. Daily Tax Log

For example, if one of your students is audited and has claimed the lessons he has taken with you as a business or educational expense, even if he has paid in cash, the IRS will want to see that that money was deposited into your business account. If you use your own personal account to conduct business transactions, you should seriously consider opening a separate business account to simplify record keeping.

It is extremely important to keep records of all bank deposits. If you deposited forty-five thousand dollars into your account and only claimed forty thousand as gross income the IRS would want you to explain each and every deposit to find the missing five thousand dollars. A discrepancy may be as simple as a bounced check that was deposited twice or a transfer from another account, but be sure to record this information. It may seem silly now, but try remembering every bank transaction from the last few years and you'll understand the importance of record keeping.

Surviving an IRS Audit

Your tax preparer should do all he or she can to remove any red flags from your return that might prompt an audit. However, a certain amount of luck is involved in the process and there is still a possibility that you will be audited.

If you keep a detailed log of mileage and business expenses, organize your receipts and file on time, there is very little need to worry about an IRS audit. Though an audit is never pleasant, if your taxes were prepared by a tax professional, you have even less to worry about. Most tax professionals help you prepare for an audit and many attend the audit for you. Ask about this when you are looking for a tax professional. By signing over your power of attorney to your certified public accountant, you allow him or her to deal with any questions that may arise. A trained tax professional can answer the questions more expediently. If there are any questions that need to be answered by you, the IRS can consult you at a later time by telephone.

Computer Software for Preparing Tax Returns

Many companies have designed software for preparing your tax return. While these programs are often very accurate and reliable, our experience is that software is no substitute for a tax professional who can work with you, dispel your fears, and give you solid advice for the years to come. It may be a good idea to use one of these programs before meeting with an accountant, but it's the tax professional who can ask the right questions and help you avoid missing any significant deductions or claiming any that you are not eligible for.

A FINAL WORD ABOUT FINANCES

No one except accountants seems to be terribly excited about getting a handle on finances. It is usually an intimidating and demoralizing prospect, put off until a financial (or marital) crisis occurs. We spent many years with our heads in the sand, imagining the worst about our finances and doing nothing. Once we shook the sand off and took a look around we discovered that preparation and planning are the cornerstones of a positive financial picture. No matter how much or how little you are making, facing up to your finances frees you from worry, builds your confidence, and by so doing, makes you a better professional.

CHAPTER TEN

CONTINUING TO GROW AS A MUSICIAN AND A TEACHER

Y ou probably have spent years reaching a certain level of competence on your instrument, aiming either for a performance or teaching career. It is a myth that completing your formal education marks the end of study on your instrument, or of studying music in general. The decision *to teach* actually marks a new beginning on your musical journey. Your own musical education is just beginning when you start to teach others.

Sitting down in a studio with an individual student or standing in front of a large classroom requires you to formulate your own teaching ideas, style and method. Whether you are a self-taught musician who has learned by ear, or a scholar of music who has obtained the highest degrees, your current teaching style reflects your background. Before now, your *style* may have been something more natural than conscious. Now it's time to "get conscious," to objectively evaluate your ideas, methods and techniques and make sure you communicate clearly with your students.

You must constantly refine, organize and update your approach so as to improve and grow as a teacher. A dedicated musician forever reaches for new goals and strives for new levels of achievement, learning different styles of music or different techniques. It requires great dedication on your part to continue to grow musically, but this important commitment to growth as a teacher and a musician keeps you motivated as a player and an instructor. Staying motivated keeps your teaching style energetic and fresh. You keep your students inspired and motivated, and that is good for business, too. By staying up with current trends in music and technology, continuing to study music on your own, developing your "business side," and learning about your own strengths and weaknesses as a teacher, you become the best instructor possible. The end result is that you can motivate students to reach their own higher goals.

The idea is *not* to indiscriminately rack up college credits or attend workshops about which you care little, but to continue to learn about what interests you musically, and moreover, what interests your students. The magic comes when you can incorporate what you know to be important musically with the styles that capture particular students.

STAYING ON TOP OF CURRENT TRENDS IN MUSIC

One of the traps you can fall into is developing a style or approach that remains unchanged despite the constant musical changes that take place around you. An inability or refusal to change can cause you to grow stagnant or out of touch with your student population. For teachers involved with teenage students and/or teaching contemporary music, this is especially important. Not staying on top of the current trends or technology in today's music puts deserved distance between you and students. While your musical ideals and methods may be sound ones, if students cannot relate them to something that sounds familiar or interests them, your methods may prove unsuccessful. Students may even interpret your unwillingness to incorporate newer concepts as a personal affront. Being able to teach concepts in the context of familiar music makes your points relevant and, therefore, more effective.

Staying "Up" on Current Styles of Music

Most students are truly eager to enhance their knowledge of musical concepts and willingly work on the traditional music you assign each week. However, when they get home and go off to a weekend party, most are not likely to listen to string quartets or orchestral music. More likely they tune into the latest musical trend or popular style to hit the charts. While this music may seem unrelated to your teaching, the fact that students are hearing it on a daily basis is important and relevant. It is a good political and professional move if you can expand your knowledge of contemporary music. Going beyond that and investigating qualities, techniques, and songs of certain styles, groups or players further advances your standing with many students.

Have students record examples of their musical influences or favorite artists for you. This gives you a better sense of what motivates them musically. Once a student delivers a tape of their favorite music, listen to it and use the information to relate better to the student. That may be as simple as saying you enjoyed a particular song or group. Better yet, refer to musical passages in relation to musical concepts you are teaching. Better still, you can transcribe and teach entire songs. (See page 129 for more ideas on using popular music in your teaching.)

Research contemporary music using radio, music video TV stations, record stores, and music magazines that list top-selling albums. Try to put aside any judgment you may have about the music and listen for what you *can* relate to or use in lessons.

The best way to hear contemporary music, of course, is to hear it live. Check your newspaper and listen for news of artists coming to your area. If you are truly dedicated and brave, you can even go with a few of your students to a show of particular interest, underscoring your open-mindedness and willingness to hear what is important to them. Always inform your students about artists coming to the area who you think showcase your instrument well. You may know that the keyboard player from The Chili Dogs was classically trained at Julliard, even though you think their total sound leaves something to be desired.

Keeping a current music library. Start a library of current music by having students record their favorite contemporary music for you. You can categorize each tape by the student's name or style of music recorded on the tape.

Recording music directly from top-forty countdown shows is another way to keep an updated library of contemporary music. You can begin to organize a collection of weekly top-forty tapes. You can then refer to these tapes to determine what music stays popular long term. These selections make good examples of songwriting, performance and recording techniques that you can discuss in detail with students.

Use the information from top-twenty shows to determine what music is worth purchasing on CD for your listening pleasure or for lesson material. Using a CD to refer to a selection is easier than using a tape, since you can go directly to the selection you want. Remember that if you purchase music for educational purposes, you may be able to deduct the cost as a business expense. Refer to chapter nine for more financial information and always consult with your accountant or tax specialist.

Understanding and Using Current Technology

Spanning the history of contemporary music over the past few decades are real changes in technology that have influenced the current generation of musicians. From advances in electronic instruments and amplification to recording techniques and MIDI, each change meant new challenges for musicians entering the field. As instructors, part of your responsibility is to investigate and become exposed to these trends and to prepare your students for what may lie ahead. Depending on your own involvement with these advances, you can simply pass on your knowledge about the significance (or insignificance) of these trends or actually give students hands-on exposure.

A great deal depends on what and whom you teach. Teaching more traditional instruments or music to certain student populations limits the need to involve yourself directly in the technological advances of the day. However, even in these circumstances you should be knowledgeable about what those advances could mean to your students. Perhaps they will one day record and need to be aware of recording advances. They may find themselves in recital and faced with dilemmas concerning miking and sound reinforcement.

Even though these situations might be a small part of what you are involved with in teaching students, they are important and should not be overlooked. Reading music equipment catalogs, or musical periodicals should give you plenty of information about current trends in technology. If you find a particularly helpful article, photocopy it and pass it out to students as supplementary lesson material. If you become aware of a new technology and want more information, contact the manufacturer directly and request information on the product. Look for interviews with people who incorporate this technology into their music. Staying abreast of advances does not necessarily mean purchasing each new product, but knowing what is happening out there allows you to pass that valuable information along to your students.

Almost every teacher can benefit from having an electronic keyboard in the studio, as well as composition software, for teaching theory if nothing else. Plus, there is a lot of music education software for drills in rhythm, listening, note reading, etc. You can research the most helpful for your instrument and pass along that information to your students.

The need to stay aware of and involved in the advances in technology is greatest for teachers who instruct students on instruments used in contemporary music, especially drums, bass, keyboard and guitar. Even wind and brass instruments are becoming more advanced, incorporating MIDI and other technology. So almost everyone involved in music should be aware of the trends in technology.

Take a trip to the nearest music store that is well equipped with the most current equipment. Visit the store with the intention of trying out new equipment. Try to get the salesperson to explain differences between models and brands. Research different equipment offered by various companies through magazines that feature contemporary music and technology. Many salespeople try to sell you on the line of products their store carries. If you have some knowledge of other products, get the salesperson to describe differences or particular features of all the various products. Have the salesperson provide some hands-on learning, if possible. Remember, even if you are not in the market for a particular item, one of your students may be.

The knowledge you gain from these field trips can help you give students insight into what to look for in their product search. Be sure to point them to the same articles or interviews you used in your research. Many times your students are very knowledgeable about different areas of technology, so do not hesitate to ask for their opinions or to swap information about new advances. Be cautious of endorsing one product to students, lest they buy it and have a bad experience with it. It is far better to discuss a few models and let the student do his or her own research before making the final decision.

CONTINUING YOUR EDUCATION AS A MUSICIAN AND AS A TEACHER

While there are lots of ways to keep up with music informally, you should also try to continue your formal education to the extent that time and money allow. It may not be realistic right now for you to pursue a higher college degree but don't misinterpret that as a call to inaction. There are many ways you can continue to take advantage of the educational opportunities happening all around you.

Look at your musical knowledge realistically and determine where your weakest link lies. Work at strengthening that particular link. Many musicians are so insecure about their shortcomings that they avoid working on them altogether, thereby making any problem worse. This sets up a vicious circle because after twenty years of playing by ear, a professional feels silly learning the fundamentals. Remember that your students will become handicapped in the same areas you are, so you owe it to them as well as yourself to bring those areas up to speed. Also, work from your strengths. If you find, for instance, that you possess an affinity for rhythm, try learning some difficult or obscure time signatures to pass along to your students.

Using Colleges, Universities, Conservatories and Workshops

You may have reached a point in your life where you want to pursue a formal or advanced degree in music, or finish one you started years ago. People often balk at the idea of going back to school full-time, but you do not have to make the commitment all at once. Break it up into doable parts. First make the decision to call the schools in which you are interested and ask them to send you a catalog. Your other decisions will follow naturally. We applaud anyone who takes this step any time in their life.

You don't have to be a full-time student to reap the benefits of the institutions of higher learning you may have right in your own backyard. Call the admissions office for a catalog and "let your fingers do the walking" through their course offerings. Many universities let you take a number of courses without being a fully matriculated student. Chances are, there are opportunities for more advanced study on your particular instrument. Try to stretch yourself stylistically by working in unfamiliar styles. Look into courses in alternative instruments that give you insight into your own. You can even go back and sit in on a basic or advanced music theory course to see how they are teaching it and to jump-start yourself. Though it may be repetitive for you, history of music and music appreciation courses are fun and a relaxing way to be "on the other side of the desk" temporarily and get you thinking musically again. In some cases, it takes some fancy footwork to be able to audit or sit in on a course, but it can be well worth the effort, both through the benefit of the course work and the people you may meet in the process. (The dean of the music department is probably not a bad person to know professionally.)

Course work in a great number of disciplines other than music can help you personally and professionally as well. Think about taking a course in childhood development or child psychology to help you work with those young students. Courses in education can help you think through your lesson plans and identify different types of learners. Some colleges offer courses in music technology or music business that can help you and also provide you with information for your students. Poetry classes can help you with those lyrics. If you have always wanted to write, take a creative writing course. Just being a student can help you get in touch with your own students.

Consider joining various music associations as commitment to continued growth and professionalism. ASTA (American String Teachers

Association) and MTNA (Music Teachers National Association) are examples of organizations committed to growth and professionalism in the field of music education (see "Resources" at the back of this book).

Workshops are often offered through music associations, colleges, community music programs and the like. Even area high schools with strong music programs sometimes sponsor guest artists or clinics for band members or jazz ensembles. Call your local high schools to find out. Consider attending summer enrichment programs offered through music colleges and conservatories. Contact your area college music departments to get on their mailing list so you are aware of any such events.

Though you may think that they are geared only for young musicians, many of these programs attract professional and teaching musicians. In fact, some colleges offer programs specifically for music teachers. These programs offer courses in subjects pertinent to today's music educators, such as music technology. Remember that any progress you make in your own education ultimately augments your teaching ability and musicality.

Continuing Your Own Private Lessons

Another source of inspiration that is often overlooked is continuing to take your own private lessons. A tough lesson to learn is that there is probably *someone* out there who is more proficient on your instrument than you are. Though you may not take lessons weekly, it is a good idea to meet with your own teacher once a month or so. You can also use private lessons to hone a particular style, and you can even trade lessons with another teacher. For instance, a classically trained singer can trade lessons with a rock vocalist and both can benefit and continue to serve a more diverse student population.

Taking private lessons on a different instrument is another way to propel yourself right back into the beginner's seat and experience how it feels for your beginning students. Learning another instrument gives you insight into your own and can even give you concrete skills for your own teaching. Most teachers should have some keyboard knowledge, for instance.

Regardless of your principal instrument, consider taking voice lessons to supplement your learning. Voice lessons help you with confidence and presentation and help you teach ear training as well. Using your voice as an instrument gives you new respect for all those singers out there. Encourage all students, particularly those who play contemporary styles, to consider voice lessons, because a player who can also sing is eminently more employable.

Continuing to Learn Through Performance

One of the greatest advantages of a musical life is learning through doing what you love. Getting together with people to play music, whether it is paid or not, is an integral part of continuing to grow as a musician.

Make playing music together a part of your lessons. Don't just listen to students or play *for* them to illustrate the correct way of doing something; play *with* them. This serves a twofold purpose: It gives students experience playing with a more advanced player, and it gives you the opportunity to play.

Outside of lessons, opportunities to perform provide a great deal of learning for you. Continue to work in the style that excited you most about music in the first place. Rehearse with your jazz trio weekly. Keep that community orchestra seat warm. Play for money, but also play for fun.

Besides your regular performance opportunities, we wholeheartedly encourage you to take a few musical risks. Fight complacency and play music you are unfamiliar with. Play shows and community benefits. Play classical and play rock-and-roll. Even if you don't play a traditional rock instrument, sit in with a rock band and explore the versatility of your instrument (ever hear a viola miked?). If you are a contemporary player, try hooking up with a community big band. Play with all types and all levels of musicians to stay in touch with the simple fact that *music is fun*.

Continuing to Learn Through Self-Study

Reading this book is just one of a number of ways you can help yourself do a better job of teaching. There are lots of ways you can continue your education all by yourself. You can conduct research on any aspect of music on your own if you are so motivated. If it is ragtime piano, yodeling or rap rhythms you want to research, your students, local schools and universities, music stores and your local library most likely have treasures galore to unearth. You can listen, read, transcribe and practice yourself into expertise.

Subscribe to magazines and other periodicals that deal with your branch of music or particular instrument. If you are a contemporary guitarist, for example, several national magazines are written especially for you. Many music teacher associations publish newsletters (see "Resources"). Mainstream contemporary music magazines keep you up-to-date on what's happening in the world of music and newspapers inform you about the local music scene, critique new albums and spotlight certain artists. Another way to learn about a particular style or era in music is to read the many available autobiographies and biographies (authorized and unauthorized!) of musicians.

USING RECORDING TO EVALUATE YOURSELF

One simple piece of equipment that can really upgrade your skills as a teacher and as a musician is the tape recorder. From simple cassette recorders to eight- and sixteen-track studio set-ups, you can learn a great deal about your own style by listening to yourself play. Use the tape recorder to record live performances to play back later. Record practice routines, compositional ideas and rehearsal sessions. Play back recordings and critique them, identifying positive and negative aspects of your playing. Look for weaknesses in time, overused phrasing or motifs and lack of dynamics. Also give yourself credit for those things you do well and use that information to work from your strengths.

A less usual and more challenging way to use the tape recorder is to tape yourself teaching lessons (or videotape yourself!). Use the tapes to evaluate where you could answer more clearly, where you lose patience, where students need to be taught differently. As with performance, look for aspects of your teaching that are successful and those that need work. Many performers are self-conscious about hearing themselves play, let alone teach, so try to put that fear in perspective and use this important tool. Remember that you are trying to identify, acknowledge and perfect your teaching style.

KNOWING YOURSELF AS A MUSICIAN AND A TEACHER

When you get into this business of teaching music and find that there is a good lifestyle to be had, we are happy to report that you may come across dilemmas you never thought you'd encounter. You may be surprised once you get going that unlike portrayals in the movies, you are not scratching out a living, eating bread crusts and drinking too much coffee. Your dilemmas are the same as those experienced by all successful and ethical business people who are committed to their fields.

One dilemma is time management. You may not believe the day will ever come when you have more students than you can handle, but it may happen. At first, teaching musicians tend to take on every single student they can, always certain that the bottom of their teaching business is going to fall out. Even though your list of students may be ever-expanding, days are set at twenty-four hours. Decide ahead of time what seems like a reasonable amount of time in any given day to be teaching and remain fairly rigid about it. Having made a commitment to your continuing education and personal growth, make space in the schedule for that. Though you are tempted to take on as many students as you can, remember that you owe it to the students you *have* to do a top-notch job. When creating a waiting list is necessary, be reassured that teachers who have a waiting list enjoy a fair amount of clout in the musical community, since that is indicative of their ability to retain current students and simultaneously attract new ones.

Through the process of getting to know yourself and your teaching style, you will no doubt identify the populations with which you are most effective and those you can't work with well. If you know in your heart that you are not the best teacher for a particular student, it is your responsibility to pass that student along to someone else. Perhaps you have decided that you don't work well with children, or that your jazz skills are not marketable to jazz enthusiasts. The most important and difficult students to pass along are those with whom you have worked for a while whose skills begin to outpace yours. If you are not up to it, extremely talented students need to be passed to someone who can stay ahead of their progress and inspire them. It is hard not to let ego interfere in these situations, but it is essential.

Another aspect of knowing yourself and your teaching style is identifying what you really do well. Some teaching musicians go so far as to identify themselves by that specialty. "Michael Knox, Piano Teacher, specializing in classical study for serious young people" or "Mildred Jones, Electric Bass for adult learners." While you may limit yourself in this manner, you can certainly get the word out about your area of expertise.

SOME FINAL WORDS ABOUT CONTINUING TO GROW
Part of planning for the business of teaching music is to plan to stay in it. With this end in mind, you must set aside time and conceptual

space for your continued musical growth. Take time to stay current, and be open-minded about your students' musical tastes. Try to look at your continued musical education as a break from teaching and an opportunity to examine and augment your own practice as a player and a teacher. Finally, remember that working on your personal musicianship eventually benefits your students.

SOME FINAL WORDS

We hope you have found in these pages some suggestions that will keep you excited about music, will make the business side of teaching more manageable and will improve your interactions with your students. If you want to teach music, we can assure you from experience that there are many ways to do so. Too many people head down one road and, finding it rocky, turn back discouraged and convinced that it can't be done. We encourage you to head down several roads simultaneously, and when they get rocky, rest but don't retreat. We have discovered over the years that in teaching music, as in life, perseverance pays. Having found real happiness in a life filled with music, we wish you the same.

RESOURCES

American Academy of Teachers of Singing (AATS)
75 Bank Street
New York, NY 10014

American String Teachers Association (ASTA)
1806 Robert Fulton Drive
Suite 300
Reston, VA 22091

Canadian Music Educators' Association (CMEA)
16 Royaleigh Avenue
Etobicoke, Ontario M9P 2J5
(416) 244-3745
Fax (416) 235-1833

International Association of Jazz Educators (IAJE)
P.O. Box 724
Manhattan, KS 66502
(913) 776-8744

Keyboard Teachers Association International (KTAI)
361 Pin Oak Lane
Westbury, NY 11590-1941

Music Educators National Conference (MENC)
1806 Robert Fulton Drive
Reston, VA 22091
(703) 860-4000
Fax (703) 860-1531

Music Teachers National Association (MTNA)
Carew Tower
441 Vine Street, Suite 505
Cincinnati, OH 45202-2814
(513) 421-1420
Fax (513) 421-2503

National Guild of Piano Teachers (NGPT)
P.O. Box 1807
808 Rio Grand
Austin, TX 78767
(512) 478-5775

INDEX

Discover How To Make More Money Making Music!

Songwriter's Market Guide to Song and Demo Submission Formats — Get your foot in the door with knock-out query letters, slick demo presentation, and the best advice for dealing with every player in the industry! *#10401/$19.95/144 pages*

Hot Tips for Home Recording — Discover the tricks to recording a polished, professional demo! Musicians acquainted with recording technology will learn how to lay down basic tracks, add vocals, and mix to get exactly the sound they want. *#10415/ $18.99/160 pages*

Creating Melodies — You'll be singing all the way to the bank when you discover the secrets of creating memorable melodies — from love ballads to commercial jingles! *#10400/$18.95/144 pages*

Making Money Making Music — Cash in on scores of ways to make a profitable living with your musical talent (no matter where you live). *#10174/$18.95/208 pages/ paperback*

Music Publishing: A Songwriter's Guide — Get a handle on your songwriting career! You'll get the advice you need on types of royalties, subpublishing and much more! *#10195/$18.95/144 pages/paperback*

The Craft of Lyric Writing — You'll sell more songs when you learn the tricks to writing lyrics with universal appeal. *#10015/$19.95/292 pages/paperback*

Successful Lyric Writing — Write the kinds of lyrics that dazzle music executives with this hands-on course in writing. Dozens of exercises and demonstrations let you put what you've learned into practice! *#10015/$19.95/292 pages/paperback*

Networking in the Music Business — Who you know can either make (or break) your music career. Discover how to make and capitalize on the contacts you need to succeed. *#10365/$17.95/128 pages/paperback*

Beginning Songwriter's Answer Book — This newly revised and updated resource answers the questions most asked by beginning songwriters and inspires you to get started in the music business. *#10376/$16.95/128 pages/paperback*

Who Wrote That Song — If you're a music buff, you'll love the 12,000 songs listed here! Each listing includes title, composer, lyricist, and publication year. Where appropriate, listings also reveal who made the song popular, others who recorded it, and who sang it on Broadway or in the movies. *#10403/$19.95/432 pages/paperback*

The Songwriter's Idea Book — If your muse tends to sleep on the job, discover 40 winning strategies proven to spark your imagination and get you back to writing. *#10320/$17.95/240 pages*

88 Songwriting Wrongs & How To Right Them — Expert advice will help you fix what's wrong with your song, avoid common pitfalls, and apply sound solutions to your songwriting. *#10287/$17.95/144 pages/paperback*